The LOUISVILLE, CINCINNATI & CHARLESTON Rail Road

Railroads Past & Present

GEORGE M. SMERK, EDITOR

A list of books in the series appears at the end of this volume.

INDIANA UNIVERSITY PRESS

Bloomington & Indianapolis

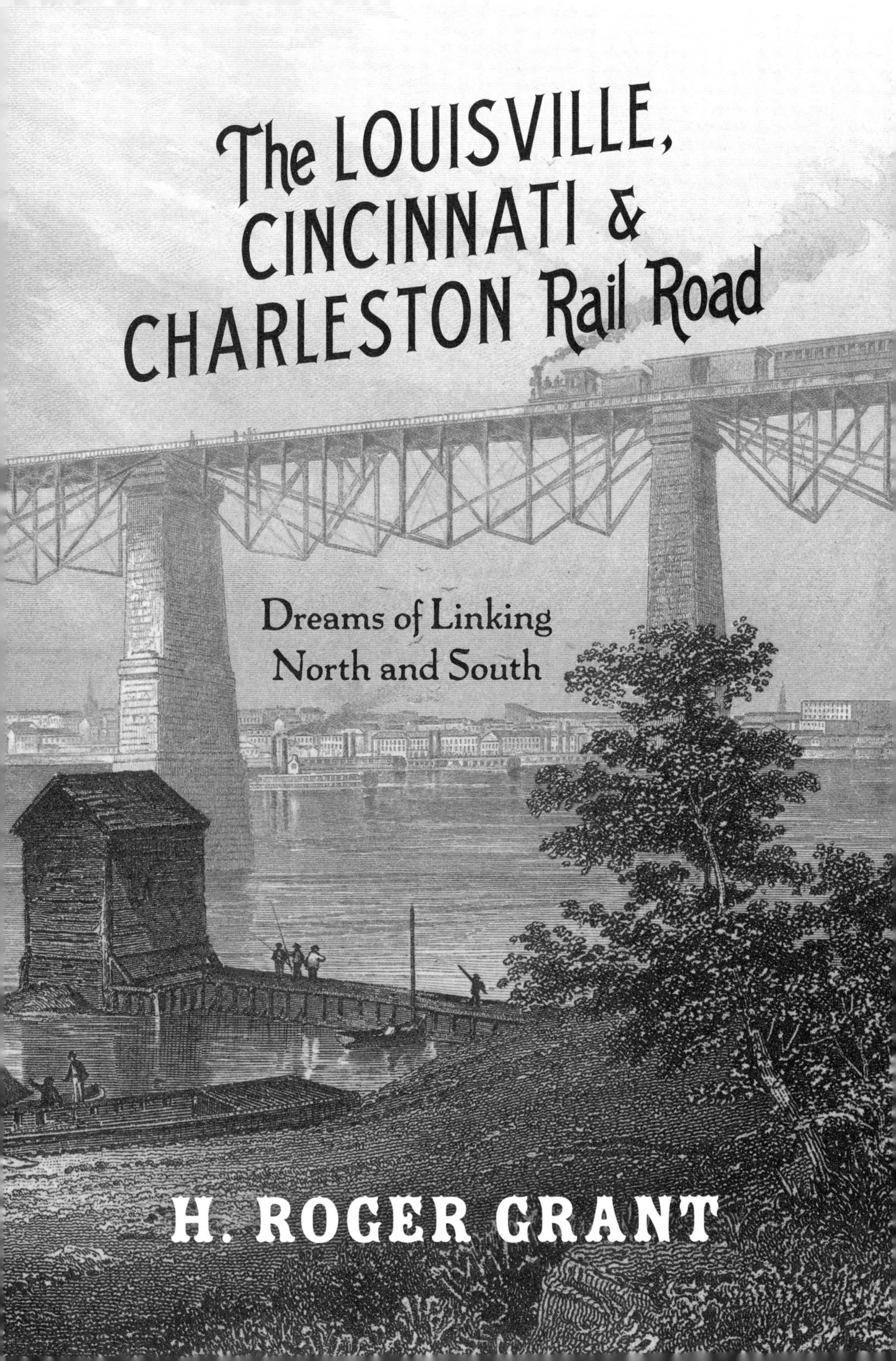
The LOUISVILLE,
CINCINNATI &
CHARLESTON Rail Road
Dreams of Linking
North and South
H. ROGER GRANT

This book is a publication of

Indiana University Press
Office of Scholarly Publishing
Herman B Wells Library 350
1320 East Tenth Street
Bloomington, Indiana 47405 USA

iupress.indiana.edu

Telephone orders 800-842-6796
Fax orders 812-855-7931

∞ The paper used in this publication meets the minimum requirements of the American National Standard for Information Sciences–Permanence of Paper for Printed Library Materials, ANSI Z39.48–1992.

Manufactured in the United States of America

Cataloging information is available at the Library of Congress.

ISBN 978-0-253-01181-7 (cloth)
ISBN 978-0-253-01187-9 (ebook)

1 2 3 4 5 19 18 17 16 15 14

JOHN T. MOON, II

1953–2012

Contents

PREFACE ix

ACKNOWLEDGMENTS xiii

1 SLOW, DIFFICULT, AND DANGEROUS TRAVEL 1

2 A RAIL ROAD? 23

3 KNOXVILLE, 1836 44

4 SURVEYS, FINANCES, AND CONSTRUCTION 69

5 CRISIS AND CONTRACTION 100

6 WHAT HAPPENED 120

7 WHAT MIGHT HAVE HAPPENED 152

NOTES 165

INDEX 183

Preface

PROFESSIONAL HISTORIANS AND INTERESTED AMATEURS HAVE long explored a variety of railroad topics, including the organization and construction of the earliest American lines. This interest in the Demonstration Period of steam railways, which spanned the 1830s and 1840s, may be attributed to that human desire to know about the beginnings of things. This is more than an idle curiosity, being a valuable way to learn how remote events shaped later cultural, economic, political, and physical environments. The antebellum era was an exciting and expansive time in the nation's history, including the transport sector, when the agrarian republic was evolving into an industrialized nation. It would be railroads, rather than canals, roads, and waterways, that created a remarkable revolution in domestic transportation.

Although aspects of the proposed link between Charleston and Cincinnati have been discussed in scholarly monographs, doctoral dissertations, and masters' theses, no book-length study consolidates the pertinent primary and secondary sources. This ambitious – perhaps too ambitious – Louisville, Cincinnati & Charleston Rail Road (LC&C) of the late 1830s and early 1840s deserves attention. After all, this projected railroad was one of the first seriously attempted trans-Appalachian interregional projects. It held a close connection to what was briefly the longest railroad in the world under a single management, the 136-mile trans-state South-Carolina Canal & Rail-Road. Opened in 1833, this pioneer carrier demonstrated the practicability of an infant railroad technology. If the LC&C had begun operations as planned, it would have been both America's longest railway and its largest single private corporation. Even though only about 10 percent of the hoped-for LC&C was completed by the mid-nineteenth century, a direct route between the southern Atlantic Ocean coast and the mid–Ohio River valley was eventually established under a single management, attesting to the soundness of that audacious initial proposal.

If this most daring project of the 1830s had been completed by the 1840s or somewhat later, it surely would have had a wide-ranging impact on its service area. As a path-breaking developmental railroad, the LC&C would have bolstered economies of the three cities at its extremities, most of all Charleston. The road also could have altered the political landscape of the nation, even affecting southern secession. Strong, enduring bonds of commitment might have been forged by a carrier that created and sustained rapid, safe, and predictable commercial intercourse between the Old South and the Old Northwest (or what contemporaries called the "West"). Moreover, patterns of interstate migration may have been changed significantly, allowing whites from the Old Northwest and other northern areas, who frequently held antislavery views, to relocate to border and southern states. Some of these new residents might be attracted initially by railroad construction jobs and then operating, maintenance, and management positions, and others would seize opportunities in farming, lumbering, mining, and commercial and professional endeavors. But, alas, that did not happen; the iron rails of the LC&C became only one part of an extensive network of intrastate South Carolina lines.

As with most railroads, whether early or late, large or small, successful or not, several individuals sparked the drive. For the LC&C its greatest champion was the nationally prominent Robert Y. Hayne, a man with a passion for a Charleston-to-Cincinnati railroad. No wonder this beloved South Carolina politician played a pivotal role in organizing the greatest railroad convention in the South prior to the Civil War. In July 1836 hundreds of delegates from multiple states assembled in Knoxville, Tennessee, to consider this nearly 700-mile proposition. This railroad convention became a widely discussed and long-remembered event.

The Louisville, Cincinnati & Charleston faced numerous and ultimately fatal obstacles. Without question, the courageous efforts to turn the ocean-to-river plan into reality graphically reveals that railroad undertakings were capital intensive, potentially controversial, and extremely risky. A perfect storm of sorts derailed completion, most notably a deep and long-lasting depression triggered by the Panic of 1837, Hayne's own unexpected death, and growing opposition from Kentuckians, some influential South Carolinians, including John C. Calhoun, and others. Ultimately, though, a railroad, the Cincinnati Southern, constructed by the municipal government of Cincinnati, Ohio, spanned part of the distance envisioned by proponents of the LC&C, and the remainder of the Charleston-Cincinnati-Louisville trackage came about from several separate undertakings. After 1894 the Southern Railway, then newly organized, gained control of this route between Charleston and Cincinnati, effectively realizing those dreams conceived at the dawn of the Railway Age. The labors of the Knoxville Railroad Convention therefore were not discarded into the trash bin of history. Even a dozen years after the Knoxville assemblage, a meeting of internal proponents recognized the significance of the grand Atlantic Ocean to Ohio River vision. "The persuasive eloquence of the gifted and lamented Hayne was not without its beneficial influence in awakening the public attention to the vast importance of bringing into more intimate intercommunication the new and enterprising States of the West, with the older sisters of the Atlantic."

Acknowledgments

ALTHOUGH I HAVE STUDIED SEVERAL MODERN RAILROAD companies, I never expected to examine a largely failed carrier from the antebellum period. It would be contacts made through the Lexington Group, a seventy-year-old transportation history organization, consisting of academics, librarians, and railroad industry professionals, that led me to prepare this examination of the Louisville, Cincinnati & Charleston Rail Road (LC&C). Two Norfolk Southern Corporation employees, the late John Moon and William (Bill) Schafer, got me involved, and their supportive efforts resulted in the Norfolk Southern Foundation awarding me a handsome research grant. During the course of my work John provided guidance, including making joint trips to research centers, locating pertinent materials, and reading an early draft of the book manuscript. Others at Norfolk Southern offered assistance, including company archivist Jennifer McDaid and assistant corporate secretary Mary Ann Mullady. And my colleague Richard Saunders Jr., a prominent railroad historian, kindly supplied me with a copy of his MA thesis on the LC&C that he completed in 1964 at the University of Illinois. As with every research endeavor there are others, particularly institutions, that deserve acknowledgment. The list includes: Calhoun County Museum, St. Matthews, South Carolina; Calvin M. McClung Historical Collection, East Tennessee History Center, Knoxville; Cincinnati Historical Society and Museum Center, Cincinnati, Ohio; Special Collections, Clemson University; National Archives, College Park, Maryland; R. M. Cooper Library, Clemson University; South Carolina Archives and History Center, Columbia; South Caroliniana Library Archives, Columbia; Southern Railway Historical Association Archive, Kennesaw, Georgia; and University of Tennessee Library, Special Collections, Knoxville. I also wish to thank William (Bill) Klugh of Clemson, South Carolina, for providing access to his Simpson family collection of manuscripts and published materials.

Unlike earlier research projects, I examined online numerous books, journals, trade publications, and newspapers, allowing me to reduce my research travels and to broaden the scope of my work. Services provided by Clemson University Libraries and the John W. Barriger III National Railroad Library in St. Louis, Missouri, gave me opportunities to access varied research materials. And the late Craig Miner, professor of history at Wichita State University, provided guidance through the maze of electronic sources.

As with earlier book projects my wife, Martha Farrington Grant, read the evolving manuscript on several occasions. As in the past she made her perceptive comments, significantly improving the quality and readability. And with my previous four books with Indiana University Press, staff members have been professional and supportive through the publication process, creating wonderful and enduring working relationships. I am appreciative, too, of the financial commitment that members of the Lemon family have made to my Kathryn and Calhoun Lemon Professorship. Their generosity has contributed to an academic environment that is pleasant, satisfying, and productive.

H. Roger Grant
Clemson University
Clemson, South Carolina

The LOUISVILLE, CINCINNATI & CHARLESTON Rail Road

Slow, Difficult, and Dangerous Travel

1

ROADS

Before the Railway Age Americans faced limited travel options. Nearly always they were slow, difficult, and potentially dangerous. There was little need to question the sardonic judgment made more than a century ago by Henry Adams. This historian and man of letters wrote that persons "struggling with the untamed continent in 1800 seemed hardly more competent to their task [of road improvements] than the beavers and buffalo which had for countless generations made bridges and roads of their own."[1]

Although poor land transportation knew no geographical bounds, residents in interior sections of the Old South and the Old Northwest[2] experienced severe challenges when they made overland treks by foot, on horseback, or in an animal-powered vehicle. No wonder, then, that from the earliest settlements through the antebellum decades the promotion of internal betterments, including roads, became a popular focus. Improvements to land transport seemed imperative for progress; people wanted to move more rapidly, reliably, and securely. "To persons who have reflected upon the subject of internal improvement, there is no maxim of political economy better understood than that agriculture and commerce will improve, and civilization and happiness spread in promotion as the facility of conveyance increases," wrote a thoughtful Robert Mills, architect, civil engineer, and member of the South Carolina Board of Public Works, in 1821. "Where men are kept asunder by forests, morasses or inaccessible mountains, their knowledge must be circumscribed and their conveniences few. In proportion as the difficulty of communication is removed, the spirit of enterprise increases." Yet in antebellum America the federal government did little to coordinate, design, fund, or construct domestic transportation improvements, although discussions and debates repeatedly occurred in Congress, state legislatures, courthouses, and elsewhere.[3]

Most of the nation, including the Old South and the Old Northwest, was crisscrossed with trails, animal (often made by bison migrating to feeding areas) and Indian, that served as the "corner-stone of land travel in America." These pathways, usually only twelve to eighteen inches wide and often worn a foot or more deep, connected navigable bodies of water, offered practical ways to skirt mountains, lakes, and swamps, and forded streams where waters were shallow. Just as Indians walked great distances, intrepid settlers and later residents did the same. So-called ankle wagons, namely a person's two feet, served as a popular means of transport. Contemporary accounts during the formative decades of the Republic and even later reveal that individuals walked considerable distances just as religious pilgrims had made extended journeys on foot throughout medieval Europe. In America it might be a walk between Charleston, South Carolina, and the Upstate, perhaps to the old Cherokee trading post at Oconee Station, or between Lexington, Kentucky, the gestating "Athens of the West," and such Ohio River destinations as Louisville and Maysville, Kentucky, or Cincinnati and Ripley, Ohio.[4]

Lucius Verus Bierce, a recent graduate of Ohio University, made a remarkable 1,800- mile trip on foot in several stages from Athens, Ohio, and back during late 1822 and early 1823. He frequently walked 20 to 30 miles a day and carried a knapsack "weighing seventeen and half pounds." Early on in his journal Bierce mentioned the common woes of such travel. "I began to feel the effects of my choice of the mode of traveling – one blood blister on my foot, tired, headache, and to cap all most awfully downhearted – perhaps homesick." Another somewhat less intrepid walker was Parmenas Taylor Turnley, a young Tennessean, who also undertook a long-distance walk. In June 1841 he traveled the 418 miles from Greeneville, Tennessee, to Winchester, Virginia. Although he rode 55 miles in a stagecoach, most of his fifteen-day journey was on foot, hiking an average of about 30 miles daily. After walking the nearly 30 miles from Greeneville to Elizabethton, Tennessee, on his first day, he noted in his diary, "It was a pretty hard day's walk, as the sun was intensely hot." Later entries revealed other discomforts, particularly blistering feet and fatigue.[5]

Such treks were nearly always fraught with difficulties and dangers. It might be spring "freshets" that flooded streams, wild animals, venomous snakes, pesky plants (particularly poison ivy), or the annoyance of mosquitoes, flies, and other insects. Then there were matters of weather – heat, cold, rain, snow, hail, fog, and wind. Early on, Euro-Americans might be attacked by Indians. Such ambushes (and killings) along the Buffalo Trace (also known as the Kentucky Road or Vincennes Trace) between the Indiana river settlements of New Albany and Vincennes prompted the federal government during the War of 1812 to dispatch soldiers to protect travelers. There also could be robbers, who were notorious along the walkway

(later roadway) between Natchez, Mississippi, and Nashville, Tennessee. Called the Natchez Trace, this important route had been cobbled together from a series of linked animal and Indian paths. Nearly all primitive traces lacked overnight accommodations, and so food and camping equipment, which nearly always included a heavy iron cooking pot, became essential for extended journeys. And reports of walkers getting lost along trails were not uncommon; after all, their routes might be merely "blazed" paths with the occasionally marked tree.[6]

Walking in early-nineteenth-century Europe closely resembled the practice in the United States. This gent is on a hike in the Yorkshire region of England, but likely he is not on an extended journey. In America a long-distance walker would have his knapsack that included an iron kettle, sleeping gear, food, and other necessities. The background in this sketch reveals one of the first steam-powered coal trains.

Author's collection.

Travel times were less of a concern. They were slow, but not that slow when compared to most inland watercraft and later canal boats. A healthy adult male could walk several miles per hour, depending upon terrain, trail conditions, weather, and personal limitations, especially if possessions or goods were being carried.

While some travelers dreaded a walk, especially over long distances and through rugged terrains, some enjoyed all or parts of the journey. When walking it was possible to reach precisely the desired destination, and at minimal cost. Moreover, walking generated a rhythm of thinking. "The passage through a landscape echoes or stimulates the passage through a series of thoughts," remarked a student of walking. An individual could also notice the attractive, even breathtaking aspects of nature. As historical geographer John Jakle put it: "To walk was to allow more time to see and to hear and otherwise imprint the landscape on the memory."[7]

Trails normally were shared by horseback riders. And some of these travelers led small caravans of pack horses or mules. Speeds for lone riders were faster – as much as 40 or 50 miles per day – and movements were less physically strenuous, although the rider needed to care for his animal. Yet dangers lurked. Trouble could result from their mounts stepping into watery holes or other depressions and breaking or injuring their legs. Horses might become spooked by snakes, animals, or the weather, bolting away in an uncontrollable gallop. Equipment problems could also ensue; slipped saddle girths were common annoyances. Plus the awful physical condition of these traces remained. "Nothing can exceed the road for badness in some particular places, the mud being belly deep to our horses, & the banks of the Creeks almost insurmountable, from their steepness & slippery nature, particularly Richland Creek, which bank was very high & almost perpendicular, & slippery as ice," related a traveler on a Tennessee road in 1795. "An old man in ascending it, after his horse had got almost to the top began to slide backward, & at length fell over & threw him down the precipice into the mud & water, where both man & horse stuck so fast that it was with great difficulty they were extracted."[8]

Nevertheless the importance of trails and primitive roads led individuals and neighborhood groups to provide minimal maintenance and to seek modest improvements. It might be removal of boulders, seasonal underbrush, and debris or construction of primitive bridges across the most difficult impediments. Sometimes residents hitched up their animal teams to their wooden or iron plows to make furrows, allowing for easier identification and better drainage of the pathway.[9]

The utility of trails led to a bold proposal. As the Railway Age dawned, an imaginative contributor to the recently launched *American Railroad Journal* suggested building "foot railroads." "Those inventions are the most important which enable all classes of society to make the best use of their personal strength. [Foot] railroads for the use of individuals, like a foot path, will do this." This writer believed that it was unrealistic to construct turnpikes, canals, and especially railroads that could directly serve extended sections of a predominately agricultural nation. "Large railroads must necessarily be confined to great channels of communication; they require too great capital to be extended to every village." With creation of a network of trails that would be relatively level, not only would walking be faster and less difficult, but individuals could use what he called "carriages," a type of the wheelbarrow. "Probably the families that go to country stores, do not carry generally more than 100 lbs. weight;

and most commonly they do not carry more than 50 lbs. But suppose that it is 100; then there is a carriage of 50 and a load of 100 lbs. The force required to move this on a level railroad, will be only a small fraction more than that required to raise half a pound over a pulley." This futurist closed with these thoughts: "It will appear then, that foot railroads will be a vast public benefit; an advantage not to the rich only, but chiefly to the laboring classes."[10]

The creative concept of the foot railroad never materialized, but wider and better trails – actual roads – did. If conditions, including weather, were satisfactory, a person on horseback usually could travel successfully along an old animal or Indian trail, but a road was preferable. There was also the necessity of conveying goods, those larger and heavier items that a walker or horseman could never manage. It would be the two-wheeled cart, pulled by horses, mules, or oxen, that enjoyed early and widespread usage, by both farmers and urbanites. A version of the common cart, at first with two wheels and then four, allowed teamsters to move shipments between watercraft and warehouses and other nearby destinations. Such uncushioned carts were uncomfortable for drivers, slow, and inherently small-scale. Appearing, too, were four-wheeled wagons and the Conestoga, with the latter's distinctive sway-bellied design that for decades served as the preferred conveyance for heavy loads. A Conestoga wagon was pulled by two, six, or even eight horses, mules, or oxen. Yet these larger vehicles did not significantly reduce the high costs of freight haulage, largely because of the labor and time involved. Even on the "best" roads, speeds were painfully slow. In the 1820s it took an average of three days for a Conestoga to travel the 90 miles between New York City and Philadelphia, but some contemporaries considered such a wagon to be a "flying machine."[11]

Travelers who did not care to walk or ride horseback might take a stagecoach. By the 1820s the Concord stage had been widely adopted and continued to be improved. This four-wheeled vehicle consisted of a strong, round-bottom body suspended on sturdy braces and mounted on rugged gearing. Passengers, who usually numbered eight or nine, took interior seats or occupied the single space next to the driver. A rear platform and portions of the roof accommodated baggage, light freight, and mail. But the journey by stagecoach might be less than pleasant. It could be more than a bumpy ride; it might face delays (at times lengthy) because of road conditions and mechanical breakdowns. These coaches were repeatedly subjected to great strains due to wretched roads and to overloading. There was always the risk of having disagreeable or drunken travel companions, and all seated close together. Occasionally there were highwaymen and troublesome Indians who took their toll on passengers. Stagecoach drivers might consume strong spirits, and an inebriated or semi-inebriated driver hardly made for a safe passage. Apparently drink "heightened their courage for venturing upon the rough roads."[12]

Whether travel involved a farm cart, Conestoga wagon, or Concord stage, journeys over American roads were consistently trying. This was particularly true in wet periods, during spring thaws and after heavy rains. This common saying rang true: "Be sure to choose your rut carefully. You will be in it for a very long time." Contemporary newspaper reports, travelers' accounts, personal diaries, and other sources described the difficulties and hardships of journeys on antebellum roads and continued to do so for decades to come.[13]

In 1822 the *Georgian,* a Savannah newspaper, captured the essence of travel in the Southlands. "The roads in the upper part of the state are in a dreadful situation. A letter from a correspondent states that between Milledgeville and Augusta, he passed not less than 126 waggons [*sic*] loaded with cotton, twelve of which were fast in the mud, and two or three upset." The report continued: "The stage between Augusta and Milledgeville was in continual danger of upsetting." Or as Christopher Schultz, who early in the nineteenth century visited sections of the region, reflected, "If the mud does not get quite over your boot tops when you sit in the saddle they [Southerners] call it a middling good road." Observed another writer in the 1820s, "The rich inhabitants of the back country of South Carolina and of those parts of North Carolina and Georgia which trade with Charleston, are obliged, at great expense, to transport their produce and receive in return, their supplies; weeks, and not infrequently, months have elapsed before places not more distant, in a direct line, than one hundred and twenty miles, could effect these communications, and then, and at all times with great expense." The narrator added: "Travelers fare as badly as goods, for if they move at all faster, it is still with a slow tiresome pace, consuming time that might be profitably employed." A minister, who moved his family from Virginia to Alabama by wagon in 1818, had a similar tale of woe. He experienced "nine weeks traveling over broken roads, and exposed to every danger" and called Alabama's roads "infernal." These commentaries reinforce the belief that no section of the country had poorer roads than the American South.[14]

In the Old Northwest residents likewise struggled with their network of roads that during wet weather travelers described repeatedly as "muddy quagmires." Then during dry periods they became dusty and remained rutted. Ohio was typical. In 1811 Charity Rodman Rotch mentioned in her diary about her journey to Massillon, Ohio. "Reach'd Shartlers Inn on the 27th [of May] a very comfortable Log house, and kind people perhaps 12 miles from Lancaster [Ohio], in the morning rode two miles to Tarlton, & stopt at Lybrands Inn on – of getting a pr. of horses, the *mud* now being too deep for ours, to convey us comfortably." Somewhat later, in 1834,

Marianne Parker Dascomb wrote to friends in New England about her Buckeye State trip. "At five o'clock we took stage for Elyria, which is ten miles from Oberlin – road very bad from ruts and mud. We were in constant danger of overturning. Once when we came to a ditch in the road the gentlemen got out and took down a fence, so that we could turn aside into the adjoining field and ride around the obstacle." And a good summary of road conditions appeared in the *Cincinnati Directory* of 1819: "In no part of the United States are good roads more wanted [than in western Ohio]. During the winter months the ways are so soft and the mud so deep, that travelling, especially with loaded wagons, is very laborious, tedious and disagreeable. In a country so populous, rich and beautiful, such vile and disagreeable roads are degrading to the taste, public spirit, and enterprize of the inhabitants."[15]

While there were efforts to enhance the hodgepodge of badly constructed and poorly maintained wagon roads, there was that poster child of the modern roadway, the National Road (or Cumberland Road or Great Western Road), an ambitious project that became the first federally planned and sponsored internal improvement. Although authorized by Congress in 1806, construction did not begin until five years later. This "Grand Portage" between the Atlantic seaboard and the trans-Allegheny West, along a route that was highly politicized, began at Cumberland, Maryland, where it connected with turnpikes to Baltimore and Washington, D.C., and extended westward to the Ohio River at Wheeling, Virginia. Once the road reached the mighty Ohio in 1818, a Bostonian commented that "such a work could never have been accomplished by individual enterprise; and many have thought ought not to have been by the public. There can be no doubt, however, but that the public at large have reaped a benefit more than equal to the expense." Later the National Road passed through a corner of Pennsylvania and crossed Ohio and Indiana before stalling miles from its announced destination of St. Louis (or possibly Jefferson City, Missouri). To a degree this roadway resembled the cardiovascular system of a living body; the main artery had a network of mostly capillary ruts branching out into the hinterlands. Until being overtaken by the iron horse (and to a lesser degree by canals), the National Road was alive with traffic, including settlers traveling west and livestock being driven east.[16]

The National Road, with its graded and rocked surface, graceful stone-arched bridges (perhaps more elegant and costly than needed), cast-iron mileposts and tollhouses with their strong metal gates, impressed the traveler, but it was a unique long-distance thoroughfare. Roads backed by state governments and private investors were more common. In the 1820s South Carolinians saw the opening of a strategic wagon road, financed in part from public coffers, that spanned the state between Charleston,

Columbia, and the North Carolina border. And in 1828 this artery continued through Asheville, North Carolina, to the East Tennessee town of Greeneville. In marshy places this roadway and others like it were "corduroyed," being built with slabs of pine timber. But the humid climate caused rapid decay, necessitating nearly constant wood replacements. A signature early travel way in Georgia, known as the "Old Federal Road," but initially the unimproved Middle Cherokee Trading Path, stretched from Athens northwestward to the Tennessee River Valley north of present-day Chattanooga. Unlike the National Road, this misnamed roadway received no federal funding, being supported by local governments and individuals. Similarly the Wilderness Road, made famous by the trail blazing of the legendary Daniel Boone, likewise developed without federal support, emerging in the latter part of the eighteenth century as the principal avenue for settlers from Virginia and Atlantic coastal regions to reach Kentucky. More a walking and horse trail than a road, this route started in extreme western Virginia at Block House in present-day Washington County and passed northwesterly through the strategic Cumberland and Pine Mountain Gaps of the Appalachians and continued to Harrodsburg, Kentucky, southeast of the falls on the Ohio River (Louisville). A fork extended to Boonesborough, on the bank of the Kentucky River southeast of Lexington. For years the Wilderness Road, often steep and rough, could be traversed only on foot or on horseback. But in 1796, with funding from the new state of Kentucky, conditions improved, allowing for wagon transport and for farmers to drive their livestock – cattle, hogs, and sheep (and horses and mules, too) – to market, mainly in the Carolinas. During the late eighteenth and early nineteenth centuries private turnpike construction spearheaded the quest for better roads in New England and the mid-Atlantic states, but in the South, Virginia most of all, public assistance aided these turnpike companies. That state's efforts produced two important toll roads, the Staunton and Parkersburg Road and the Northwestern Turnpike, the latter connecting Winchester with the mouth of the Little Kanawha River.[17]

Widespread interest in making better roads continued, but money for improvements was universally scarce. Governmental bodies, usually townships and counties, commonly dealt with these needs by permitting taxpayers to "work off" their yearly road assessments. In Georgia, for example, counties had long required all able-bodied men between the ages of sixteen and forty-five (or their paid substitutes) to labor on public roads fifteen days annually or pay a hefty fine. However, these events, which frequently became festive neighborhood occasions fueled by ample jugs of corn liquor, customarily accomplished little of practical value. States, too, became involved. As early as 1785 the Virginia legislature required three days of annual road maintenance from every male who was at least

This artist's sketch portrays the Cumberland Gap, located near the borders of Kentucky, Tennessee, and Virginia, which served as a strategic part of the Wilderness Road. Walking was the earliest way that travelers exploited this natural opening through the Appalachians. Later this well-known geographic feature caught the attention of surveyors who correctly saw this depression as a practical passageway for a railroad line.

Courtesy of the Library of Congress.

sixteen years old. But partying also plagued the meaningful implementation of this statute. No matter the legal demands, road workers, even those with good intent, usually lacked the skills, equipment, or availability at the best time of the year to fashion decent roads. Yet sometimes funds were found for grading and ditching and applying river gravel or crushed stone, supervised by experienced overseers, that produced acceptable results. Then the untrained could contribute.[18]

New technologies and construction techniques promised to end the curse of bad roads. Two advances were especially noteworthy. By the 1830s, layers of crushed stone, applied with a bonding agent, produced the highly desirable macadamized road, a process developed about 1820 by John Loudon McAdam, a Scottish road surveyor and engineer. But the expense in preparing proper surface drainage and applying by hand the correct dimensions of stones, together with substantial material expenses, often deterred such undertakings. During the antebellum decades only a limited mileage of roadways in the Old South and the Old Northwest claimed this superior construction. Then there were plank roads. In the 1830s and 1840s this approach to improving roads swept parts of Russia and Upper Canada (Ontario) and also found support in the United States. Proponents believed they had a better way to facilitate land travel, especially through marshy locales. They proposed laying heavy hardwood planks across wood stringers, fastened with iron spikes or wooden pegs, to create a solid surface over the wettest and hence muddiest stretches. This was a refined version of the long-employed corduroy road, with its split-log construction that placed the flat sides downward. Plank roads, though, were never a panacea. The continual expense of upkeep became their glaring shortcoming, even though these usually state-chartered plank-road companies collected tolls. If not repaired, surfaces, weakened from use and decay, menaced travelers. "[A plank road] was a comfort at the outset," commented a contemporary traveler, "and a nuisance at the end." Still, they were preferable to no surfacing at all.[19]

Although improved roads existed, a comprehensive network of reliable thoroughfares before the Civil War failed to cover adequately either the Old South or the Old Northwest. In many places it would not be until after World War I that all-weather roads predominated, when public expenditures were propelled by the growing agitation of motor vehicle owners. By the 1920s Americans had assimilated the automobile into their lifestyle and relied on trucks for the delivery of a major portion of their short-haul goods. "It is to be regretted that the early settlers could not have lived to witness the triumph of the twentieth century," remarked an Ohioan in 1924, "and ride over the wonderful roads that we enjoy today."[20]

RIVERS

The natural waterways that flowed from the eastern continental divide offered numerous varied transport opportunities. There were those streams, tidal near their mouths, that emptied directly into the Atlantic Ocean. Notable ones were the James River that facilitated water transport from the sea to the fall-line at Richmond; the Savannah River that also allowed vessels to ascend to the fall-line, in this case at Augusta, Georgia; and the Altamaha River, likewise in Georgia, that with its two principal tributaries, the Ocmulgee and Oconee, permitted boat travel to the fall-lines at Macon (Ocmulgee) and Milledgeville (Oconee). More rivers entered the Gulf of Mexico, including the Chattahoochee-Apalachicola and the Coosa-Alabama, and extended to upstream fall-lines. The problem was that the navigable waters of these Atlantic- and Gulf-flowing rivers did not reach great distances back into the hinterlands. The major exception was the complex and interconnected Ohio-Mississippi river-drainage system that dominated interior water transportation. From the earliest days of Euro-American settlements and then into the early republic these two mighty streams became the jugular veins of the continent. North of the Ohio River, waterways tended to be short and shallow, although there were anomalies. The Muskinghum River (later canalized with dams and locks) permitted freight and passengers to move from its mouth at Marietta northward to Zanesville, a distance of about 75 miles, and there provided a connection with the National Road. The larger and much longer Wabash River, which drained two-thirds of Indiana, allowed transport deep into the interior and later provided water for the largely parallel Wabash and Erie Canal between Fort Wayne and Terre Haute. This 475-mile river became "the highway of [Indiana's] maturity." But the Wabash was usable only during periods of high water; it was a fickle stream. It would be to the south where major streams flowed into the Ohio River, notably the Cumberland and the Tennessee. The former was somewhat less valuable as a water highway, mostly due to relatively low water levels, but this stream linked Nashville with the Ohio River east of Paducah, Kentucky. The largest tributary to the Ohio was the mighty Tennessee River. From its source in East Tennessee, formed by the confluence of the French Broad and Holston Rivers, the Tennessee flowed more than 650 miles through Alabama, Tennessee, and Kentucky before emptying into the Ohio not far from the mouth of the Cumberland. Early in the nineteenth century Colonel Stephen Long of the U.S. Engineering Corps considered the Tennessee a "medium of commercial intercourse" and equal, if not superior, to the Ohio River. The Tennessee, nevertheless, presented problems for navigation, most of all whirlpool and rock hazards caused by such colorfully named places as the Boiling Pot, Kettle, Suck, Tumbling Shoals, and Muscle Shoals. Furthermore the river did not run directly into the Mississippi, creating an excruciatingly long travel route to that primary waterway.[21]

From time immemorial boats plied these river corridors, making for easy transport, at least when compared to overland travel. What was called the Canoe Age involved a variety of mostly small boats. Indians, afterward joined by explorers, fur trappers, and traders, and then early settlers, found the dugout and the birchbark canoe practical ways to exploit these streams for personal travel. Yet there existed craft with good carrying capacities. Skiffs or bateaux measured 12 to 14 feet long, contained room for two passengers, and had the capability to accommodate several hundred pounds of cargo. Pirogues were more impressive, being 35 to 40 feet long with space for as many as fourteen or fifteen occupants and several thousand pounds of freight.[22]

By the nineteenth century the flatboat and the keelboat would dominate interior river travel. Numbering in the thousands, these craft were easy to build and inexpensive, and they enjoyed a wide range of movement. Immigrants preferred flatboats. They wanted a cheap and practical way to reach their downstream destinations and probably had no intention of returning to their points of departure. Farmers and merchants also employed flatboats to get their products – animals, pork, lard, flour, produce, whiskey, lumber, and the like – to market. Writing from Cincinnati in 1834, an English lad told his parents, "There are flat boats that go from hear to New Orleans. Tha carry 7 or 8 hundred barrell of flower each. It was one of these kind of boat I left Zanesville in." In another case a teenager recalled, "[At Paducah] my uncle purchased two flat boat loads (one of lime and the other corn and oats) and started me off in charge of said boats and contents, for Memphis, where in due time I arrived and where I spent most of the winter, in selling what was placed in my charge." Some travelers opted for flatboats for personal transportation. "In descending the Ohio and the Mississippi, at that time, it was customary to purchase a flat boat," recounted Guillaume Tell Poussin, a former French minister to the United States who in 1817 journeyed from Pittsburgh to New Orleans. "Embarking on this, it was necessary to trust to the strength of the current to convey you to your destination. This was certainly not a very expeditious method of traveling. From sixty to seventy days were consumed in this part of the journey." Depending on river current strength, speeds varied, ranging from a few to 6 or 7 miles per hour, and 75 miles or more might be covered in a day. Those individuals who sought to return upstream before the steamboat era usually traveled overland; a flatboat, unable to move against currents, offered only downriver travel.[23]

The common flatboat was simplicity personified. "The only claim of the flat-boat to rank as a vessel was due to the fact that it floated upon water and was used as a vehicle of transportation," opined an observer. The craft featured a flat bottom and a straight prow and measured about 30 or 40 feet in length and a dozen feet in width. Sizes, however, varied. Flatboats that floated down the principal rivers were much larger, described as being "generally from forty-five feet to sixty feet in length and eighteen to twenty feet wide." Roughly sawed lumber made up the component members. Most were equipped with a primitive roof and used handmade oars for steering; some sported sails.[24]

For onlookers a flatboat held a certain fascination. "No uncommon spectacle to see a large family, old and young, servants, cattle, hogs, horses, sheep [and] fowls," wrote a traveler along the Ohio River, "bringing to recollection the cargo of the ancient ark." Flotillas of passing flatboats could make an indelible impression with scores of rafts passing in a single day.[25]

A more sophisticated and versatile version of the flatboat was the keelboat (or poleboat). This cigar-shaped vessel contained a more complex structure. As the name implies, the keelboat was constructed on a keel and had ribs like a ship. This long, narrow craft measured about 50 to 75 feet or occasionally longer and 10 to 15 feet in width, and featured prows and "running boards" on each side from end to end to facilitate poling upstream. Usually a roof covered much of the boat to shelter the thirty to fifty tons of freight and the Spartan living quarters. Occasionally a keelboat might have a dozen crewmen and fifty or more passengers. The narrowness of the keelboat permitted it to navigate more than the largest rivers, allowing its usage on such streams as the Congaree, Kentucky, Licking, and Wabash Rivers. Speeds downstream varied by currents, but upstream rates were much slower, usually less than 2 miles per hour. In that direction a keelboat crew considered a daily movement of 20 miles as an exceptional run.[26]

Notwithstanding the limitations of the keelboat or other primitive vessels, shippers reaped attractive cost advantages over road transport. Early in the nineteenth century land movements of goods per ton-mile cost about five times more than moving them upstream. And a staggering price differential existed for floating them downstream: a factor of about twenty-four.[27]

However, anyone who made a trip on a flatboat, keelboat, or any type of craft took risks. Dangers infested the waterways: fast currents (especially after snow melts and spring rains), seasonal ice floes, eddies, whirlpools, snags, and floating debris. More so than keelboats, flatboats were difficult to control. "[Flatboats] can be managed only slowly and with difficulty, and are not, therefore, well adopted to avoid the obstacles which suddenly present themselves; they cannot at all contend with the current," noted a contemporary source. "Their pilots are seldom well acquainted with the habits of the river." Occasionally there was a human threat. "The outlawed criminals and the desperate adventurers from civilization stalked about the shores or prowled with light canoes among the bayous and creeks," commented an early student of river transport, "watching for chances to plunder, even if murder was necessary to aid them."[28]

At last the steamboat appeared. This vessel brought about a revolution in river transport, becoming the water equivalent of the railroad locomotive. After decades of experiments with steam engines in Britain, the United States, and elsewhere, a major breakthrough for their use on water occurred early in the nineteenth century. On August 17, 1807, a 150-foot-long vessel, unimaginatively named *Steam Boat,* the work of inventor Robert Fulton, churned its way up the Hudson River at the amazing rate of 5 miles per hour, much faster than any keelboat could battle a fast-moving current. And it was Fulton who was the first American to operate steamboats commercially. Quickly these boats appeared on major rivers, the Great Lakes, and coastal waters. A notable journey involved the Fulton steamboat *New Orleans,* which in October 1811 traveled from Pittsburgh, Pennsylvania, down the Ohio-Mississippi system to the Crescent City. More significant for steamboating in the trans-Allegheny West were trips made by the *Enterprise.* In 1815 this vessel made two round trips from Pittsburgh to Louisville and then proceeded from Pittsburgh to New Orleans, and returned under its own power.[29]

Soon the Steamboat Age became established. Within five years of the travels of the *Enterprise,* the Ohio-Mississippi network saw an ever-increasing number of steamers – seventeen were in operation on western waters by 1816 – and by the 1830s hundreds of these vessels appeared on navigable waterways. On the Tennessee River, for example, high waters during the spring of 1828 allowed the *Atlas* to move past the various obstacles, including the dangerous currents near Chattanooga, to become the first steamboat to dock in Knoxville. Its owners were greeted on their arrival "by a dinner and by speeches and honorably toasted," and they gladly accepted a cash prize from businessmen for their historic achievement. The clamor for more steamboats led to their widespread construction. By the mid-1820s sixty boats had been built in Cincinnati, and a decade later the total reached 164; boatyards in Louisville, Pittsburgh, and other river towns were busy as well. The rapid development and expansion of steamboating led to these exaggerated conclusions: "Steam navigation colonized the west! It furnished a motive for settlement and production by the hands of eastern men, because it brought the western territory nearer to the east by ninth tenths of the distance." Added this impressed observer, "It has advanced the career of national colonization and national production, at least a century!" He was right in that personal travel experiences improved, movement of freight accelerated, and transportation costs dropped.[30]

Steamboats found in the West and South differed significantly from their counterparts on eastern rivers, the Great Lakes, and the Atlantic and Gulf coasts. Most were stern-wheelers – not equipped with side-paddle wheels – and were propelled by lightweight, high-pressure engines whose compact boilers tolerated muddy river water. Unlike their larger brethren, western craft featured light-draft, flat hulls and drew only a few feet of water, making shallow-water operations possible or, as one wag suggested, giving them "the ability to navigate on a heavy dew." Yet that was hardly true. "The river Savannah is lower at this time [1828] than it has been since 1819," reported a South Carolina source, "so low, indeed, in some places below Augusta, that it is easily waded across. Steam-boat navigation is completely at a stand still – produce being almost altogether transported by pole boats, and their attendant lighters." Until mid-century these western and southern steamboats burned cordwood, but later they relied on coal, which eastern boats had long used.[31]

A trip by steamboat usually made for a comfortable journey. Some vessels, including those that operated on major western waters, provided impressive accommodations. Although the first deck housed the boiler, engine, and things mechanical and accommodated most of the cargo, the second deck of these multilayered boats offered a more pleasing environment, containing salons and staterooms. The furnishings of these public and private spaces might be opulent, with European carpeting, crystal chandeliers, and other eye-catching accessories. The main salon contained the dining room and frequently a bar and gambling tables, with the latter two commonly placed near the bow. The typical steamboat included a third level, appropriately called the hurricane deck since it was open to the elements. With only the presence of smokestacks and the elevated

pilot's house (and occasionally masts and sails to take advantage of favorable winds), the view from this part was largely unobstructed. In good weather passengers enjoyed a vantage spot to watch the passing scenery.[32]

"Bound Down the River," a lithograph by the famed firm of Currier & Ives, realistically depicts nineteenth-century river commerce, featuring the growing number of steamboats and showing the persistence of flatboats.

Courtesy of St. Louis Mercantile Library at the University of Missouri–St. Louis.

At times passengers grumbled about their steamboat journeys. For one thing, the hurricane deck was not the place for everyone. One traveler on the Ohio-Mississippi system strongly objected to "being covered with black sparks, or greased by some horrid invention in the neighborhood of the funnels." Some passengers fussed about the constant noise and vibrations. John C. Calhoun, U.S. senator from South Carolina, disliked the "tremor from the machinery, the puffing of the waste pipe," and the "endless thumping of the billets of wood on their way to the furnace." Others, though, found soothing the regular "paddle, paddle, puff" sounds of the steam engine. Complaints about sleeping accommodations, food, and other on-board services were hardly rare. The naturalist John James Audubon was not pleased with his trip in 1843 from Louisville to St. Louis. "A crazy, dirty little craft, which was provided with but twelve berths or sleeping shelves, furnished with scanty and dirty bedding. The food was detestable – salty meats, rancid butter, coffee and tea without milk."[33]

Nevertheless, a journey by steamboat was a "modern" experience. "The traveler could be cocooned completely; a protective, transportation environment encased him," suggested one scholar. "Many travelers knew the country not by what they saw, but by what they were told in the comfort of the steamboat salons."[34]

Steamboats hardly solved the challenges of antebellum transportation. While under normal conditions this waterborne transport moved with acceptable speeds and offered passengers accommodations superior to any other form of long-distance domestic travel, dangers lurked. Pilots had to wrestle with swift currents and eddies, treacherous shallows, shifting channels, submerged sandbars, sawyers, snags, and other obstructions. Writing in the 1820s, a commentator observed that "frequent delays from mishaps or shallowness of streams, the danger of wreck" hampered steamboat travel on South Carolina waters. And schedules could be erratic. In 1838 a Camden, South Carolina, newspaper reported that the steamboat *Thomas Salmond* made a "quick trip" from Camden to Charleston in sixty hours, but later it reported sarcastically: "Dispatch Extraordinary – A sensation produced by arrival here of Boyd's boat 'Belle' from Charleston in the unprecedented time of one hundred forty days on the trip." Traveling the Palmetto State's Santee and Wateree Rivers could be exceedingly slow or nearly impossible. Moreover, steamboats could sink, have their high-pressure boiler explode, or catch fire and burn to the waterline. Their somewhat fragile nature helps to account for the building of nearly six thousand steamboats from 1811 to 1880 in boatyards along the Ohio River. And rivers did not always flow in the most desirable direction. "If only the tenn. [*sic*] went as the crow flies from e. tenn. to Mobile or directly to the Miss," lamented a Knoxville, Tennessee, merchant. Water levels, whether high or low, regularly caused problems; vessels were always at the mercy of short- and long-term changes in stream volumes. Rivers might flood or evaporate. As an advocate for the proposed Louisville, Cincinnati & Charleston Rail Road reminded Kentucky lawmakers in 1839, "During the past summer, the unusual drought had reduced them [rivers] below the point of navigation, and as soon as the usual season arrived for the rains of the fall, a frost of peculiar severity has bound them in fetters of ice." The timing of these low-water periods usually coincided with the harvest season of the late summer, making streams unreliable for most craft, especially steamboats. Benjamin Franklin said it well: "Rivers are ungovernable things." Still there existed a plethora of useful waterways. Testified Frenchman Guillaume T. Poussin, in an 1836 commentary: "One of the most curious circumstances is, no doubt, the abundance of its [America's] vast and navigable rivers, its great bays, straits, and lakes, all of which contribute to a coherent interior navigation system incomparable to that of any other continent." Such commodities as bacon, beef, flour, lard, pork, rope and hemp, tobacco, and an assortment of manufactured products traveled by steamboat and other river craft.[35]

CANALS

A remarkably better form of land transport was the canal, or technically the "still water" canal. The concept of the post-Revolutionary-era canal came from outside the United States, in this case from England and several European countries, being an example of technology transfer from one continent to another. Even though not a home-grown transportation form, canals in America were the epitome of the modern. Enthusiasm (and building) occurred in two distinct waves, namely from the 1790s into the early years of the nineteenth century and then after the War of 1812, especially following the completion in 1825 of the 363-mile Erie Canal. The opening of "Clinton's Folly," which held the honor of being the longest manmade waterway in the world, proved to be anything but a folly; Governor DeWitt Clinton of New York sensed the value of this well-positioned artery. Some observers have described this New York State "ditch" as being "the most decisive event in the history of American transportation." Scholars may disagree, but there is consensus that this spectacularly successful canal accelerated the economic maturity of the Empire State, and in the process became the American "school of general engineering." No one would challenge the contention that the trans–New York waterway threw the nation into a spasm of canal fever. By 1850 this frenzy of construction had produced approximately 3,700 miles of "artificial rivers."[36]

The heartland of the canal came to be New York, the Mid-Atlantic states, and sections of the Old Northwest. Ohio, for one, became interlaced with hundreds of miles of these relatively shallow ditches, commonly supporting a width of 40 feet and a depth of 4 feet. In 1832 Lake Erie at Cleveland was joined with the Ohio River at West Portsmouth by the state-sponsored Ohio and Erie Canal, nearly as long as the prototype Erie Canal. Several lateral canals augmented this impressive 308-mile engineering feat. But this transportation triumph missed Cincinnati, the state's largest city. Nevertheless the canal facilitated trade throughout a large section of the Buckeye State and additional destinations, including New York City via Lake Erie, the Erie Canal, and the Hudson River. Yet civic boosters in the "Queen City of the West" were displeased with this Lake Erie to Ohio River artery; they wanted their "own" canals. And with state aid they got them. Sixty miles of the Miami and Erie Canal opened between Cincinnati and Dayton in 1829, although it took another two years to finish the lock complex that permitted canal boats to descend to the Ohio River. In 1845 the 160-mile Miami Extension Canal opened through western Ohio and tied into the Wabash and Erie Canal, a beneficiary of Indiana's 1836 $13 million internal improvements program and one of the longest canals in the world. At the Manhattan, Ohio, connection, the Miami waterway forged direct access to Toledo and Lake Erie, becoming the second trans-Ohio north-south waterway and a fitting capstone to canal mania in the Buckeye State.[37]

Cincinnati got still another waterway, the 21-mile Cincinnati and Whitewater Canal. Organized in 1837 and begun two years later, this publicly backed artery soon linked the Queen City to the Whitewater Canal, which by the late 1840s had penetrated Indiana for 76 miles from

Lawrenceburg on the Ohio River to Cambridge City on the National Road. Commercial interests in Cincinnati endorsed this Whitewater project; they wanted an alternative connection with the expanding network of Hoosier State canals and feared that Lawrenceburg might displace their city as the entrepôt for the growing commerce of southeastern Indiana.[38]

Construction of canals in the Old South, or for that matter below the Ohio and Potomac Rivers, paled in comparison with what had taken place in the Old Northwest. The central and southern Appalachians were found to be too rugged or too expensive to cross. Yet there were concerted efforts to do so. The premier project in the Southlands was the long-struggling James River and Kanawha Canal, successor to the late-eighteenth-century James River Company. The goal was to connect the James River tidewater with the Ohio River via the Kanawha River, creating a southern version of Pennsylvania's 322-mile, $15 million Main Line of Public Works (a mongrel system of canals, railroads, and inclined planes) and the less successful Chesapeake and Ohio Canal, a waterway that stalled at Cumberland, Maryland, 184 miles from Georgetown (District of Columbia) on the Potomac tidewater. Construction of the Virginia canal moved slowly at best. Work began about 1800, and with remarkable persistence this undercapitalized internal improvement reached Lynchburg, 146 miles from Richmond, in 1840, and eleven years later it was extended to Buchanan, making for a nearly 200-mile waterway with its ninety-eight locks and twenty-three dams. Until the outbreak of the Civil War work continued beyond Buchanan but only sporadically. "The James River and Kanawha Company received tepid legislative support [and failed as planned]," concluded historian John Majewski, "because it lacked a big city to champion its cause." Ultimately this ambitious public works project of the Old Dominion forged a mixed route to the Ohio River. Sixty miles of channel betterments along the Kanawha River to its mouth on the Ohio River at Point Pleasant together with 208 miles of improved turnpike roads over the mountains created a connection between ocean and river. Notably, secession killed any possibility of having a canal reach its intended destination. In 1861 a French-Belgian investment consortium backed out of its proposal to buy the waterway and finish it.[39]

South Carolina ranked second to Virginia in canal construction. Unlike the Old Dominion, the Palmetto State would not have a dominant artificial waterway. The pioneer Santee Canal was closest to the James River and Kanawha Canal, but far shorter. Agitation for a safe, direct water route to Charleston by connecting the Santee River (which entered the Atlantic Ocean about 50 miles north of the city) with the Cooper River started in 1786, although work did not begin for another six years. When completed in 1800 the 22-mile project bolstered the Charleston economy, allowing upcountry planters better access to the city and its port for their cotton and foodstuffs, and providing an avenue for Charleston merchants to transport their goods to upcountry customers. The project, though, revealed the difficulties of the new canal-building technology with needs for everything from excavation equipment to water-tolerable mortar, taking years for the refinements to be achieved.[40]

The strategy of canal enthusiasts in South Carolina involved mostly river improvements with the installation of several state-sponsored short canals to allow watercraft to pass major impediments, usually found at the fall-lines of the several ocean-flowing streams. The most useful portage, the Columbia Canal (also called the Saluda Canal), dated from the early 1820s and linked the Congaree River below Columbia with the Broad and Saluda Rivers above the city. Measuring 6.5 miles in length and having limited lockage, the Columbia Canal became the most heavily utilized (and successful) of all canals in the state.[41]

Before the triumph of the railroad, additional canals dotted the Southern landscape. In Georgia the 15-mile Savannah and Ogeechee Canal by 1830 linked the navigable Savannah and Ogeechee Rivers, but the coming of the iron horse ended efforts for an extension to the Altamaha River. North Carolina claimed the 9-mile Roanoke Canal, completed in 1831, allowing commercial boat traffic to bypass the falls of the Roanoke River at Weldon. And there was the 20-mile Dismal Swamp Canal, a deep "ship" canal that tied Elizabeth City, North Carolina, located on the Pasquotank River, with Norfolk, Virginia, on the south bank of the Elizabeth River.[42]

Still there were truly grandiose plans for canals south of the Ohio River. As early as 1808 Albert Gallatin proposed, in his much discussed (and often rancorously debated) *Report of the Secretary of the Treasury on the Subject of Roads and Canals,* artificial waterways extending from the Tennessee River through Georgia to the Atlantic Ocean. If completed this massive waterborne transport undertaking would have been the Erie Canal of the South. Later proponents of long-distance canals, which would span the southern Appalachians, claimed the customary advantages, including the advancement of agriculture and other commercial pursuits. Greater utilization became a recurring theme. Canals in the Southlands would be shut down for "only about thirty days in each year," being dramatically different from the Erie Canal, Ohio and Erie Canal, and other waterways in northern climes where winter ice closed commerce for extended periods. From 1840 to 1848, for example, no cold weather–related service interruptions occurred on the James River and Kanawha Canal except for twelve days in 1845.[43]

Canals offered distinct advantages. These watercourses (perhaps in conjunction with slack-water canals and river improvements) appeared to be sensible solutions to the conundrum of how to reach distant markets cheaply, reliably and safely, especially for freight. Large quantities of goods, including some of the heaviest, could be shipped at prices well below what teamsters charged; antebellum freight rates usually ranged from fifteen to twenty-five cents a ton-mile by wagon, but five cents or less by canal boat. At the beginning of the nineteenth century it was claimed that transporting a ton of goods 30 miles into the interior of the country cost almost as much as sending the same shipment to England. Early on, nearly every canal offered regular passenger service, with passenger packets and freight boats that might accommodate fare-paying riders. These travelers universally welcomed a smooth, quiet ride, much different from what they could expect on a horse or in a wagon, carriage, or stagecoach. Canal boats moved at a steady pace of about 4 miles per hour, except during locking and other delays. And they could move day and night, a practice that was either impossible or risky on a trail or primitive road, although oil lamps and glass reflectors and better roadways might permit stagecoach travel during nighttime hours. Also canal boats at times operated on more frequent and more reliable schedules than stagecoaches, enhancing their conveyance and popularity. Mentioned, too, was that the removal of heavy freight wagons from public thoroughfares reduced expensive and time-consuming road repairs.[44]

The perceived value of canals went beyond the economic, comfortable, and convenient. A harbinger of what became a repeated argument used by advocates of a transmontane railroad between the Atlantic Ocean and the Ohio River involved the intangible of the republican mission. This meant uniting the nation, preserving freedom, and promoting human progress. On July 4, 1825, Thomas Ewing, a Lancaster, Ohio, politician, uttered such a theme when he spoke at the commencement of work on the Ohio and Erie Canal at the Licking Summit. "[This canal] will unite the East and the West, the North and the South, by identity of interest, by frequency of communication, and by all the ties that can connect human beings in the bonds of friendships and social intercourse." His patriotic rhetoric continued: "The union of the states will be as firm as the everlasting hills; and from this great epoch in our history, we may dismiss all fears of the dismember of the American republic." Canals then could do what the open waters of the Atlantic Ocean had done since colonial times, becoming the principal highway that linked the northern and southern colonies.[45]

But canals that served regions of the Old Northwest, Old South, or elsewhere were hardly ideal forms of transportation. Significantly, they were expensive to build and maintain, and they could not be constructed in certain terrains. Locks, aqueducts, dams, culverts, weirs, and occasional tunnels were costly; rodents and floods damaged or eroded banks, and raging waters carried away aqueducts, breached dams, and destroyed locks. Occasionally residents, especially farmers, objected to the nearby presence of feeder reservoirs, fearing outbreaks of deadly "fevers." Canals did not operate continuously, especially in the North. These waterways were also susceptible to problems caused by heavy rains and drought conditions, producing either too much water (and damage) to the infrastructure or too little to allow for the free movement of packets and boats. It was not unusual for a sudden cloudburst or some other act of nature to put stretches of canals out of service for weeks, even months, before repairs could be made. Congestion at locks might cause prolonged stoppages as well. And irresponsible behavior by "canal boys," lads who rode the horses or mules that pulled the boats, and by other canal workers might cause disruptions.[46]

A journey could become a living nightmare. As on steamboats, it might be crowds, crying babies, obnoxious children, vile males, and sickly travelers. It could be poor food and drink and close, uncomfortable, and dirty sleeping quarters. And the smell of animal effluvia wafting from the towpath bothered, even sickened, many. In the 1840s a passenger on the packet *Express Mail,* which operated on the Cincinnati and Whitewater Canal, did not savor his journey. "Some twenty of us are crowded into the small cabin and of all the miserable stenches from chewing, snuffing, smoking, spitting tobacco, we were ever compelled to witness, this is the nearest beyond the possibility of exaggeration. A good portion of the time, some one is sawing on an old fiddle, while others are whacking down their cards, amid the most horrible profanity imaginable." Much then could prevent a delightful trip.[47]

Still passage on a canal packet or boat often was a pleasant experience. "With a lively jerk as the horses fell into a trot, away we went, the cut-water throwing up the spray as we rounded the Penitentiary hill, and the passengers lingering on the deck to get a last look at the fair city of Richmond, lighted by the late rays of the setting sun," reminisced a passenger on the James River and Kanawha Canal. "As the shadows deepened, everybody went below. There was always a crowd in those days, but it was a crowd for the most part of our best people, and no one minded it. Everything seemed as cozy and comfortable as heart could wish. I brought to the table – an excellent one it was, – a school boy's appetite, sharpened by travel, and thought it was 'just splendid.'"[48]

A BETTER TRANSPORTATION TOMORROW

By the dawn of the Railway Age the overall quality of transportation in the Old South and the Old Northwest remained poor. *If* the steam railroad had not made its debut until later in the nineteenth century, a combination of reliable roads, improved rivers, and additional canals could have shattered more of the isolation that plagued these regions. Some physical barriers could not have been easily overcome or compression of distances readily achieved. There also existed opposition from the federal government (and from other sources, too) for financing most major projects. Politically powerful "strict constructionists" had an aversion to public debt and a suspicion of centralized authority. President Andrew Jackson angered internal improvement advocates when he vetoed the Maysville Road (Kentucky) bill in 1830 and squelched the proposed "National Turnpike to New Orleans," a wagon road between Washington, D.C., and the Louisiana entrepôt. His actions and those of fellow Jacksonians who railed against Washington involvement placed the burden on state and local governments and the private sector for most betterments.[49]

Fortunately, a new day for individuals starved for better transportation was about to dawn. Railroads, more so than canals, could supplement nature's passageways or surmount its limitations. The remarkable steam-propelled railroad could operate almost everywhere and in nearly any kind of weather and at speeds much faster than alternative forms of transport. Before the advent of the iron horse travelers could move no more rapidly or more efficiently than those who had traversed the roads of ancient Rome or the canals of imperial China. Moreover the railroad could run on regular schedules, function with relative safety, and carry equipment tailored to the needs of its customers. For even the casual observer the difference in transportation technologies offered a sharp, vivid contrast: the slow-moving mule on a towpath and the smoke-belching iron horse on a set of iron rails. Simply stated: railroads offered an amazingly attractive alternative to all existing forms of transport.

Railroads also brought about a redirection of freight and passenger traffic in much of America from a predominately north-south orientation to an east-west routing. Still, a strong desire to unite North and South appeared at the start of the remarkable Railway Age, and it persisted long after the Civil War.

A Rail Road?

2

BEGINNINGS

No one knows the exact origin or date of the first railroad.[1] It is probable that in the sixteenth, seventeenth, and eighteenth centuries mechanics and tinkerers in Great Britain and on the continent, especially in the German states, made the earliest developments. "Its invention, like most other valuable inventions of the present day [1829]," as an early student of railroads opined, "is the result of gradual improvement." Fortunately, a free-flowing transfer of technology from the Old to the New World laid the foundation for the most significant invention in the development of modern society: the railroad. It mobilized, drove, and advanced the Industrial Revolution. During the Railway Age observers of the American scene likely agreed that the railroad seemed ideally suited for what Alexis de Tocqueville, that perceptive French visitor in the 1830s, called the "restless temper" found in the sprawling republic.[2]

Although it is impossible to date the "first" railroad, it is known that activities in Great Britain by the mid-1700s had led to the construction of widely scattered private "plateways," "tramways," or "waggonways" that served collieries and slate and stone quarries in England, Scotland, and Wales. These primitive affairs fit the standard definition of a railroad: an overland right-of-way with a fixed path consisting of paired wooden rails that are elevated to support self-guided vehicles on flanged wooden wheels (wheels with projecting rims or collars). For more than two centuries an assortment of Lilliputian carriers used animals (horses, ponies, mules, and oxen), gravity, human traction, and occasionally wind to propel these cars to a nearby river, canal, or tidewater port. These bulky cargoes then moved wholly or in part by water transport to their final destinations.[3]

Just as it is not possible to date initial tramway operations in Britain or elsewhere, it is hard to pinpoint when and where the first railroad appeared on American soil. A good candidate for that honor would be the

Beacon Hill Railroad (BHR) in Boston, Massachusetts, one of approximately twenty-five "wooden rail-roads" that dotted the eastern seaboard prior to the 1830s. In 1805 this pygmy pike, which consisted of about one-fifth of a mile of track, began to shunt cars filled with dirt and rock so that a real estate development company could pare down historic Beacon Hill to fill in nearby tidal marshes. In reality the BHR was a contractor's railway designed for heavy "cut-and-fill" work, replicating what some British builders had installed to facilitate work on bridges, lighthouses, and tunnels. Although details about the short-lived BHR are scarce, at least one commentary exists: "There was a Rail Road running in a southwesterly direction from the top of the hill. It struck Cedar Street a little to the South of Mt. Vernon Street, and struck Charles Street on the east side." Added the brief narrative: "It was used with a large pulley at the top fastened to each set of cars, and one set of cars went up while the other went down, both being attached together. There were branch rails at the top and the bottom. It would be difficult to say how many men and teams there were."[4]

More is known about another Massachusetts wooden tramway, the Granite Railway (GR), sometimes called the Quincy Rail Road or the Quincy Granite Rail Road. In 1823 a patriotic organization, formed to honor the fiftieth anniversary of the Battle of Bunker Hill of June 17, 1775, decided to erect a gigantic 220-foot granite (syenite) obelisk on neighboring Breed's Hill in the Charleston section of Boston. In order to transport materials to the work site, the initial strategy was to load stone at a quarry in West Quincy and haul it overland by wagon the three miles to the Neponset River for placement on barges for movement to Charleston Harbor. On March 4, 1826, the General Court of Massachusetts granted a charter to organizers of the GR for conducting "general transportation," although stone blocks would be the sole commodity transported. This document holds significance, attesting to the founding of the first railroad to be constructed under a state charter and hence supporting the claim that the GR was the "first railroad in America." Later in 1826 this 3-mile wooden tramway, which had cost about $11,000 per mile, opened between the quarry and the river and functioned as its backers had intended. For the next quarter century the GR made modest updates and continued to provide a practical means to haul stone for area building projects. Throughout its existence a combination of horses and gravity (the latter aided by chains and ropes) provided locomotion; steam never came to the little carrier. The company's wooden cars on their iron wheels rumbled over wooden rails with iron bar caps ["strap rail"], which measured 2.5" × 0.625", that workers had fastened to a "continuous foundation of granite bocks [which rested] on a base of dry stonework." The GR possessed a lightly graded right-of-way, having several sections with different inclinations to manage the hilly terrain.[5]

Commentators praised the early operations of the Granite Railway. In January 1829 William Jackson, a member of the Massachusetts Charitable Mechanics Association, told colleagues that "the construction, uses and advantages of the Quincy Rail Road, I presume, are familiar to most of those who hear me." He noted that "the cars upon this road carry from four to five tons. Two cars are considered as a load for one horse, traveling at the rate of 3 miles an hour. This is for continued operations through the day. If the horse, however, is put to its utmost capacity, such as is frequently the case with the truck horses of this city [Boston], he can carry double this load." Concluded Jackson, "Many apprehensions were entertained that our severe frosts and deep snows would injure and obstruct its operations. But the frosts have done no harm to the road, nor has the snow." And he made this apt observation: "The success of this Rail Road is fortunate, not only because it accomplishes the object for which it was designed, but because it serves to give confidence to calculation for other and more extensive roads."[6]

The importance of the GR continued to be recognized. "This unique project first demonstrated in America the engineering advantages of rail transport," observed the American Society of Civil Engineers later in the century, "and introduced many technical features, such as switches, the turntable and double-truck railway cars." The long-term experiences of the British with wooden railways and the triumph of the Beacon Hill Railroad contributed to the success of the GR.[7]

When it came to wooden railways, the Mason-Dixon Line was no demarcation. Although primitive tramways sprang up in Massachusetts and other parts of the North, they also existed in the South. A noteworthy installation, the Falling Creek Rail Road (FCR), appeared in the Richmond, Virginia, area and likely was the first American railroad to haul hazardous materials and the first to provide a passenger service.[8]

To serve the new Brown, Page, and Burr gunpowder facility on Falling Creek south of Richmond, its owners about 1810 constructed the Falling Creek Rail Road. Built of wood and powered by a gravity and rope return system, this tramway extended for about a mile between the gunpowder mill and the powder magazine, structures that needed to be physically separated because of the threat of a catastrophic explosion. The most impressive feature of the FCR was an "immense trestle about 75 feet high" that crossed a valley that stretched for nearly a quarter of a mile. Although an explosion destroyed the mill and stopped powder production in 1819, the wooden railway remained. Former mill hands in the neighborhood ran it "for their own amusement making excursions on the road." In time a deteriorating superstructure ended these casual passenger operations. Nevertheless, the FCR and others like it revealed the practical advantages of having a railroad, even in its most primitive form.[9]

Additional wooden railways were considered, but most remained "paper" entities. At least one was suggested in the Carolinas. In 1820 a "timber" railroad was proposed to link the Cape Fear River in North Carolina with the Greater Pee Dee River in South Carolina, "because a canal between the two streams was impracticable." No construction occurred on what would have been an amazingly long wooden road.[10]

INFANT STEAM

Development of the steam locomotive closely resembles that of the latter-day automobile in the complexities associated with its origins and formative years. Experiments with steam-powered transport long predated the debut of George Stephenson's historic *Locomotion No. 1,* a remarkable piece of machinery that on September 27, 1825, chugged over the rails of the 26-mile Stockton & Darlington Railway (S&D) in the English Midlands. From the mid-eighteenth century onward inventors throughout Britain had built experimental steam carriages to operate on public roads, but alas they were nearly universal failures. A more successful steam conveyance, a "driving carriage," made its debut at the dawn of the nineteenth century, being the handiwork of mining engineer Richard Trevithick, whom fellow Cornishmen affectionately called "Captain Dick." But following an impressive road trial this 5-ton contraption caught fire in its shed and was destroyed. Thereafter the intrepid Trevithick turned his mechanical skills to his "traveling engine," which he designed to run on rails. In February 1804 this machine, distinguished by its massive flywheel, was tested on a tramway owned by the Pen-y-Darren Ironworks near Merthyr Tydfil, Wales, and it made an impressive showing. The remarkable steam engine propelled a train of five cars loaded with 10 tons of pig iron and seventy people for 9 miles at speeds of up to 5 miles an hour. The obvious shortcoming of this experimental trip involved the heavy damage done to the light track structure of iron rails on stone blocks. Still Trevithick had accomplished much. "It proved conclusively that a smooth wheel could grip a smooth rail with the adhesion needed to haul a load," noted a student of early British railways. "It also demonstrated mechanical power in a compact and portable form."[11]

Although Trevithick continued to experiment with steam-powered locomotives, he drifted away from the invention of the age, focusing on high-pressure stationary engines. What is also noteworthy about this inventive genius was his impact on other individuals who shared his passion for steam, including William Hedley, George Stephenson, and William Symington. Trevithick's advances prompted these men to forge ahead, solidifying the claim that Britain was the cradle of railroad and locomotive technology.[12]

The brightest stars in development of what became the revolutionary steam locomotive were George Stephenson and his son Robert. In the mid-1820s it would be the Stephenson genius that made the Stockton & Darlington a resounding success and the carrier that became the transition between the wooden, animal-powered tramway and the general-purpose steam-operated railroad. Their Stephenson and Company of Newcastle produced the pioneer motive power for the S&D. "Inventor of Railways," George Stephenson was not, but he was the "Father of Railways." Importantly, both men believed that railroads would become the transportation of the future, serving as common carriers and not just as private avenues to haul coal, stone, and other bulk commodities.[13]

The Stockton & Darlington triumph led to the Stephensons winning the right to command a much larger project, the 35-mile Liverpool & Manchester Railway (L&M), a private corporation chartered in 1826. This first-ever intercity passenger carrier, which opened in 1830, became the prototype for the modern railroad. Moreover, it competed with, not supplemented, the existing canals and turnpikes. Yet railways in Great Britain came to be strikingly different from their counterparts in the New World. The L&M and subsequent British roads benefited from being heavily engineered. Low grades, wide curves, and bridges, tunnels, and viaducts characterized these lines as they crossed an undulating landscape.

The Stephensons did more than shape the L&M, which opened with a gala ceremony on September 15, 1830; they sought to perfect a much better locomotive. This they did. At the famed Rainhill trials, which stretched over a seven-day period in October 1829 on a section of straight and level track 9 miles east of Liverpool, the Stephensons demonstrated the high performance of their *Rocket* locomotive. This machine reached the blistering speed of 30 miles per hour and eclipsed its three steam competitors: *Novelty, Perseverance* and *Sans Pareil.* A fourth locomotive, the *Cycloped,* which performed poorly, was a bizarre horse-treadmill contraption. It would be the *Rocket,* with its 0-2-2 type wheel arrangement, horizontal, multitubular boiler, and steam cylinders directly connected to the driving wheels, that took the coveted prize of 500 pounds sterling. This model for the modern steam locomotive paved the way for a wide range of motive power that appeared during the all-important Demonstration Period of the 1830s and 1840s in transportation-hungry Britain, Europe, and the United States. By 1831 the Stephenson company had supplied the L&M with seventeen good-performing locomotives. When the senior Stephenson predicted before his S&D and L&M achievements that "I will do something in coming time which will astonish all England!" he hardly understated his intentions. He hit the mark again when he subsequently prophesied that railroads "will become the great highway for the King and all his subjects."[14]

In time residents of Britain and elsewhere realized the contributions made to the world of transportation by Stephenson and his fellow countrymen. A sense of national pride spread through the kingdom. Appropriately, British historian George Macaulay Trevelyan considered railroads "England's gift to the world." Knowing individuals willingly accepted this interpretation.[15]

DEBUT OF AMERICAN STEAM

At the same time Americans were tinkering with primitive steam-powered railways. The most widely publicized activities were associated with John Stevens, a wealthy, well-educated resident of Hoboken, New Jersey. When it came to transportation, Stevens was first involved with steamboats, including his triumphant *Phoenix* that in 1809 plied the waters between Hoboken and Philadelphia. Then he turned to railroads, publishing a tract in 1811 called *Documents to Prove the Superior Advantages of Railway and Steam Carriages over Canal Navigation.* Stevens did more. In 1825 he built a circular wooden track on his rambling Hoboken estate, Castle Point, and ran a 16-foot "steam wagon" of his design; the conveyance worked reasonably well. Stevens might claim that he operated the first steam locomotive ever to run on rails in America, although other demonstration steam railways appeared during the 1820s. Even though the Stevens experiment was little more than a toy, it pointed the way to far bigger things. The "prehistory" of railroads in America was about to end.[16]

During the late 1820s and early 1830s small demonstration railroads caught the public's attention. Entrepreneurial individuals traveled about to show off their miniature trains and to make money in the process. "The ladies and gentlemen of Camden [South Carolina] and its vicinity are respectfully informed that a circular railroad will be laid down in the old Methodist Church," reported the *Camden Journal* of January 29, 1831, "giving the public a specimen of the Liverpool & Manchester Rail Road, England, on which a steam engine will be placed and put in operation by steam and draws a splendid car." The cost for a ride: "50 cents; children, half price."

It is certain when the first commercial steam locomotive took to American rails, and a canal company was responsible. In 1823 the privately operated Delaware and Hudson Canal Company (D&HCCO) received charter rights from the states of Pennsylvania and New York to provide a practical and economical way to transport anthracite coal from mines in northeastern Pennsylvania to emerging markets, particularly in New York City. After struggling for several years the D&HCCO in 1828 opened a 108-mile waterway from near the Hudson River at Eddyville (up Rondout Creek), New York, through Port Jervis to Honesdale, Pennsylvania.

This construction won acclaim for its two massive stone aqueducts over the Delaware River. Unfortunately the terminus at Honesdale was not suited for coal transport. The artery needed to reach mine sites at Carbondale, Pennsylvania, but the barrier of the local Moosic Mountains, which reached more than 2,000 feet in height, made that impractical.[17]

A railroad, though, could provide access. The owners and advisors agreed that a 16-mile line made sense, and they gambled on steam locomotive technology. Production by Robert Stephenson and Company had substantially increased, including eight locomotives being built in 1828 and 1829, and so the company turned to this experienced manufacturer. The D&HCCO agreed to buy a Stephenson locomotive, the *Pride of Newcastle* (sometimes called the *America*) and also the *Stourbridge Lion,* a product of Stephenson competitor Foster, Rastrick, and Company of Stourbridge, England. Although details are sketchy, the *Pride of Newcastle,* which on January 15, 1829, was the first engine to reach American shores, apparently never operated. Four months later the *Stourbridge Lion* landed at the Port of New York and soon reached the canal's rail line. Immediately testing was underway, and the results were long remembered. "The locomotive, having no train behind it, answered at once to the movement of the hand, and there being no doubt as to the result, a motion was had at once in which there was not any evidence of distrust," recalled the man at the throttle, Horatio Allen, civil engineer and former associate of the D&HCCO's chief engineer John B. Jervis. "Soon the straight line was run over, the curve was reached and passed before there was time to think as to its not being passed safely, and soon I was out of sight in the three miles' ride alone into the woods of Pennsylvania." It would be Allen who had faith in the rapid advancement of iron horse technology. As he wrote in 1828, "I am fully of the opinion too that the present Locomotive Engine is an imperfect machine compared with what it will be 10 or 12 years hence."[18]

Although Allen had made a successful first run, *Stourbridge Lion* proved too heavy for the flimsy strap iron that capped the wooden rails and the lightly built viaducts of green hemlock; it never entered revenue service on the D&HCCO. The company had badly miscalculated the burden of the British-built "walking beam" locomotive, underestimating the weight by a goodly percentage. The alternative for the D&HCCO was to rebuild the track structure, emulating lines in Britain, but the price tag was too high and the time was thought to be too long. Management wanted to tap immediately the lucrative New York City coal market. All was not lost, however. Later the boiler of the *Stourbridge Lion* was utilized as a source for stationary steam power. Fortunately for investors the coal railway – known for years as the Gravity Rail Road – with several upgrades to its physical plant, functioned with impressive profitably, relying on gravity and teams of ponies for propulsion. No power changes occurred until late in the nineteenth century.[19]

"THIS GREAT AND PUBLIC SPIRITED UNDERTAKING"[20]

Disappointment with the *Stourbridge Lion* on the railroad division of the Delaware & Hudson Canal Company did not dim American interest in the novel technology. Neither did it lead to lengthy delays in placing steam locomotives on American rails. Within an amazingly short period – by December 1830 – a steam-powered common carrier, the South-Carolina Canal & Rail-Road Company (SCC&RRCO), informally called the Charleston and Hamburg, Charleston and Augusta, or South Carolina Railroad, began to serve the immediate Charleston vicinity, and this fledgling Palmetto State road expanded rapidly.[21]

Historian James Dilts has identified the Baltimore & Ohio Railroad (B&O) as "the nation's first railroad," but this pioneer carrier relied on horses, not steam, for its initial motive power. Launched in 1827 and designed to link Baltimore with the Ohio River, the B&O opened in sections, although modestly at first, and would not reach its Wheeling, Virginia, destination until 1853. Nevertheless Baltimoreans, who bet on railroad technology, took pride in their gestating project. This was especially so when on New Year's Day 1830 a horse-drawn car took company directors over a short stretch of the newly completed standard gauge (4 feet, 8.5 inch) line between Pratt Street, Baltimore, and the Carrollton Viaduct. A week later the road opened a mile and a half of track to the public, and by May welcomed travelers and shippers to the 14-mile section between Baltimore and Ellicott's Mills, a flour-milling village nestled in a gorge of the Patapsco River. These were small steps, but commercial interests held high hopes that the Maryland metropolis could compete with East Coast rivals for the trade with the West. Most knowledgeable citizens did not believe that a canal – even the projected Chesapeake and Ohio Canal – could achieve such ends. "*Depend upon it you will never see a canal between this city and the Ohio River*" (italics in original), proclaimed a contributor to a Baltimore newspaper in early 1827. "You must look for some more permanent mode of intercourse; that mode must be a *rail road,* with locomotive and stationary engines, inclined planes, etc."[22]

The South-Carolina Canal & Rail-Road Company also came into being in 1827, although it received a revised charter a year later. Paralleling the motivations of the B&O, sponsors of the SCC&RRCO, predominantly members of the Charleston business elite led by merchant Alexander Black, who chaired the Chamber of Commerce Special Committee on Rail Roads, sought to strengthen the city's weakening economic position. Unlike supporters of the Baltimore project, the Charlestonians were not fully committed to a fledgling railroad technology. The charter granted by the General Assembly authorized "a Rail Road or a Canal, or a Rail Road and Canal from the city of Charleston, on the most practicable routes, to each of the towns of Columbia, Camden and Hamburg."[23]

The technology of railroading, notwithstanding the publicized success of the Stockton & Darlington, remained experimental and uncertain, but looked promising. Unlike what the B&O faced, construction of a trans-state railroad to Hamburg (nee Fort Moore), a settlement opposite Augusta, Georgia, on the fall-line of the Savannah River, could be made over comparatively level terrain. The descent into the valley of the Savannah River, however, would be a challenge, as would be the swamps and marshes that dotted much of the South Carolina Low Country. Fortunately, only one major river, the Edisto, needed to be bridged if the line left Charleston between the Ashley and Cooper Rivers. Extensions to either Columbia or Camden were also authorized, although crossing the Congaree River would be expensive, and the line would traverse some rough country.[24]

The motivation of Charlestonians was clear: stiff business competition affected their seaport city. Where Baltimore felt the sting of rivalry from New York and Philadelphia and wished to alter existing trade patterns, Charleston needed to battle a thriving Savannah, which benefited from being near the mouth of the extensive Savannah River drainage system. Luckily for Charlestonians the North Carolina ports of Beaufort, New Bern, Morehead City, and Wilmington and those of Brunswick and Darien in Georgia posed far lesser commercial threats. "*Charleston will* and *must* be the great commercial mart of the surrounding states" (italics in original), pronounced the Charleston Chamber of Commerce on the eve of construction of the SCC&RRCO. "No local jealousies can interrupt her march to wealth. No rival competition impede her progress to her 'Destined Elevation,' if her citizens be but faithful to *their own interest* and seize with a becoming energy those advantages which *providence* has placed at their disposal, and cultivate those vast resources of trade which lay invitingly within their reach" (italics in original).[25]

Most Charlestonians strongly favored gaining the trade of the immediate hinterlands and therefore bolstering their local economy. Then there was that desire to break through the land confines to the Savannah River. Traffic, most of all cotton – "white gold" – could be snatched from points above Hamburg/Augusta and transported directly to Charleston, thus circumventing the 140 miles of riverway to Savannah. It seemed possible that a large share of the upcountry Georgia and South Carolina commerce could be captured. There was a pressing need to act; Charleston was in the doldrums or, as some believed, in a permanent state of decline. Yet Charleston had flourished in colonial times and into the early decades of the Republic. During the American Revolution the city was the leading southern port, and only Baltimore, Boston, New York, and Philadelphia were comparable in wealth and prestige. Toward the end of the 1810s, however, conditions deteriorated. A crude barometer of the economic well-being of Charleston comes from import duties collected at the port's custom house. In 1817 the amount totaled $1.6 million, but a year later revenues plunged to $738,000, and in 1819 they stood at only $549,000. No major up-ticks followed. Although the impact of the Panic of 1819 and decline in the fertility of area cotton lands contributed to the downturn, failure to bounce back as the national economy improved in the early 1820s was troubling. Just as revealing were statistics showing the value of domestic exports. In 1816 they totaled nearly $11 million, but following the panic they dropped noticeably, leveling out to about $7.5 million annually in the 1820s. And the population was stagnant, hovering around 25,000 inhabitants. "The present great depression of commerce and the enormous distress pervading almost every portion of the community," editorialized the *Charleston Courier* in 1827, "are daily becoming matters of deeper concern and higher consideration." A year later the newspaper reported that the Chamber of Commerce found no improvements in the general health of the city; in fact, conditions had worsened. "Charleston has for several years past retrograded with a rapidity unprecedented. Her landed estate has within eight years depreciated in value one half. Industry and business talent driven by necessity have sought employment elsewhere. Many of her houses are tenantless and the grass grows uninterrupted in some of her chief business streets." And the closing sentence: "This may be a melancholy picture, but is nevertheless true." The Charleston claim as the "Commercial Emporium of the South" might vanish forever.[26]

What could be done to jump-start Charleston's moribund economy and spur lasting growth? Residents and their supporters had long sought to enhance interior water transport. Their major accomplishments involved improvements to river navigation and construction of the Santee Canal. Collectively these expensive betterments helped trade. By the end of the 1820s South Carolina claimed that it had opened 1,200 miles of waterways to vessels of various sizes, including steamboats, and a similar mileage of in-river and canal transport for smaller craft. Then there was the lauded Santee Canal. As the Canal Era began, agitation developed for a still-water canal to link the Santee and Cooper rivers, providing Charleston direct, safe access to interior sections of the state. South Carolinians knew well that the Santee River route via the "Sea Island Passage" was fraught with coastal water dangers. Although the General Assembly in 1786 passed "An Act to Establish a Company for the Inland Navigation from Santee to Cooper River," extensive delays followed. Not until 1800 did the first boat pass through this 28-mile privately owned canal. The Santee proved to be somewhat of a disappointment, failing to transport the anticipated volume of goods. During the extreme droughts of 1816 and again in 1818 and 1819 water shortages shut down operations. Even so, later in the nineteenth century the federal government made this generalized, albeit flawed, statement: "The canal was opened to commerce in the year 1800 and operated with more or less success down to the year 1840."[27]

Charlestonians exhibited interest in additional canal and river improvement projects. One involved a 110-mile canal between their city and Columbia. Although a bill was introduced in the General Assembly in 1821 for such a waterway, it failed to garner much support, and the idea soon died. Probably existing and proposed river improvements killed the proposal. Later that decade there was talk, triggered by Robert Mills's *Statistics of South Carolina,* published in 1826, about a fanciful scheme to unite the Atlantic Ocean and the Ohio River through a combination of canals and river betterments. Mills believed that it was feasible to use the Green River, a branch of the Broad River (which becomes the Congaree River near Columbia and then the Santee), to reach the French Broad River in North Carolina. "The Green river extends to a point in the Blue ridge, where this mountain is very low and narrow; on the opposite side of the mountain rises the French Broad, a large branch of the Tennessee," wrote Mills. "It is confidently presumed that the Atlantic and western waters may be united here by a navigable canal with great comparative ease." Mills's thinking foreshadowed what would become agitation for a transmontane railroad along a similar route.[28]

It would be the railroad option that helped Charlestonians realize their economic goals or, as some believed, at least reduced the rate of decline. This was something that the Mills canal scheme would have struggled to achieve. Just as the iron horse would benefit Baltimore and later Boston, the latter having no realistic chance of creating a direct water route to the Hudson River, Erie Canal, or Lake Ontario, other coastal cities by the 1850s came to rely on rail connections to penetrate the West. The large and daring investments made by Baltimoreans in the B&O and Bostonians in the Western Rail Road of Massachusetts turned out to be wisely placed.[29]

South Carolinians adopted the railroad, at times with a frantic intensity. And in the process there came the matter of choosing the propulsion. Interest in the steam locomotive dated from almost the official beginnings of the SCC&RRCO. Not only did a representative of the B&O attend the Railhill trials, as did Horatio Allen, later chief engineer for the SCC&RRCO, but Ezra Miller, a wealthy Charleston merchant, mechanical wizard, and SCC&RRCO director, also watched the *Rocket* strut its stuff. The South Carolina company wanted to know its options, including motive power, and Miller liked what he had seen in England. In fact, this Charlestonian later helped to design his road's first steam locomotive – namely the boiler – and to arrange its purchase.[30]

As the South-Carolina Canal & Rail-Road Company took shape across the Palmetto State, it did not become a canal in whole or in part, but rather a steam railroad. The thinking of Ezra Miller, a staunch advocate of external-combustion power, shaped that monumental decision, as did these cogent observations made by Horatio Allen: "There is no reason to expect any material improvement in the breed of horses, while, in my judgment the man is not living who knows what the breed of locomotives is to place at command." The future in the minds of Miller and Allen (and others, too) belonged to the mechanical horse, not the fleshy kind. Yet some conservative backers thought that horse power would be preferable, a safer option to steam. Railroads admittedly remained experimental, and their dependability and capacity to manage stiff grades was yet unproven.[31]

Although some Charlestonians and other South Carolinians felt an uneasiness about the steam locomotive and believed that the Savannah River could be reached by a canal or a combination of canal and railroad, the principal survey in the late 1820s, directed by Horatio Allen and partially financed by the federal government under terms of the General Survey Act of 1824, became one that was designed for a railroad. Fortunately, there existed a dry ridge that extended more than 90 miles between the Edisto River and the western portion of the state, permitting an easy grade, or what railroaders would later call an "air-line" route. And this topography facilitated the rapid construction of much of the trans-state road. Problems, though, remained: negotiating the Savannah River valley and finding an entrance to the boat landing at Hamburg.[32]

As with the vast majority of railroad proposals over the course of nearly a century, debate erupted about the best path or paths the iron horse should follow. As early as 1828 there was support for a branch that would connect the main line with the Santee River. This trackage, its advocates believed, would divert traffic from the Santee Canal to Charleston, providing shippers faster, better, and cheaper service. "It gives an outlet to market, for the produce of all the country watered by the tributary streams of the Santee; and the mountain boats can deliver their cargoes upon your rail-way." Backers of the SCC&RRCO wisely concentrated on the main stem, although its charter allowed extensions to Columbia and Camden, appendages that later would be built.[33]

Even with the chosen course and not one that geography would dramatically hinder, right-of-way adjustments became necessary. Some desired property was unavailable or too expensive, but donated or inexpensive real estate provided workable options. A few land owners objected to having a railroad in their neighborhoods, complaining about danger and noise of the proverbial machine in the garden. "Engines would run over and kill the little negro slaves," warned a cotton planter from the Barnwell District, "also that the noise of the trains, such as the blowing of whistles and ringing of bells would seriously disturb the quiet and repose of the citizens and under no circumstances would such a nuisance be tolerated by a respectable community." What the Barnwell District resident did not say – but a worry to slave owners – was that a railroad might tempt their human property to take the "cars" and flee to freedom.[34]

With land problems solvable, the SCC&RRCO began construction and the selection of cutting-edge motive power. The locomotive that pulled the earliest trains, the *Best Friend of Charleston* (or sometimes called the *Rocket of America*), had the honor of being the first American-constructed steam locomotive employed in regular commercial service. Its very name symbolized the hopes of Charleston and South Carolina. Admittedly, the B&O rightly claimed the first iron horse, the *Tom Thumb* (not so named at the time), an experimental steamer built by the wealthy New York manufacturer Peter Cooper that ran briefly in August 1830. Yet the *Tom Thumb* was hardly comparable to the SCC&RRCO locomotive.[35]

Instead of being a product of British manufacture, the *Best Friend of Charleston* was the handiwork of a domestic company, the West Point Foundry Association. The owners of this small New York City machine shop realized that railroads were taking hold with amazing speed and doubted if Britain could satisfy demand. An expanding market was developing, and the West Point Foundry was prepared to respond. Already the firm had similar product lines, including boilers and other heavy metal fabrications, and easily made the transition to steam locomotives. The actions taken by the West Point Foundry showed that American ingenuity was equal to any revealed by the British.[36]

The *Best Friend* was small and simple. This 4-ton locomotive offered the most elementary steam locomotive wheel arrangement, having a 0-4-0 design.[37] However, by the end of the 1830s this configuration would be abandoned, except for engines constructed for switching duties. Instead builders embraced the 2-4-0 and the soon enormously popular 4-4-0 or "American Standard" styles, which provided greater pulling power and better handling over flimsy, curvy, and steep track structures. The American railroad infrastructure continued to be known for its low capital input. With its vertical boiler, dual-angled cylinders, and direct inside connections to the wheels, the *Best Friend* possessed innovative design features. It was a "cab-in-front" locomotive, giving the engineer excellent

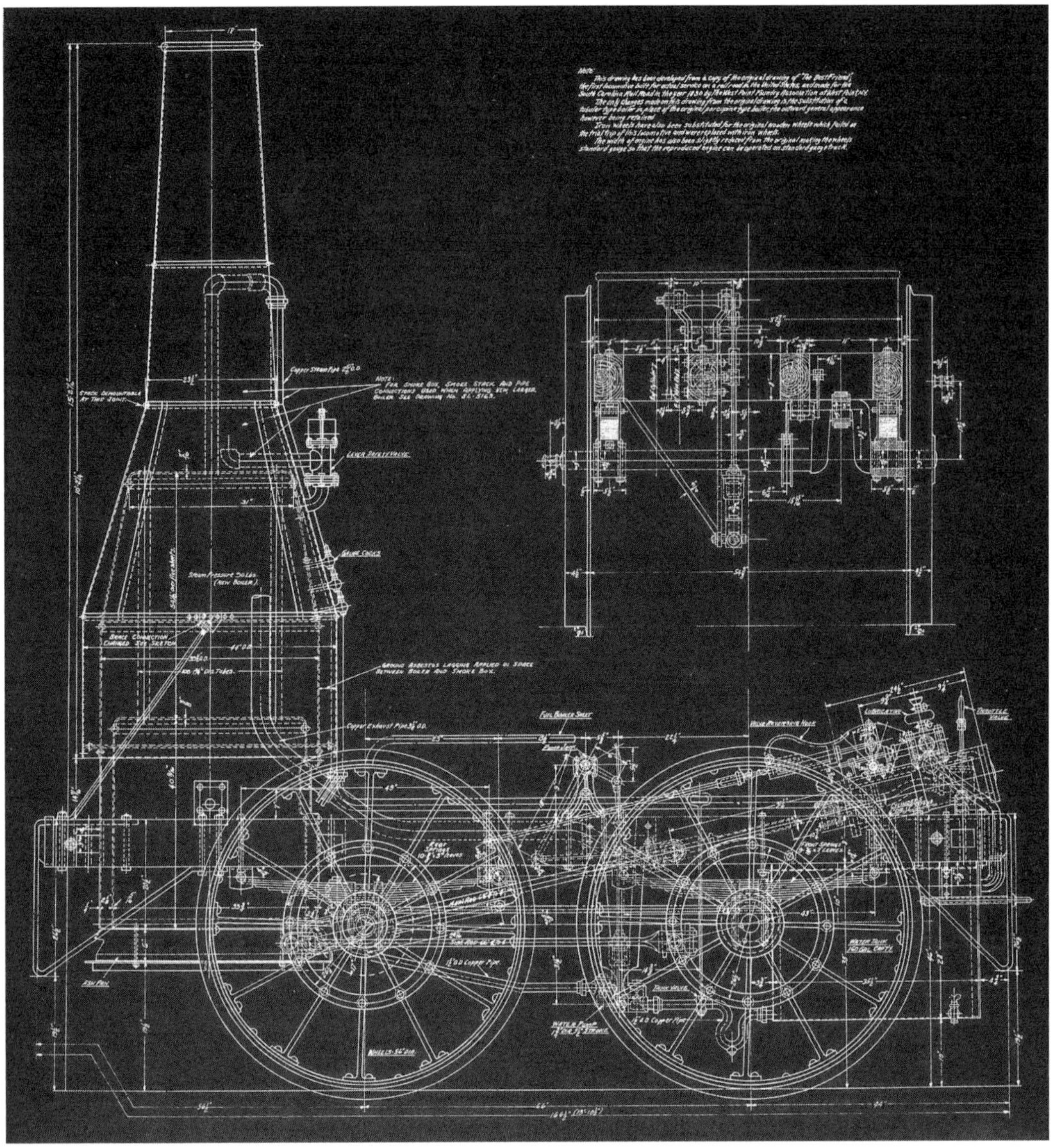

visibility of the right-of-way, even though he lacked an enclosed cab, while the fireman worked at the rear of the locomotive. The *Best Friend* was also a "tank engine," featuring an onboard supply of water that sported a feedwater heater. The placement of these components balanced the upright boiler.[38]

The *Best Friend* claimed another distinction. On Christmas Day 1830 this unique piece of motive power, which had arrived in Charleston in late October, became the first steam locomotive to power a regularly scheduled passenger train on American rails. (On a trial run that previous August the tiny *Tom Thumb,* weighing less than one ton, had pulled a passenger carriage over the 13-mile B&O.) The West Point product performed well. The trip of approximately 6 miles handled 141 riders, and hundreds more watched at trackside. The *Charleston Courier* excitedly reported that the train "flew on the wings of the wind at the speed of fifteen to twenty-five miles per hour, annihilating time and space leaving all the world behind."[39]

What became a hallmark of the SCC&RRCO, spearheaded by chief engineer Allen, and backed by other railroad proponents in South Carolina, was the willingness to take risks. Acquisition of the *Best Friend* had been a wise move, and this locomotive type seemed destined to meet foreseeable needs. In fact, the company soon acquired a companion locomotive, the *West Point.* But disaster struck on June 17, 1831, when the boiler of the *Best Friend* exploded. The fireman, a railroad-owned slave who did not understand the function of the safety valve and who reportedly found the sound of the escaping steam an annoyance, tied down the releasing device. This tragic mistake led to his eventual death. Although the boiler became so-much scrap metal, the running gears remained intact. Soon the locomotive was rebuilt with a replacement boiler and refinements, and the company appropriately named the restored machine the *Phoenix.*[40]

After the destruction of the *Best Friend* the pioneering SCC&RRCO became safety conscious. The company required that a flatcar or "barrier" car, filled with bales of cotton, be coupled behind all locomotives in passenger service. This operating procedure would hopefully protect riders from a boiler explosion, safeguarding them from scalding water and flying metal and other airborne debris. And the safety valve was moved beyond the reach of any person on the engine.[41]

Although a barrier car (later eliminated) and a repositioned safety value were minor advancements, the SCC&RRCO under the leadership of Horatio Allen showed remarkable creativity. Allen, who remained chief engineer until 1835, designed the *South Carolina,* an eight-wheeled articulated steam locomotive that entered service in February 1832, being the first of what would be four of these unusual West Point Foundry products. The boiler, according to locomotive expert John H. White Jr., "was made on a radical plan with two barrels at each end. A common firebox at the center provided a perch for the engineer. A single cylinder at each end mounted at the bottom of the smokebox was another highly original feature of Allen's design." Added White, "Allen's pioneering plan was for a very light style of engine which had a long wheelbase to spread the load for a weak track that could not sustain heavy axle loading. But the plan suffered from a bit too much inventiveness. The double enders proved a colossal failure. Most spent more time in the shop than out on the road." By 1838 the company had retired all of these bizarre iron horses and cannibalized various parts for other uses.[42]

Fortunately, the railroad saw its fleets of 0-4-0s and recently introduced 2-4-0s, built by the Stephenson and the American Mathias William

This detailed drawing of the 4.5-ton *Best Friend of Charleston* outwardly looks simple, yet it possesses a complex assortment of parts and physical arrangements. As with the earliest British-built engines, the *Best Friend* featured wooden wheels with cast-iron hubs and wooden spokes. In order to hold the wheel together, workers at the West Point Foundry added a thick wrought-iron band that they fitted tightly around the rim. They then installed a much heavier flanged tire over this band. By the standards of the early 1830s the *Best Friend* was a state-of-the-art steam locomotive. It took time before manufacturers could produce and machine heavy castings and fabricate large boiler plates.

Courtesy of Norfolk Southern Corporation.

The Southern Railway, which traced its corporate linage back to the South-Carolina Canal & Rail-Road Company, constructed a replica of the *Best Friend of Charleston*, tender, and two coaches. For decades the railroad displayed this historic train at fairs and other celebrations.

Courtesy of Norfolk Southern Corporation.

Baldwin companies, performing adequately and impressing the public with speeds that at times exceeded 25 miles an hour. The latter locomotive type was more powerful, and its tenders helped to provide better traction, allowing for higher speeds and greater pulling power. Also the tracking qualities of the 2-4-0s far surpassed those of the original locomotives.[43]

Since major, even radical, experimentation characterized the 1830s, it was hardly surprising that the SCC&RRCO did more than just innovate with its motive power. The railroad also did so with its track structure. Directors decided to fix its 5-foot gauge rails (which became the dominant width in the South) on a piled roadway, rather than installing them directly on a graded surface. This occurred for several reasons. Allen and his colleagues believed that costs would be lower, in part because of an ample supply of cheap or donated southern yellow pine. The argument also went that the expense of replacing decayed pilings would be less than that of replacing crossties that rotted on the ground. In no way did Allen or other American railroaders wish to embrace the British-style of construction – namely straight and level lines; they responded to the curvature of the terrain, building a railroad as cheaply as possible. Moreover, the South Carolina road needed to cross extensive wetlands along the eastern section of the projected route, and a piled roadway made sense. And pilings, it was thought, would produce a solid foundation, creating a "uniformity of surface" for train movements. Admittedly this "railroad-on-stilts" approach, not unknown to the railway world during the Demonstration

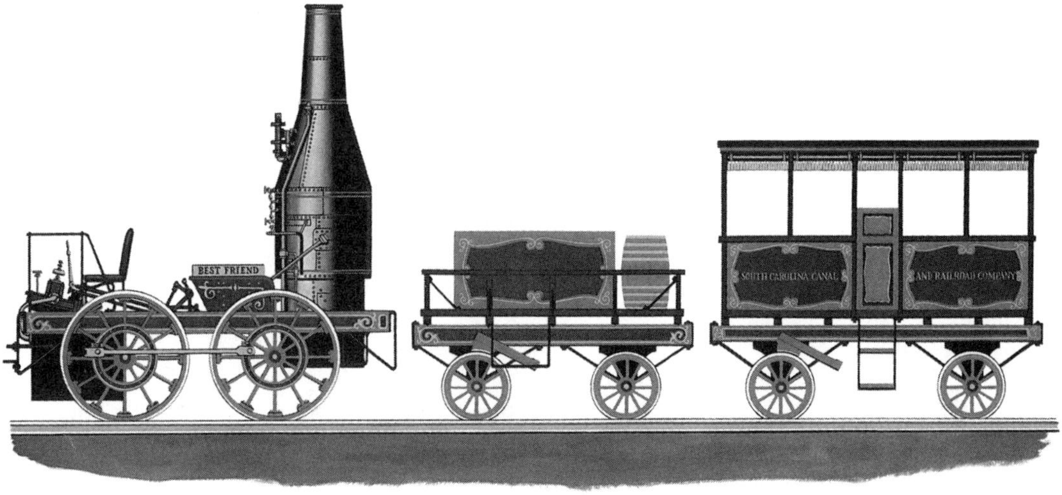

Best Friend of Charleston, 1830

Period, seemed logical and practical. In the case of the SCC&RRCO it was relatively inexpensive, according to the *American Railroad Journal,* "varying little from $5000 per mile."[44]

Lamentably the SCC&RRCO adopted a defective construction concept. Not long after the single-track road reached the banks of the Savannah River in autumn 1833, it became apparent that the piled roadway was wanting. Laborers had encountered difficulties driving the pilings, facing dangerous quicksand or seemingly impenetrable "hard pan" clay. Although the pine pilings possessed strength, they were subject to more-rapid-than-expected deterioration. It would take years before chemical preservatives became available that retarded the decay process. Also this wooden superstructure was vulnerable to fires. So the company, never flush with funds, started the expensive and time-consuming task of placing track on a graded roadbed. By late 1835 about 75 miles had been "embanked," an undertaking that continued until the end of the decade. Amazingly, the New-York & Erie Rail Road (Erie) embarked on a "rail-road-on-stilts" approach not long after the SCC&RRCO had demonstrated its impracticality. The company installed about 100 miles of this wooden superstructure through the Southern Tier counties of New York. In the process the Erie wasted nearly a million dollars. In another instance the 177-mile trans-state Ohio Rail Road also opted for a wooden superstructure. "Posts at least 10 inches in diameter are driven into the earth in 2 rows," noted an observer in the late 1830s. "Those in each row are 5 feet apart, center to center, and the distance between the 2 rows is 7 feet 4 inches." But before failing, this Buckeye State carrier installed about 100 miles of pilings and placed 29 miles of attached superstructure through

After having studied previous drawings, an artist created this rendition of the *Best Friend of Charleston* with its train, including a tender for cord wood and boiler water and a passenger car.

Courtesy of Norfolk Southern Corporation.

Following the boiler explosion on the *Best Friend of Charleston* in June 1831, mechanics and carpenters rebuilt the locomotive with significant refinements. The railroad appropriately named the locomotive the *Phoenix*.

Courtesy of Norfolk Southern Corporation.

the Black Swamp region between Fremont and the Maumee River near Toledo.[45]

By the mid-1830s the SCC&RRCO could not claim perfection, but with its improved steam motive power and revamped track structure it had solved two fundamental problems. The road continued to be hampered by the expense and bother of the steam-powered 3,800-foot-long inclined plane near Hamburg (later reduced in length and then eliminated in 1852). Although this installation performed adequately, it became the weak link in the chain of operations. There also existed a heated debate over extending track to the Charleston docks, allowing for the seamless flow of cargoes to coastal and transoceanic vessels. A victory occurred, but the company was forced until 1839 to use horses, not steam, to connect the outer limits of the railroad (Line Street) into the city. Many Charlestonians worried about wood embers causing fires – the scourge of American cities – and they believed that the iron horse would frighten their horses and produce a noisier urban environment.[46]

It is not clear what overall economic impact the SCC&RRCO had on Charleston and its service territory. Without question the railroad offered more dependable and rapid freight and passenger service. But did the presence of the trans-state line divert traffic from Augusta? More cargoes surely went to the South Carolina seaport, although relatively high freight rates deterred some shipments. Still Charleston merchants firmly established themselves in interior markets of the Palmetto State. Not to be overlooked were general betterments and rising land values along the railroad and in Charleston. "New buildings are rising up – others are in a course of repair for the reception of the vast stock of goods that are now or soon will be on the way to our shores," crowed the *Charleston Courier.* "Real property has advanced." Samuel Melanchthon Derrick, author of the only academic study of the SCC&RRCO, however, was less positive about the railroad's financial well-being. "The records of the company for the first ten years of operation show that a number of unexpected difficulties were encountered which forced the expenditure of considerable sums, hampered the business of the road, and in general prevented it from producing the results that were anticipated."[47]

THE FUTURE

What became apparent to everyone who knew the South-Carolina Canal & Rail-Road Company was that railroads were the best way to shatter the isolation that plagued much of interior America. As Nicholas Wood, a renowned British civil engineer, prophesied in his path-breaking treatise on railroads that first appeared in 1832, "The public attention is, at the present moment, powerfully attracted by the importance of Rail-roads; immense investments of capital have been made, and expenditures far more enormous are contemplated, throughout every part of the United States, for the construction of these important roads, which are destined to revolutionize the inland commercial intercourse of the civilized world." Public opinion grew that transportation by roads, rivers, and canals was too slow and often undependable for a rapidly growing nation. But there emerged that fascinating alternative – the steam-propelled railroad. As early as 1830 a Pennsylvania journalist envisioned lightning speeds. Steam locomotives, he predicted, "would in all probability soon enable persons to travel upon Rail Ways, at the rate of a mile per minute." Railroads were more than potentially fast; they were seen as having other attractive features: impressive carrying capacity, seldom fazed by inclement weather and the potential for being built almost anywhere. If a 136-mile railroad could expedite passengers and freight in a reliable fashion, a much longer railroad, based on existing technology, was a reasonable and desirable possibility. Similarly, the financial picture of this innovative South Carolina railroad looked promising, even though there had been a nearly $200,000 cost overrun in building and equipping the road. The value of stock in this mostly privately owned carrier (the City of Charleston contributed about a third of the start-up funds) rose from $102 in June 1833 to $125 two years later, and "even then was in the hands of persons who showed no disposition to sell." Backers recalled that the initial stock subscription books, opened on March 17, 1828, had filled quickly, allowing the project to proceed with sufficient capitalization. A subsequent long-term loan from the state also eased financial pressures. Then, too, the company benefited from its railroad monopoly status, allowing it to charge handsomely for its services.[48]

The impending railroad revolution prompted repeated discussions throughout the country about construction of long-distance lines. Although support remained for building much shorter roads to connect communities with navigable waterways and canals and to penetrate nearby hinterlands, railroads early on were seen as being capable of providing linkages between far-away end points. In 1835 rail advocates in New Orleans, Louisiana, for one, explored the possibilities of an iron roadway to Nashville, Tennessee, realizing that trade on the Mississippi River could be siphoned off by any number of strategically built railroads. They fretted that their city might lose its status of major entrepôt and become a rural backwater. These Louisianans were hardly alone; residents of other cities, whether on the Atlantic coast, Gulf of Mexico, or Great Lakes, and even inland, voiced similar concerns. This fear of decline served as a powerful motivating force for railroad proposals.[49]

By the mid-1830s a workable technology and a positive financial climate augured well for future railroad construction. The remarkable 136-mile trans–South Carolina road, which was *not* small, localized, or specialized, became a first link in what ultimately would develop into a Southern railroad network. Its promoters should be honored for rejecting the dominant contemporary view that favored short "tap" railways. The South Carolinians did not see rails as timid things, merely joining a stand of timber, mine, or quarry with the nearest canal, navigable river, lake, or ocean harbor. And they were smart not to have opted for a hybrid canal and railroad system. As historian Albert Churella has written about the Pennsylvania State Works: "Any freight that moved across the state required three transshipments, from rail to canal at Columbia, from canal to railroad at Hollidaysburg and back to canal at Johnstown. These transshipment costs constituted a significant expense for the private transporters who operated over the route." Concluded Churella, "In the final analysis, the Main Line of Public Works did not – and could not – restore Philadelphia's role as the nation's leading port, and neither did it resurrect the commercial fortunes of the city's merchants." The success of the SCC&RRCO, which at the time of its opening claimed the longest railroad in the world under one management, convinced many residents of the Palmetto State and elsewhere that railroads were no longer "new, crude and doubtful" and that long-distance projects were practical. By the end of the 1830s a growing number of American carriers operated collectively nearly 1,500 miles of "iron-ways," and, notwithstanding the harsh depression triggered by the Panic of 1837, another 1,330 miles would be added by 1840. No wonder, a French visitor reported, "Steam, with the Americans, is an eminently national element, adapted to their character, their manners, their habits, and their necessities. With them it is applied as much to extend their liberty as to augment their physical welfare." It is hardly surprising that the SCC&RRCO lost its status as the world's longest railroad under a single management. On March 9, 1840, the Wilmington & Weldon Rail Road in North Carolina celebrated the opening of its 161-mile line, allowing it to boast, albeit briefly, that distinction. Americans were determined to have an extensive transportation system. The Railway Age had begun; the nation was on the verge of becoming railroad crazy.[50]

3 Knoxville, 1836

RAILROAD CONVENTIONS

While not all railroad projects conceived during the Railway Age resulted from special conventions, many did. As late as the first decade of the twentieth century – the twilight era of railroad construction in America – promoters and enthusiasts, at times in large numbers, repeatedly gathered to discuss and organize schemes for steam railroads or for rural trolleys and electric interurbans. Yet as the nineteenth century progressed, the impact made by these railroad conventions diminished. Declared a contemporary: "Railroads were not likely to be prodigiously advanced by conventions." But prior to the Civil War these assemblages were common and occasionally attracted hundreds of delegates and interested observers. Inevitably they were prolific in oratory and resolutions. "There have been railroad conventions without end," editorialized the *New York Herald* in 1859, hardly an exaggerated statement.[1]

Conventions made sense. They offered forums to discuss the pros and cons of a specific railroad proposal. These gatherings, moreover, reflected the democratic spirit of the maturing republic. Participants were commonly elected by communities, counties, legislatures, or private organizations. They congregated in public places – meeting halls, churches, or other buildings – and in appropriate locations, usually the town or city on the projected route. These railroad conventions paralleled such contemporary assemblies as the nation's first presidential nominating convention, organized by the Anti-Masonic Party in 1832, or the landmark woman's rights convention that took place sixteen years later. Whether railroad or otherwise, conventions universally attracted the attention of the press and the general population. Once decisions had been reached, it was hoped that the enthusiasm generated could be translated into tangible results; organizers considered the "hoopla" factor important.

The phenomenon of the railroad convention can be traced to the dawn of the Railway Age. In August 1828 perhaps the first gathering of iron-horse enthusiasts to take place in the South occurred at the Chatham County courthouse settlement of Pittsboro, North Carolina. About two hundred delegates from the village and surrounding areas endorsed a proposal made by Joseph Caldwell (1773–1835), the progressive first president of the University of North Carolina. In a series of articles, which appeared in the *Raleigh Register,* Caldwell called for a trans-state railroad, extending from the port of Beaufort through Raleigh and Lexington to the Tennessee border. Much talk but no concrete action followed the Pittsboro meeting.[2]

On August 27, 1831, an early railroad convention occurred in the western Virginia courthouse town of Abington. Delegates from Virginia and Tennessee – "all were outnumbered by those from eastern Tennessee" – explored building a 322-mile double-track railroad between Lynchburg, Virginia, a community soon to be served by the James River and Kanawha Canal, and Knoxville, Tennessee, a potentially strategic river port. A convention-appointed committee optimistically reported that "it is not only practical to construct such a road between the two points, but that the stockholders will derive a handsome profit on the sum expended on the work." The committee did not worry particularly about funding, believing that it could be raised from the "redundant capital in the northern cities, belonging to our own people, and from that recently introduced by European capitalists." But the estimated cost of $4.5 million [$95.4 million in 2012 dollars] and the state of Virginia's commitment to an array of turnpikes, canals, and river navigation improvements killed the scheme. Yet a railroad advocate at Abington thought that efforts to improve these other transportation arteries, while noble and needed, were misguided, arguing that a railroad would increase property values and therefore generate taxes that could be invested in other betterments. It took nearly a generation before locomotive whistles pierced the relative silence in southwestern Virginia; trains of the Virginia & Tennessee Rail Road began to roll between Lynchburg and Abington in 1856.[3]

Only a month after delegates converged on Abington, Virginia, seventy-six representatives, consisting of "an unusually large number of the prominent leaders in business and public life" from thirty-three counties of Georgia, gathered in centrally located Eatonton to consider internal improvements: turnpikes, canals, and railroads. But these men focused on the latter, being inspired by the developing South-Carolina Canal & Rail-Road and sensing that the iron horse would come to dominate intercity transport. On September 27, the second and final day of the convention, delegates endorsed surveying for a grand network of rail routes. These included lines between Savannah, Augusta, Eatonton, and the Chattahoochee River; Savannah, Macon, and Columbus with a connection to the capital at Milledgeville; Savannah to the head of navigation on the Flint River; and Augusta, through Athens, to the northwest boundary of the state. Although the Eatonton meeting directly led only to the chartering of the Augusta & Eatonton Rail Road Company in December 1831, it set the tone for railroad building later in the decade. By the outbreak of the Civil War this railroad commitment gave Georgia the second-largest mileage in the South, an iron grid of more than 1,400 miles. As was commonplace throughout much of America, taxpayers made substantial financial contributions; there was insufficient private capital to build these Peach State rails.[4]

A convention, albeit modest in nature, that would have a bearing on the future Louisville, Cincinnati & Charleston Rail Road (LC&C) took place in Asheville, North Carolina, seat of Buncombe County and the trade center of western North Carolina. Nearly a year after the Eatonton assembly twenty-eight delegates from North Carolina and Tennessee – twenty from four counties in North Carolina and eight from four counties in Tennessee – met on September 4–5, 1832, to consider what was called the Knoxville & Southern Rail Road. This proposed company would connect the Atlantic tidewater with the Tennessee River at Knoxville, run through Asheville, and utilize the natural advantages provided by the valley of the French Broad River. South Carolina was considered vital to the success of such a railroad, explaining why Buncombe County selected Michael King of Charleston to be a delegate and why King chaired the proceedings. Surveys were suggested and money raised, but little of consequence resulted.[5]

Although Knoxville did not become the western terminus of either the "Abington Rail Road" or the proposed Knoxville & Southern, it became the site of perhaps the largest and most talked about railroad gatherings held in the South during the antebellum years. Delegates considered the proposed Louisville, Cincinnati & Charleston Rail Road a line that would bind the three cities of its corporate name and potentially become the showcase railroad of the nation, if not the world. The opening date of the convention was July 4, 1836 – the most patriotic day in the calendar – and the location was the Church Street Methodist Church. The participants, who represented nine states, discussed how a railroad might be built between the Atlantic Ocean and the Ohio River, or what proponents called: THE NOBLEST ENTERPRIZE OF MODERN TIMES (capitalization in original). As with most formal discussions about a hoped-for railroad, whether in the 1830s or later, the idea preceded the gathering in this gestating Tennessee metropolis.[6]

Coinciding with the time when the earliest railroads appeared in England, bold proposals circulated in the United States. The basic railroad technology existed, but potential builders faced extreme challenges. Lines that crossed mountains or major hills, for example, needed to employ inclined planes; contemporary steam locomotives lacked the ability to ascend heavy grades. Nevertheless the rate of technological improvements impressed knowledgeable observers, especially believers in the potential of overland steam transport. Few would disagree that advancements were occurring at a blistering rate. "What will the morrow bring?" asked a railway enthusiast about 1830. And he answered rhetorically, "I see a gridwork of rail-roads hauling people and goods with speed and safety. Other forms of transport will then be largely eclipsed. Canals will be drained and rail-roads installed in their once water-filled beds."[7]

The precise origins of the idea for an ocean-to-river freight and passenger railroad, which would pass through East Tennessee and Kentucky or some other intermediate route, are uncertain. Charleston, it was widely reported, was the source. After all, this historic port city was about to burst forth with commercial activities spawned by a trans-state railroad. With completion of the South-Carolina Canal & Rail-Road (SCC&RRCO), residents expressed a preference for long-distance rather than short "tap" railways, believing them to be the practical means for obtaining economic growth and stability.

Charlestonians had their eyes cast on the transmontane West. At a meeting of the board of directors of the SCC&RRCO held in the city on May 17, 1831, members took notice of a railroad convention scheduled for the Scott County, Virginia, courthouse village of Estellville (renamed Gate City in 1890) that planned to consider an Atlantic Ocean to interior railroad. "That the question to be there discussed in regard to the selection of an Atlantic sea port as an out-let for a very extensive, and productive portion of the western country, involves topics of the highest and most permanent importance to this city [Charleston]," namely a railroad connecting the Ohio River near its confluence with the Mississippi River with the Atlantic Ocean. Horatio Allen, chief engineer of the SCC&RRCO, assured interested individuals in Charleston, Estellville, and elsewhere that based on his own studies it would be possible to construct such an ambitious line. Allen envisioned at least two possible routes. One would begin at Camden, South Carolina, a projected branch along the gestating Charleston to Hamburg road, and continue to the Catawba River valley and then follow the Nolichucky and Holston Rivers to the Tennessee River and finally parallel the Cumberland River to near its mouth.

Another would start at Hamburg and proceed along the Savannah, Tugaloo, and Little Tennessee Rivers to the Tennessee River and then to the Cumberland River. What the Estellville meeting confirmed was the desire for a railroad to serve this landlocked region where commercial agriculture was taking hold and where farmers longed for a dependable and inexpensive way to send their products to distant (and profitable) markets. Those who met at Estellville took this sentiment to the railroad convention held not long thereafter in Abington, 40 miles away.[8]

In the early 1830s other South Carolinians contemplated a railroad connection between Charleston and the "West." Joel R. Poinsett (1779–1851), diplomat and Charlestonian, who served as a delegate to the Knoxville Railroad Convention, took time in 1833 to write an eight-page pamphlet in which he considered the advantages offered by his home city to become the principal outlet for products originating in the nation's vast interior. The connection would be forged either by river improvements and canals or by a railroad.[9]

Near the time of the Knoxville Railroad Convention, though, Ebenezer Thomas (1775–1845) sought to put to rest the question of the origins of the Louisville, Cincinnati & Charleston. Thomas had lived in Charleston for sixteen years, where he had been a dry goods merchant, bookseller, and editor of the *Charleston City Gazette.* Then he moved to Cincinnati, Ohio, and took charge of the *Cincinnati Daily Evening Post.* Thomas contended that *he* alone had fathered the mammoth plan; in fact, he collected letters from fellow Cincinnatians to support his claim. Morgan Neville was one. On December 24, 1835, this head of the Ohio Insurance Company wrote Thomas, saying, "You are the first person from whom I heard the suggestion of the practicability and expedience of a railroad communication between this city and Charleston. The idea then appeared to me to be a visionary one, and consequently made but little impression on my mind. The late movements on the same subject have brought the conversation which passed between us to my recollection. I think it took place upwards of five years since." And Neville penned an important postscript: "On further reflection, I believe it was in 1829–30, that you were attempting to create a feeling in favor of your Charleston Rail Road *project*" (italics in original). In his memoirs Thomas boasted that he had considered a railroad long before its publicized appearance in Great Britain, proposing a "railroad, for carrying freight and passengers near the close of eighteen hundred and twelve, or the beginning of eighteen hundred and thirteen." Even though poor land transportation plagued the U.S. military during the War of 1812, no contemporary record confirms his extravagant statement. If true, nearly everyone would have thought the idea as far-fetched as sending a man to the moon.[10]

Notwithstanding Thomas's assertions, other contemporary enthusiasts pondered the possibilities of constructing exceptionally long railroads. One visionary was William C. Redfield, a New Yorker who had earlier experimented successfully with steamboats. In 1829 he wrote a widely disseminated tract (revised a year later) that he called *Sketch of the Geographical Rout [sic] of a Great Railway by Which It Is Proposed to Connect the Canals and Navigable Waters of New-York, Pennsylvania, Ohio, Indiana, Illinois, Michigan, Missouri, and the Adjacent States and Territories.* In this forty-eight-page publication Redfield advocated a bold scheme to construct a railway between the Atlantic Ocean and the Mississippi River. Apparently his faith in steam engines and his unpleasant memories of arduous journeys between Connecticut and Ohio shaped his thinking. Redfield went so far as to suggest a fantastic plan to push a railroad to the Pacific Ocean. Then by the mid-nineteenth century numerous grandiose schemes had been recommended, including additional proposals for a transcontinental artery. Beginning in the 1840s Asa Whitney, a prosperous merchant who had widely traveled abroad, launched an unrelenting quest for such a Pacific railway, and he attracted considerable attention. There was a growing public enthusiasm for his transcontinental vision and a realization that conveyances by water and beasts of burden were really not practical to accommodate long-distance transport needs, the former being limited in scope and the latter in capacity.[11]

Less grand but more realistic than a transcontinental railroad was probably the first proposal calling for a rail connection between Charleston and the Ohio River. In 1828, a year before Ebenezer Thomas's claim of originating such a plan, Stephen Elliott, a true futurist, sensed the value of such a route, suggesting in the *Southern Review,* published in Charleston, that a railroad could bring the commerce of the West to his city "in six days, produce might be taken from the confluence of the Ohio and Mississippi to this city, and in five days a return cargo be delivered at the same point." Although a man of letters, "a profound and elegant scholar," Elliott understood the world of business and commerce, having served as president of the Charleston-based South Carolina State Bank.[12]

The highly vocal Thomas, who failed to acknowledge Elliott's proposal, never became *the* sparkplug in what became the plan for the Louisville, Cincinnati & Charleston Rail Road (originally the Cincinnati & Charleston Rail Road). Rather the three individuals who did much to guide the project before and during the 1836 Knoxville assemblage were Daniel Drake (1785–1852), Robert Young Hayne (1791–1839) and James Gettys McCreary (J. G. M.) Ramsey (1797–1884).

Daniel Drake was one of the truly talented residents of antebellum Cincinnati. Contemporaries often referred to him as the "Franklin of the

A leader in the drive to build a transmontane railroad was Dr. Daniel Drake, a Cincinnati physician and humanitarian. As a public-spirited resident of the "Queen City of the West" he became interested in the promotion of internal improvements, including canals and railroads.

Courtesy of Cincinnati Museum Center.

West"; historian Richard C. Wade called him "Cincinnati's best known citizen." This New Jersey native received an excellent medical education, graduating from the University of Pennsylvania in 1815. He did not remain in the East, moving to frontier Cincinnati, where he became renowned for his professional activities, organizing the Medical College of Ohio, establishing a hospital for river boatmen, and launching the *Western Journal of the Medical and Physical Sciences.* Drake wrote several books and treatises, including *The Natural and Statistical View or Picture of Cincinnati* and one on the prevention and treatment of cholera. He also became involved in various nonmedical projects, including canals and railroads.[13]

The individual who assumed leadership of the Knoxville Convention and became the first president of the LC&C was the distinguished South Carolina lawyer and politician Robert Hayne. Described as "always the cultivated gentleman" who avoided "demagogic oratory," he was a tireless crusader for what he considered to be the public interest. After holding several elective offices, including state attorney general, Hayne won election to the U.S. Senate in 1822, and gained fame for his defense of states'

The individual most associated with the Louisville, Cincinnati & Charleston Rail Road was South Carolina lawyer and politician Robert Young Hayne. This portrait shows the young Hayne as a U.S. senator, a dozen years or so before he assumed the railroad presidency. Said a contemporary, "He had a loveable face and the manners of an accomplished gentleman."

Courtesy California State Railroad Museum, Railway and Locomotive Historical Society.

rights and free trade. Nine years after going to Washington he graciously resigned to allow his political soul mate at the time, John C. Calhoun, who had voluntarily left the U.S. vice presidency, to take his seat. But Hayne remained politically active, participating in South Carolina's notorious nullification convention, serving one term as governor (1832–34) and becoming the first intendant (mayor) of Charleston (1835–37).[14]

Drake and Hayne were gifted individuals, but J. G. M. Ramsey was a renaissance man. Like Drake a trained physician, this long-time resident of Knoxville earned his undergraduate degree at age nineteen from Washington College (today's Washington College Academy) near Jonesboro, Tennessee, and then read medical journals in the office of a local physician. Later he took a year of formal medical study at the University of Pennsylvania. Although Ramsey practiced the healing arts, he worked intermittently as a banker (following in the footsteps of his wealthy father),

This photograph of a sober Dr. James Gettys McCreary (J. G. M.) Ramsey, which was taken late in life, reveals the individual who played a major role in organizing the Knoxville Railroad Convention and who later labored for financing the Louisville, Cincinnati & Charleston Rail Road.

Courtesy of McClung Historical Collection, Knox County Public Library System.

operated a large farm, and showed a fascination for history, helping to found the East Tennessee Historical Society in 1834 and writing *The Annals of Tennessee to the End of the Eighteenth Century* (1853). And for a decade beginning in 1874 he served as president of the Tennessee Historical Society. Ramsey was a committed Presbyterian elder and a contributor to literary publications. During the Civil War this fire-eating secessionist served as a civil office holder for the Confederate government in his hometown.[15]

Throughout his adult life, even after the war, Ramsey battled for enhanced transportation for East Tennessee, focusing on river improvements and railroad construction. In the latter part of 1828 he suggested a rail link between the navigable rivers of Tennessee and the Atlantic Ocean, urging in a series of pieces that appeared in the *Charleston Mercury* for such a road and also a regional convention for discussion and promotion. He gladly supported efforts by an "association of gentlemen" in nearby Rogersville, who on July 4, 1831, launched one of the nation's earliest railroad-oriented publications, the *Railroad Advocate,* "for the purpose of encouraging and advocating the building of railroads in Tennessee." Ramsey also enthusiastically endorsed the 1832 meeting held in Asheville for that proposed, albeit stillborn, Knoxville & Southern Rail Road.[16]

FIRST STEPS

The first major event on the road to Knoxville involved Drake and Cincinnati boosters. These civic-minded men, who included prominent merchants, manufacturers, and lawyers and other professionals, wished to see the continued growth of their home city, which at the time appeared to be firmly established as the most important commercial center in the trans-Allegheny West. Having a population of 24,831 in 1830, it was far larger than Louisville (10,341), its principal rival, and St. Louis (5,882) or the still dormant Chicago (70). City fathers happily pointed out that their population had doubled regularly from one federal census to another. On August 10, 1835, a large assembly of railroad proponents gathered at the Commercial Exchange, located on the bustling public landing, to consider a railroad from the Kentucky bank of the Ohio River – either Covington or Newport – southward to Paris, Kentucky, a distance of about 80 miles. Toward the end of the session, however, Drake offered this resolution: "That a committee of three be appointed to inquire into the practicability and advantage of an extension of the proposed Rail-Road, from Paris into the state of South Carolina." The group heartily agreed.[17]

At another meeting in Cincinnati held five days later, Drake presented a reasoned argument for a railroad between Cincinnati and Charleston. He may have embraced such a bold proposal because of his knowledge of several rough surveys made in 1832 by U.S. Army officer Stephen H. Long that indicated that such an interregional railroad was possible. Drake had a plan and purpose in mind. Adding to the proposed line between Cincinnati and Paris (perhaps Lexington) and the existing South-Carolina Canal & Rail-Road, the routing would extend approximately 600 miles through the Cumberland Gap to Knoxville and follow the French Broad and Saluda Rivers to Asheville and Columbia and then to Branchville, South Carolina. Such a railroad had numerous advantages. Most of all, it would become the first direct link between the Old Northwest and the Old South, facilitating trade of a wide variety of raw and finished goods. Heretofore the Blue Ridge and Cumberland mountains had effectively walled off the cotton belt and rice plantations from the mixed agriculture – grain and livestock – to the north and northwest.

In response to critics who believed that such a railroad would fail because it would cross a sparsely populated region, backers argued that the meager population was due largely to a lack of railroad access. The road would enhance settlement by opening up vast, untapped resources in Kentucky and Tennessee, allowing for the exploitation of "iron, salt, coal, tar, turpentine and other natural productions." Market development would benefit everyone. And the iron horse would greatly enhance personal travel, movement of the U.S. mails, and rapid troop deployments. What would become a theme of the Knoxville Railroad Convention and later promotional efforts was this observation: "The north and the south would, in fact, shake hands with each other, yield up their social and political hostility, pledge themselves to common national interests, and part as friends and brethren." Drake indicated that this rail line, with connecting railroads, canals, and improved waterways and turnpikes, would become a vital artery for commerce. "Thus the proposed main trunk from Cincinnati to Charleston would resemble an immense horizontal tree extending its routes through and into ten States and a vast expanse of uninhabited territory in the Northern interior of the Union, while its branches would wind through half as many populous States on the Southern seaboard." Cincinnati, not unexpectedly, would reap much from this railroad project, bolstering its economy at the expense of rival Louisville. Hardly surprising, the Drake handiwork received unanimous support.[18]

The second Cincinnati railroad assemblage did more than endorse an Ohio River to Atlantic Ocean railroad. Participants created a "standing committee of inquiry and correspondence," consisting of seven appointed members, namely "four from Cincinnati, two from the adjoining part of Kentucky, and one from eastern Indiana." The meeting charged the body to create its own working organization and "to make an immediate communication to the governors of each of the states and territories, interested in the proposed work, requesting them to bring the subject before their respective legislatures, at their next sessions." The committee was "to adopt such measures as may be practicable to inform and interest the people living near the proposed road, relative to the subject." Enhancing its status was the recruitment of the politically savvy General William Henry Harrison, hero of the War of 1812, U.S. senator from Indiana, and future president of the United States. Although Harrison served as chair, Drake became the point man, serving as corresponding secretary.[19]

The Drake committee made an impact. Most notably, Charlestonians expressed keen interest in what would become the most daring railroad project of the 1830s. Always eager for better transportation, they understood the shortcomings of canals and the need for government to disconnect itself from these "dismal ditches." At the October 22, 1835, meeting of the Chamber of Commerce, the city's commercial organization, members appointed a study group to examine the Ohio to Atlantic proposal. And the findings were positive: citizens should move forward "promptly,

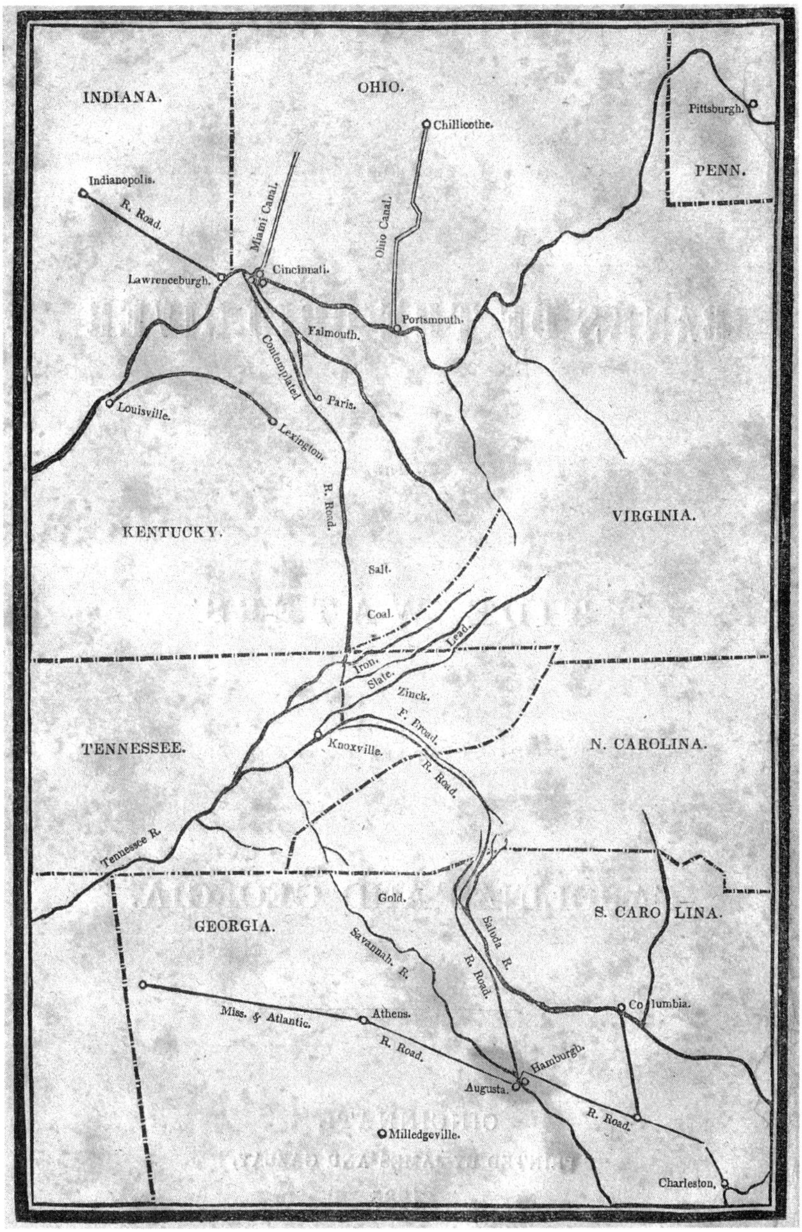

The Cincinnati proponents of a long-distance railroad from their city to Charleston endorsed publication of a small pamphlet with a long title, *Rail-Road from the Banks of the Ohio River to the Tide Waters of the Carolina and Georgia.* The work appeared in 1835 and included a rough map of the projected line. The map maker added the location of the potential raw materials that the carrier would likely carry: coal, iron, salt, slate, and "zinck."

Courtesy of Cincinnati Museum Center.

vigorously, resolutely." This they did. Public meetings followed and Robert Hayne, now mayor, took charge. "ONE and ALL," he wrote, "to signalize this happy era of returning good feeling and general prosperity – by laying the foundation of a MIGHTY WORK, which would be a BLESSING TO OUR COUNTRY – A RICH TREASURE TO OUR POSTERITY, AND IN ALL TIME TO COME, AN ENDURING MONUMENT OF OUR ENTERPRISE, WISDOM, AND PATRIOTISM" (capitalization in original). The *Charleston Courier* concurred: "What a bold conception! What a magnificent project!" Being a seismograph of public tremors, the newspaper continued to boom the project: "For if it succeeds, South Carolina will be prosperous beyond all former calculations, and the Union of the States will be as lasting as the rocks and mountains which will be passed and overcome by the contemplated road."[20]

Hayne was surely sincere with his well-publicized remarks. Yet arguably he was guilty of fostering a competitive localism, placing the goals of Charlestonians in the larger context of being a universal blessing for *all* Americans. But there was something wonderful about his repeated bursts of colorful rhetoric: "We can almost perceive the finger of heaven pointing to the barriers which have so long separated them [West and South], and reverently think we HEAR THE VOICE OF GOD, speaking through his works, commanding us to remove those obstacles, and encouraging our exertions, by the promise of abundant blessings, with which a wise and beneficent Providence, seldom fails to reward the faithful efforts of his children" (capitalization in original).[21]

Replicating actions in Cincinnati, Charleston backers passed a set of resolutions that expressed their enthusiasm, outlined their strategies and established a committee of correspondence. Joining with like-minded men from Columbia, the South Carolinians pushed to have the legislatures of Kentucky, North Carolina, Ohio, South Carolina, and Tennessee charter this Cincinnati & Charleston Rail Road (the LC&C name came later). Victories followed. Between December 1835 and March 1836 four of the five lawmaking bodies granted the requested charters. Ohio did not, being intent on adding more canals, creating additional turnpikes, and expanding its own intrastate network of railroads. These state documents contained no unusual features. Of importance, though, was that the new company would consist of twenty-four directors. Three would represent each of the five states (Ohio was included) and nine would serve as general representatives of the stockholders. Since Ohio failed to grant a charter, the size of the board was later reduced to twenty-one.[22]

There had been no organized opposition or proposal altering the chartering process in North Carolina, Tennessee, and South Carolina, but Kentucky was different. The state's general assembly demanded modifications, particularly including service to Louisville and Maysville. Most lawmakers had no great love for Cincinnati. Louisville, the dominant Bluegrass State city, was a fierce commercial rival of Cincinnati, and these men did not wish to have the economies of any Kentucky community damaged or threatened. Fortunately, the South Carolinians dispatched to Frankfort the able Colonel Abram Blanding, lawyer, banker, and former commissioner of public works for South Carolina, who worked to win legislative passage. In the minds of lawmakers the extension to Louisville would surely protect and promote the interests of the state.[23]

More action followed. The Hayne-led group formed a "board of engineers" to determine the best route or routes, required for determining costs and for generating support. An allocation of $10,000 from the South Carolina General Assembly helped to underwrite this essential field work.[24]

The agitation from South Carolina advanced what was now the Louisville, Cincinnati & Charleston Rail Road (a corporate name that reflected the importance of Louisville). And a strong grassroots movement emerged, particularly pronounced in transportation-starved East Tennessee. "For many years past," editorialized a Rogersville journalist in 1832, "our most intelligent and patriotic citizens have viewed with deep concern, the great disadvantages under which East Tennessee has labored, for the uninterrupted conveyance of her surplus productions to market." Within a few years, though, this worry turned to real hope for change. On October 20, 1835, one of several localized gatherings convened in the courthouse town of Jonesboro (not far from Rogersville), where citizens drew up a petition that endorsed the railroad and called on legislators to fund the exploratory surveys and to cooperate with the South Carolinians and other out-of-state proponents. The thinking prevailed that the existence of the already functioning SCC&RRCO enhanced chances for the success of the LC&C. It did not take long for about six hundred male voters from Washington County to sign the document.[25]

"THE GREAT KNOXVILLE RAILROAD CONVENTION"[26]

Project leaders realized that a general meeting (convention) needed to be called to discuss what had transpired and to consider what actions should follow. Everyone agreed. Because of travel distances and difficulties, a central location seemed mandatory. Knoxville became the chosen place. While hardly Cincinnati or Charleston, the city claimed a growing population of several thousand and an expanding business core. At the time the *Tennessee Gazette* said, "Knoxville has 12 mercantile stores, a drug store, a book store, three hotels, two weekly newspapers, four clergyman, five physicians, and 29 lawyers." This seat of Knox County, situated at the head of navigation on the Tennessee River, dominated commercial life in East Tennessee and would be a place that the LC&C would likely serve. Strong support for the road existed locally because of the unceasing promotional efforts of J. G. M. Ramsey and economic reasons. Residents expected that their community would become "the great commercial center between Charleston and Cincinnati." No wonder a welcoming Mayor William Wynatt thanked delegates for selecting Knoxville, and wished them a "successful termination of your labors, an enterprise so useful to our whole County, and so desirable to the inhabitants of this City."[27]

On July 4–8, 1836, what became the "Great Southern Railroad Convention" or the "Grand Railroad Convention" drew a large, enthusiastic crowd, consisting of men who wanted cheap, reliable interregional transportation. The official delegates were chosen variously. The Kentucky legislature named its representatives, but most were elected at local gatherings, with a typical one taking place at Rutledge, Tennessee. Convening on May 2, 1836, in the courtroom of the Grainger County courthouse "for purpose of expressing their views upon the subject of Internal Improvements," the assembly heartily backed the forthcoming Knoxville meeting and elected nineteen delegates. The stated requirement: these individuals must report the happenings.[28]

Organizers of the Knoxville Convention cast a wide net, involving more than the states that would actually have track built within their borders. It was believed that the north-south artery would benefit adjoining areas. After all, other states were in process of enhancing transportation, mostly with railroads, and conceivably a web of rails would feed the LC&C. The 380 delegates who ultimately participated were characterized by Hayne as having "so much intelligence and patriotism, public virtue and private worth, as to entitle their opinions to the greatest weight." The editor of the *Western Monthly Magazine* concurred, calling them "highly intelligent, influential, discreet and sober minded citizens; many of the very distinguished in the political, social and scientific circles of the country." There was no question that men such as Abram Blanding (South Carolina), John C. Calhoun (South Carolina),[29] A. S. Clayton (Georgia), Leslie Coombs (Kentucky), F. B. Fagg (Tennessee), James Gadsden (South Carolina), Richard Habersham (Georgia), Vardry McBee (South Carolina), Robert Mills (South Carolina), J. W. Osborne (North Carolina), John Pettigru (South Carolina), Joel R. Poinsett (South Carolina), Robert Wicklifte (Kentucky) and John Williams (Tennessee), in addition to those individuals who spearheaded the meeting and served as its officers, possessed stellar qualifications. No other antebellum railroad convention in the South (or perhaps the nation) could claim more distinguished participants. This eminent assemblage consisted of 9 representatives from Alabama, 55 from Georgia, 4 from Indiana, 60 from Kentucky, 30 from North Carolina, 6 from Ohio, 81 from South Carolina, 125 from Tennessee, and 10 from Virginia. These numbers were not especially representative of the anticipated service area, although this state mix never became a stumbling block for the convention.[30]

While hardly a metropolis, Knoxville adequately accommodated the throng of delegates and other visitors in a "most hospitable manner." With public houses overflowing, residents invited guests to their homes. And an acceptable meeting place was required. Fortunately, the Methodist congregation, which numbered about one hundred members, had raised $5,000 ($109,600 in 2012 dollars) for a replacement church and recently workers had completed the edifice, described as a "plain brick meeting

This drawing depicts the Methodist Episcopal Church, located on Church Street in the heart of Knoxville, Tennessee. The building, which in July 1836 accommodated the Knoxville Railroad Convention, served the local Methodist congregation until 1875.

Author's collection.

house, with a galley at the back." This Church Street Methodist Church offered the largest assembly space in town. Not surprisingly this building would be the site of other public gatherings.[31]

The first day – the glorious Fourth – focused on organization. On that Monday morning John Williams, former U.S. senator and chargé d'affaires to the Central American Federation, Knoxville resident, and avid internal improvements advocate, served as temporary chair. It then came as no surprise that Robert Hayne was unanimously elected the permanent president. Throughout the convention this South Carolinian would exercise his considerable talents and political skills with distinction and aplomb. A contemporary recalled that Hayne's rhetoric could entrance an audience for hours. Appointed secretary was another seasoned politician, a delegate from the host city and former U.S. congressman, Pryor Lea. At this point a lively discussion ensued between Drake and Thomas about the origins of the railroad plan, prompting General Leslie Coombs of Kentucky to tell fellow delegates tongue-in-cheek: "Take notice, I suggest the building of a rail-road to the Pacific Ocean, and I shall, hereafter, claim the paternity of that measure." Once more Hayne reiterated the overall value of the railroad, something that he always enjoyed.

"We offer you [the interior regions and the West] more; we open up to you a sea-port through which you may reach the markets of the world in the transportation of your vast products, your rich crops of grain and other subsistence – in such demand abroad, and almost valueless at home."[32]

Then the convention got down to brass tacks, focusing initially on the preliminary survey for this monster railroad. Abram Blanding reported with relish that it was feasible to build largely along the route previously suggested by the Cincinnati group. The core of the preliminary survey work had been conducted by Captain William G. Williams of the U.S. Topographical Engineers and Colonel James Gadsden, who served as chief engineer for the State of South Carolina, and had been funded in part by that earlier grant from South Carolina. In essence Williams, aided by several assistants, including the experienced G. F. Featherstonehaugh, stated the practicability of the railroad and estimated the cost of a double-track physical plant at $10,814.046 ($222.6 million in 2012 dollars). It was critically important to locate an acceptable crossing of the Blue Ridge Mountains, that formidable barrier between Charleston and Knoxville. Fortunately, the valley of the French Broad River made that objective possible. One path could run along Reedy Patch Creek, a tributary of the French Broad, but it might necessitate several inclined planes. Another option was the Butt Mountain Gap passage, between Greenville, South Carolina, and Asheville, which could be crossed without the use of any assisting equipment. These alternatives differed dramatically from the Allegheny Portage Rail Road in Pennsylvania. It required ten inclined planes – although acclaimed as a marvel of civil engineering – to conquer the spine of the Alleghenies between the main sections of the Pennsylvania Canal (Main Line of Public Works). Moreover, knowledgeable observers were much taken by the recent appearance of more powerful steam locomotives. Hayne, for one, told a group of Charlestonians shortly before the Knoxville Convention about the "astonishing performance of locomotive engines on the Baltimore and Ohio Railroad – overcoming *acclivity of upwards of 200 feet*" (italics in original). The expected route north from Knoxville would exploit the Cumberland Gap, "which would have to be crossed by inclined plane or a tunnel a mile in length," and proceed to Lexington through the communities of Mount Vernon, Lancaster, and Nicholasville. Later Captain Williams received a second opinion of his preliminary survey, having Major William G. McNeill of the U.S. Army Corps of Engineers, "who has had perhaps more experience in the construction of Rail Roads than any man in this or any other country," review his findings. McNeill endorsed Williams's work.[33]

Since the assembly was large, delegates, being practical men, referred the Williams report and other documents to the Committee of

Thirty-Nine. However, two days later that body was expanded by five, but the late arrival of the potentially influential delegate from Maysville, Kentucky, increased the number to forty-five. No one complained about having this select group as long as it reflected the composition of the convention. The real work took place with this Committee of Forty-Five and involved such workhorses as Drake, Hayne, and Ramsey. It was fully capable of handling detailed matters.[34]

Much of the remainder of the five-day session centered on the consideration of the advantages of the Atlantic Ocean to Ohio River railroad, costs involved, and how existing or proposed railroads might be linked to the main stem. The last issue, however, triggered heated discussion, creating a less than harmonious atmosphere. Although the convention showed no signs of erupting into a shouting match, members of the Georgia delegation fussed mightily about the routing. Its representatives submitted a report that called for the line to cut through their state by way of the Rabun Gap in the northeastern section and not through western North Carolina. The powerful and determined South Carolina delegation, led by Hayne, countered with a position paper that advanced advantages of the preliminary survey.[35]

A compromise was needed, and one followed. On July 7 the Committee of Forty-Five reported to the parent body, dealing directly with the concerns of the Georgians with this statement: "That it is important that a branch of the Louisville, Cincinnati and Charleston Rail-road should be extended, from some point in Tennessee, into the state of Georgia, upon reciprocal terms with those enjoyed by the states of Kentucky, Tennessee, North Carolina and South Carolina; and whereas an opportunity should be afforded to the state of Georgia and its citizens, to become participants in the construction and benefits of said road." This position led to this formal resolution, which the convention accepted: "An amendment should be made in the existing charters of said company, providing that the branch of the road to be extended into Georgia, shall commence at Knoxville, or at the nearest point thereto, if the road of the said company shall not strike Knoxville, to be constructed thence to such a point in the state of Georgia as said state may elect; and, for that purpose, that the capital of said company may be increased." Remarked the *American Railroad Journal*, "The Convention was in some danger of breaking up without doing anything had it not been for the compromise with the delegates from Georgia, which appeared to satisfy all parties."[36]

It could be argued that the position taken by the Georgia delegates, who found support from some representatives of the lower counties of East Tennessee, was a fire bell in the night, especially for Charlestonians. If the Georgia branch materialized, Charleston could not expect to achieve full trade benefits. The appendage, if run between Knoxville, Athens, and Augusta, could funnel freight traffic by future rail connections or by water to Savannah.

There remained a simmering unhappiness with the Knoxville compromise, prompting members of the Georgia delegation before they returned home to call for their own railroad convention. Later interested parties convened in Macon, Georgia, "for the purpose of consulting upon the expediency and the practicability of building a railroad from some point on the Tennessee River below the Suck, through Georgia, to some point on the Atlantic." At that November 1836 gathering 116 participants from thirty-eight counties and two railroads, the Central Rail Road & Canal Company of Georgia and the Georgia Rail Road & Banking Company, decided to build a state-owned road from an undetermined point on the Gulf-flowing Chattahoochie River to the Tennessee River at Ross's Landing, the future Chattanooga. (Eventually this proposal became the Western & Atlantic Rail Road.) Delegates recommended that existing and new railroads expand in the state, including a connection with the line to the Tennessee River. Yet Georgians still wanted railroad access to the Ohio River and the Old Northwest. No one at the Macon meeting or elsewhere in public gatherings objected to the spirit of an earlier legislative measure that called for such a transportation strategy.[37]

One proposal considered by the Committee of Forty-Five in Knoxville went nowhere. The suggestion: "It is the settled opinion of this Convention that the government of the United States should become a large stockholder in said road." Most delegates balked at such a financial strategy, being influenced by the Jeffersonian tradition of limited government. Men like John C. Calhoun and Robert Hayne were representative of the cult of rugged individualism and an allegiance to states' rights. These two South Carolinians had been active nullifiers, declaring the Tariffs of 1828 and 1832 null and void and authorizing state government to take the necessary action to prevent implementation. Furthermore, any expectation by backers of the LC&C that significant direct aid would come from Washington was highly unrealistic. Admittedly the precedent for such assistance existed; the federal government had invested in internal improvements, most notably in the National Road and several canals, including the long-suffering Chesapeake and Delaware Canal. Economic historian Carter Goodrich found that expenditures by state and local governments before the Civil War, however, far exceeded those made by Congress. Based on his calculations states spent about $300 million for internal improvements while their local counterparts invested about $125 million. Washington, on the other hand, contributed a mere $7 million.[38]

Although convention delegates would not rely on *direct* federal investments, the financial situation did not appear to be too daunting.

Participants believed that the project could be adequately funded through a combination of private and public investments. After all, individuals along the expanding Baltimore and Ohio Railroad had invested handsomely, and also the City of Baltimore had contributed generously; this policy of mixed private and public support worked well. Already states along the proposed LC&C had legislative bodies that looked kindly on railroad projects. Tennesseans, for one, knew that their lawmakers had passed during the 1835–36 session a measure that offered liberal aid to railroad and turnpike companies in accordance with the recently revised state constitution that "internal improvements ought to be encouraged by the General Assembly." Moreover, times were good. Land prices, especially in the South, soared; British textile manufacturers clamored for American cotton, and the domestic money supply expanded. Delegates anticipated that the federal government, buoyed by elimination of the national debt and a mounting treasury surplus, would distribute loans to the states under terms of the recently passed Surplus Revenue Act. The widespread belief existed that these funds would never have to be repaid and that the distribution program would continue, perhaps indefinitely. The time, then, seemed ripe for building an interregional railroad.[39]

Proceedings of the convention did not emphasize profitability. Nevertheless, prospects looked bright. There would be those lucrative long-distance movements of both freight and passengers. The LC&C would differ significantly from the relatively short lines that were developing in the South, roads that served a predominantly planter constituency. Therefore, fortunes would not rise and fall with the annual cotton crop. With a traffic mix of agricultural, mineral, timber, and other products and interior-bound shipments of consumer goods, particularly to the developing metropolises of Asheville, Knoxville, and Lexington, a reasonably balanced traffic flow would result.

As with all gatherings there were likely discussions that were not recorded in the official transactions or by the press. Some delegates, especially those from South Carolina with its rapidly growing slave population, surely saw another benefit, namely that this long-distance railroad could rapidly transport troops to put down a slave rebellion. In fact, a civil engineer informally told delegates that "the South, possessing a slave population, whose physical strength increases in a ratio greater than that of their owners, will, no doubt, view this additional bond of union with their white brethren as auspicious of their own safety." No matter their views toward the "peculiar institution," delegates surely agreed that the rail line could aid any potential national or regional security threat, most likely coming from a foreign invasion.[40]

On Thursday, July 7, the day before adjournment, delegates approved the work of the Committee of Forty-Five. They called for the charters granted by the four states where the LC&C would operate to be accepted, but these documents could be amended so as to permit Alabama, Georgia, and Virginia to unite with the road. That a route and estimated cost of approximately $11 million ($226.4 million in 2012 dollars) posed no insurmountable problems, and when opened, the railroad should eventually turn a reasonable profit. As with other important railroad conventions, the proceedings would be published.[41]

The activities on the next to last day involved a break for conviviality. About five hundred delegates, visitors, and residents gathered that afternoon in a grove near the old Methodist Church to enjoy a "sumptuous and elegant Barbacue [*sic*]" hosted by Knoxville town fathers. "We have never witnessed a festive entertainment, either small or great accompanied with so little disorder and confusion," crowed the *Knoxville Register.* Speeches and toasts followed. The first was given by convention president Hayne. "In his animated and eloquent manner, [Hayne] addressed his attentive audience for a few minutes upon the great objects of their assemblage, portrayed in glowing colors the advantages, both commercial, political and social, which were certain to result from a completion of the great work they had then assembled to commence." Hayne captured the sentiment of the participants with this toast: "The proposed Union between the South and the West – the banns have been published, and we are here to witness the ceremony – 'If any man can show cause why these two shall not be united together let him now speak, or forever after hold his peace.'" Daniel Drake also commented, "giving a lucid and comprehensive view of the consequence, resulting from the completion of the contemplated work." Others spoke, including probably J. G. M. Ramsey and Pryor Lea, but their identities and comments were not recorded in the *Register* or other sources.[42]

On the closing day delegates met only in the morning. But before the convention adjourned sine die about noon several resolutions were formally passed. The body essentially repeated the sentiments of the Thursday morning meeting. Significantly, the matter of Georgia was again addressed and in less positive terms: "That the company should not be compelled to construct the said branch from the main trunk, or road, until the State of Georgia and others shall have subscribed for that object, and paid over, as required, to the company, the amount required for the construction of said branch, agreeable to the provisions of the charters." Then Hayne was recognized. "After the most hearty thanks of the convention had been awarded him," reported the *Charleston Courier,* "he made a most beautiful and happy address in parting." The last person to speak before the assembly was the Reverend Mr. Isaac Anderson, a Presbyterian clergyman, founder of Southern and Western Theological Seminary (now Maryville College) and "one of the ablest men that ever preached the Gospel in Tennessee," ending with "an address to the Throne of Grace [Hebrews 4:16]."[43]

At no time during the proceedings did delegates to the Knoxville Railroad Convention question the feasibility of the iron horse as a mode of transport. Yet that was not always the case during these antebellum railroad conventions. Take what transpired in Greeneville, Tennessee, in July 1847. Even more than a decade after the Knoxville assembly, representatives from ten Tennessee and three Virginia counties, all determined to improve area transportation, quarreled over whether it was practical to build a railroad. A sizable faction backed river improvements and macadamized road construction, arguing that these betterments were attainable, "but a Railroad was not – that its accomplishment was visionary and impractical." But those who participated in the Knoxville meeting rejected the contemporary Jacksonians' skepticism of technological change.[44]

EXIT KNOXVILLE

The Knoxville Railroad Convention, this great antebellum railroad meeting, had come and gone and in some ways resembled the impact of a latter-day political convention. The invigorated delegates returned home with much on their agendas. Many made convention-related stops along the way. Representatives from the South Carolina delegation paused in Flat Rock, North Carolina, south of Asheville, to share their thoughts and experiences. The five days spent in Knoxville had energized the participants and had accelerated the movement. Yet it would take weeks before most newspapers printed accounts of what had transpired, and even months before some delegates reported to their sponsoring bodies. Take what happened in Sevier County, Tennessee. Not until September 30 did the local delegates meet with their neighbors at the Sevierville courthouse. A report was made, and the assembled backed several resolutions, with the key one being: "That the citizens of county feel a deep and abiding interest in the success of the great and grand scheme of Internal Improvement which will promote the best temporal interest of five million of the people of this Union connecting into one indissoluble bond, the whole community from *Atlantic in the South to the Great Lakes of the North*" (italics in original). Surely participants accepted the widely held belief that *all* internal improvements were a means of increasing property values and improving their quality of life.[45]

In October 1849 the largest railroad convention held in the South prior to the Civil War may have taken place in Memphis, Tennessee. This gathering, which discussed possible routes for a Pacific railroad, attracted 392 representatives from fourteen Southern and Midwestern states and also scores of observers. But unlike the Knoxville Railroad Convention,

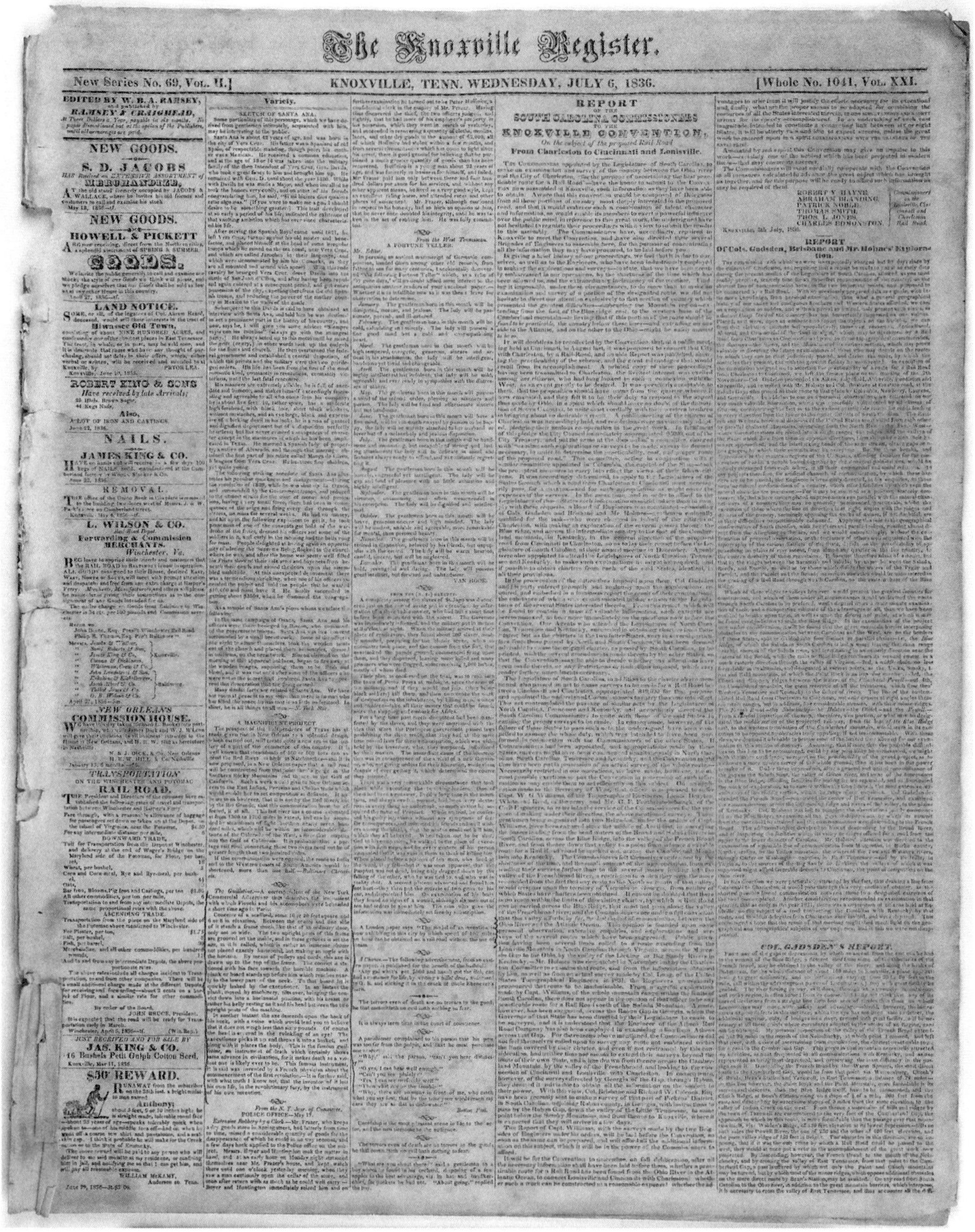
The Knoxville Register.

New Series No. 69, Vol. II.] KNOXVILLE, TENN. WEDNESDAY, JULY 6, 1836. [Whole No. 1041, Vol. XXI.

REPORT OF THE SOUTH CAROLINA COMMISSIONERS TO THE KNOXVILLE CONVENTION, On the subject of the proposed Rail Road From Charleston to Cincinnati and Louisville.

NEW GOODS.

S. D. JACOBS

NEW GOODS.

HOWELL & PICKETT

LAND NOTICE.

ROBERT KING & SONS

NAILS.

JAMES KING & CO.

REMOVAL.

L. WILSON & CO.

NEW ORLEANS COMMISSION HOUSE.

TRANSPORTATION ON THE WINCHESTER AND POTOMAC RAIL ROAD.

JAS. KING & CO.

$30 REWARD.

Variety.

SKETCH OF SANTA ANA.

A FORTUNE TELLER.

A MAGNIFICENT PROJECT

REPORT Of Cols. Gadsden, Brisbane and Mr. Holmes' Exploration.

COL. GADSDEN'S REPORT.

the precise count of delegates is uncertain. "There is hardly a doubt that many of the delegates were not delegates at all, but only visitors in Memphis or transient residents."[46]

For their part Hayne and others continued to bring attention to the proposed railroad. The same promotional messages were repeated again and again. Not long after the Knoxville convention, Hayne, as instructed by the delegates, prepared a thirty-eight-page pamphlet, *Address in Behalf of the Knoxville Convention, to the Citizens of the Several States Interested in the Proposed Louisville, Cincinnati and Charleston Rail Road,* that reviewed the proceedings and boomed the LC&C. Although new to anyone who had not followed the proceedings, little additional information was offered, but the mission was once more plainly stated:

> The main object is to **break down the mountain barriers**which now separate two entire sections of our common country – making the inhabitants of these regions almost strangers and aliens to each other; – to lay open the great West to the commerce of the South, – connect the Western waters and their tributary streams, – extending even to the upper lakes, – with the South Atlantic; – to open, by the shortest, cheapest, and most expeditious route, a direct intercourse between the vast interior of our continent, – teeming with population, and abundant in resources, – and the Southern States, and through them, with all the nations of the earth; – and by these means to mold into one common brotherhood the now estranged and alienated inhabitants of our widely extended republic [bold type and capitalization in original].[47]

It was hardly surprising that the *Knoxville Register* reported the happenings of the Knoxville Railroad Convention. Newspapers in Tennessee and elsewhere frequently reprinted all or parts of the extensive coverage found in this weekly publication.

Courtesy of McClung Historical Collection, Knox County Public Library System.

A strong feeling arose that the mission of the Knoxville Railroad Convention harmonized with growing support for railroads. Serious considerations were being given to even the most challenging construction projects. In Pennsylvania surveyors shortly entered the field to locate a 240-mile line between Chambersburg, terminus of the recently completed Cumberland Valley Railroad, and Pittsburgh, head of Ohio River navigation. Three major tunnels would be required to maintain an acceptable grade, and the estimated construction cost was set at $11.3 million, approximately the same anticipated price tag as the LC&C. Proponents of the LC&C surely smiled when they learned of the railroad mania that had erupted in the Old Northwest, including Illinois. In early 1837 that state approved an ambitious internal improvement bill that contemplated no less than 1,342 miles of railroads.[48]

The challenging work of turning the wishes of delegates at the Knoxville Railroad Convention into reality was about to commence. These public-spirited men took pride in what they had achieved in less than a week, and they basked in the favorable publicity that their sessions had generated. "The Louisville, Cincinnati, and Charleston project apparently received more general attention in the region than any similar enterprise before or since," observed historian Ulrich B. Philips in 1908. Unlike some later railroad conventions, dormant jealousies did not create lingering ill-will. This Knoxville assembly also demonstrated that these mostly southern delegates were hardly laggards when it came to the antebellum transportation revolution, endorsing a scheme of heroic proportions, perhaps in the extreme. They believed that railroads had outgrown their auxiliary relationship to rivers, canals, and other water transport and that the iron

In November 2011 the Lexington Group Inc., an organization of scholars, industry executives, and other professionals interested in transportation history, gathered for its annual meeting in Knoxville, Tennessee. At one session members learned the details and significance of the Knoxville Railroad Convention of 1836. To celebrate the 175th year of the convention, hosts Norfolk Southern and Gulf & Ohio Railroads presented attendees with a commemorative medal.

Author's collection.

horse could short-cut the long-distance roundabout waterways that dominated so much of the nation's transportation. And these individuals were not being held hostage by some Jeffersonian nostalgia about defending the yeoman farmer and fearing an urbanizing America. The sentiment of the Southern delegates was that such a giant railroad would not be detrimental to slavery; in fact, it might protect the particular institution.[49]

With hard work and a dollop or two of luck there would be trains running along the LC&C in the foreseeable future. Yet population figures alone suggested that a difficult task lay ahead. A low population density threatened any long-distance railroad undertaking, especially through the southern Appalachians. At the time there were just 15 million people living in the United States, and only about thirty places claimed populations of more than 10,000. Later in the century demographic conditions would be far more favorable for railroad promotion when the population approached 65 million and fifty cities each counted more than 100,000 residents. Still in 1836 expectations were clear: the Louisville, Cincinnati & Charleston Rail Road would reap unfathomable economic rewards and shatter spatial barriers. In the mind of Hayne and fellow delegates, "all conquering steam has indeed changed the condition of the world, and the fortunes of the human race."[50]

Surveys, Finances, and Construction

4

SURVEYS

Essential to achieving the objective of the Knoxville Railroad Convention was locating the *exact* route for the Louisville, Cincinnati & Charleston Rail Road (LC&C). The geography of this vast proposed service area meant that decision makers needed to make choices, and often their choices became contentious. Robert Hayne and his supporters strongly favored the French Broad River valley for crossing the spine of the Southern Appalachians. Such a pathway would benefit South Carolinians, both Charlestonians and residents of other important communities in the Palmetto State. Routing options included possible service to Columbia, Greenville, Spartanburg, and York.[1]

This building strategy through the Midlands and Upstate South Carolina would permit several transportation-starved counties in western North Carolina to receive rail service. As for a route through the western section of the Tar Heel State, rumors flew. Some believed that the LC&C presence would be more extensive. The longer path, it was reported, would enter the state near Rutherfordton before turning generally westward over the crest of the mountains toward Asheville and the French Broad River. So many were hopeful.[2]

Others, mostly from Georgia, who were interested in the LC&C, were not so certain about the French Broad River valley. The feeling grew that a line northward from the South- Carolina Canal & Rail-Road Company (SCC&RRCO) terminus at Hamburg along the Savannah River through northeastern Georgia – the Rabun Gap (or Miller's Gap) – to the Little Tennessee River and then in the direction of the Cumberland Gap, located near the juncture of Kentucky, Tennessee, and Virginia, would be preferred. J. Edgar Thomson, the brilliant chief engineer for the Georgia Rail Road & Banking Company (Georgia Rail Road), had a somewhat

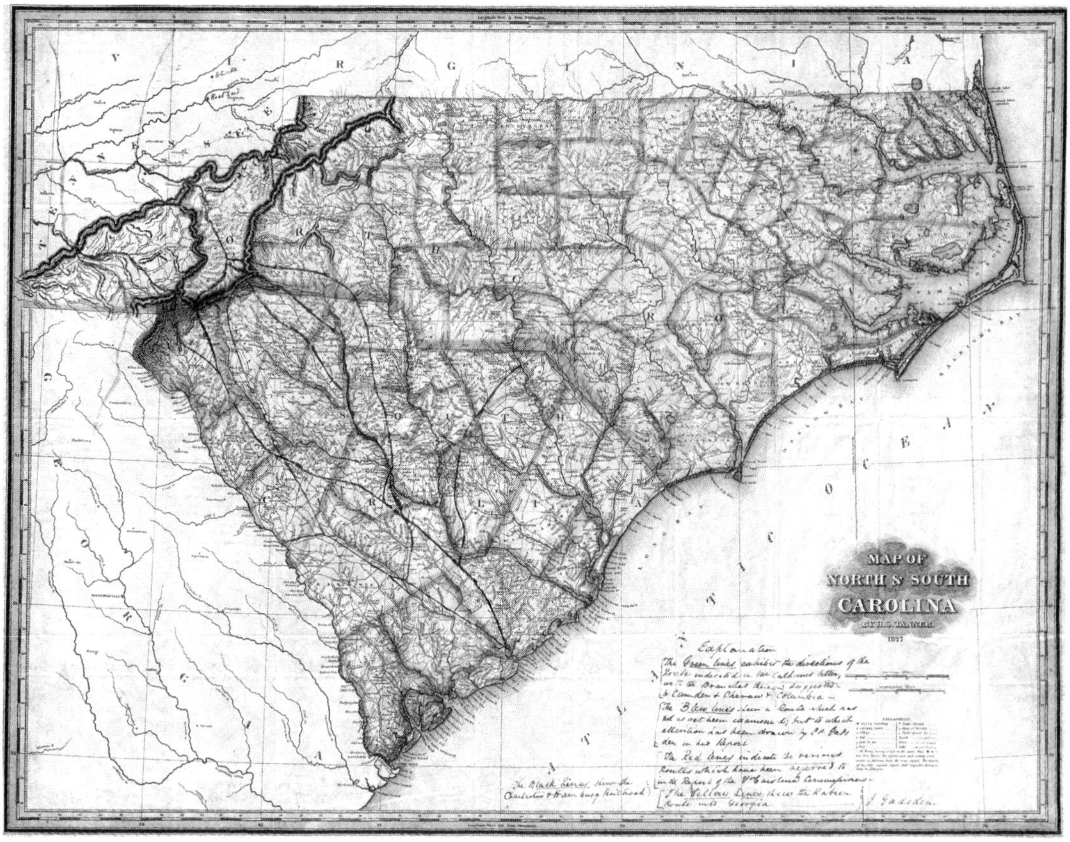

different idea, one favoring his employer. He estimated that a single track between Athens and Knoxville of approximately 200 miles was feasible and could be built at a reasonable cost. There were Georgians who contemplated another alternative, placing trackage further west and therefore avoiding some of the most rugged terrain of the region. Ross's Landing (Chattanooga) near the dangerous Suck on the Tennessee River, would likely be part of that routing design.[3]

Already instigators of the LC&C had tapped the resources of the federal government that facilitated internal improvements. Prior to the Knoxville Convention, U.S. Army engineers had conducted a crude survey (with cost estimates), but this was a general reconnaissance that offered several possible routes rather than a detailed topographical study. As the commissioners for the LC&C explained, "We have not attempted to ascertain definitively 'the best practicable route' for the said road, which could not have been done, with the means and time allowed us." The Knoxville delegates, however, expressed confidence that these army officers could determine precisely (and at what price) wetlands could be crossed, deep ravines and rivers bridged, and rocky obstacles blasted or bored. Everyone realized that difficult mountains lay athwart the route between Charleston and the Ohio River.[4]

The military personnel, who had been involved in the first examination of the French Broad River route, participated under terms of the General Survey Act of 1824, a landmark measure signed by President James Monroe. Initially this legislation was crafted to permit the federal government to make surveys for roads and canals of "national importance, in a commercial or military point of view, or necessary for the transportation of public mail." This meant that army personnel would fix routes, determine costs, and supervise construction.[5]

The military establishment applauded the survey measure for several reasons. In 1827 James Barbour, the new, perceptive secretary of war, wrote privately, "The successful introduction of Rail-Roads, into this country, is viewed by the Department as of great national importance, and especially any practicable mode of connecting the Atlantic States with the Western, whether by Rail-Roads or Canals." The secretary continued, "[Railroads and canals] offer the most sure and economical means to the Government to convey, to the different parts of the Union, the means of defense, in the transportation of men and munitions to the seat of war, wherever it shall exist." There was another perceived value: "It will give them [graduates of the U.S. Military Academy] experience and advance their usefulness to their country." Barbour realized that West Point produced more civil engineers than the army could possibly employ. The nation did not need that many men to conduct such assignments as locating and supervising the building of coastal fortifications, overseeing harbor improvements, including lighthouses and sea walls, and related construction projects.[6]

Since the time Secretary of the Treasury Albert Gallatin had proposed an interlocking network of improved transport, political conflicts had erupted over the role that Washington should play in fostering internal improvements. Neither Gallatin's proposed federal survey nor his specific recommendations for a national network of roads, river improvements, and canals won much favor from the "Virginia Dynasty" of presidents until the waning months of Monroe's second term. James Madison, most of all, fretted about federal involvement, fearing the pork barrel, corruption of government, and centralization of power. And strict constructionist Jeffersonians backed the Madison position. Yet during the Monroe administration there would be modest federal support for roads and canals, coming in the form of land grants to the states and stock subscriptions to individual companies. Secretary of War John C. Calhoun, who served in Monroe's cabinet from 1817 to 1825, deserves credit for this shift in federal policy, convincing the president of the strategic importance of improved transportation for national defense.[7]

It was fortunate for the emerging LC&C that Washington had moved toward supporting internal improvements. Having survey work done by professionals – there was an acute shortage of private-sector civil

Throughout the planning stages of the Louisville, Cincinnati & Charleston Rail Road, a variety of surveys occurred, some rough and some detailed. This annotated map, which dates from the latter part of 1836, was likely the work of Colonel James Gadsden and one that he sent to South Carolina governor George McDuffie. Apparently the report that accompanied this map has not survived. The core state map, drawn in 1822, indicates how the LC&C might be built through the Palmetto State. Each of the three lines ultimately would connect with a route through the valley of the French Broad River.

Courtesy of South Carolina Department of Archives and History.

engineers – and allowing the government to assume the financial burden pleased those associated with the developing project. Already army officers had participated in railroad surveys, starting with the Baltimore & Ohio Railroad in 1827. By 1835 they had assisted more than a dozen companies. Interestingly, the LC&C would benefit from the administrative accomplishments of Calhoun, who would be named a Knoxville Convention delegate. As war secretary this savvy South Carolinian centralized powers in his department, establishing an administrative hierarchy that enforced responsibility. These changes would have a positive impact on the future performance of the engineer corps.[8]

Following the Knoxville Convention federal assistance made possible a more complete survey, and the War Department gladly cooperated. If the LC&C opened as planned, direct military benefits would follow. In the event of war, troops and supplies could be moved more effectively between the three principal terminal cities and intermediate points, and products, especially cotton and foodstuffs, could be shipped to various domestic destinations. Backers of the railroad advanced these same arguments.

> Indeed, for all purposes of mutual protection and defense, Rail-Roads, may well supply the place of standing armies, since it enables a country acting on the defensive, to command almost immediately, the services of their *friends and allies,* whenever they may be needed: – while such Roads can never be converted to the purposes of an *invading army,* from the extreme facility, with which the intercourse afforded by them can, be cut off [italics in original].

This logic was used by military leaders, including Major General Edmund Gaines, who in the 1830s believed that railroads would "contribute greatly, incalculably, to the national defense during a state of war." Memories of poor transportation arteries that hampered troop and supply movements and nearly wrecked the national economy during the War of 1812 remained ingrained in the minds of many Americans, including proponents of the LC&C. Even the most fanatical Jeffersonian could see the value of improved transportation; a more mobile army could mean a smaller, less costly military establishment.[9]

The forthcoming field work, which took months to complete, again ignored the proposals made by the Georgians and others who objected to the French Broad River route. William McNeill led the corps of surveyors, and the likewise capable William G. Williams served as his principal assistant. Sensitive to Hayne and other like-minded South Carolinians, both men initially focused on the greatest survey (and most controversial) task, namely how best to conquer the Southern Appalachians.

The LC&C received top-notch technical assistance. Most prominent in the corps of engineers was William Gibbs McNeill (1801–53). As a lad this Wilmington, North Carolina, native considered the Episcopal clergy, but because of his love of mathematics he "expressed a wish to abandon the gown for the sword," accepting an appointment to West Point. In 1814 McNeill entered the academy and excelled at his studies. Following his graduation with the class of 1817 he began his formal military service, locating sites for coastal fortifications along the Gulf of Mexico. After passage of the General Survey Act McNeill participated in various internal improvement projects, the first being engineering work on the Summit Division of the Chesapeake and Ohio Canal and somewhat later for the James River and Kanawha Canal. In November 1828 McNeill joined an elite delegation of army engineers who visited Great Britain "to examine minutely all the railroads," and he returned "laden with much useful information." A number of assignments followed, including work for such railroad companies as the Boston & Providence, Long Island, Taunton & New Bedford, and Western Rail Road of Massachusetts. During this time his crowning achievement was the design and supervision of the construction for the Boston & Providence of the massive stone viaduct at Canton, Massachusetts, a structure that remains in use today. For several years McNeill served as chief engineer for the Baltimore & Susquehanna Rail Road. Apparently he spread his talents thinly by taking on too many responsibilities, especially with the survey duties management expected. There is no question, though, that McNeill demonstrated ability and drive throughout his professional career.[10]

As with many West Pointers, McNeill, who rose to the rank of major, resigned his army commission. Beginning in November 1837 he devoted his professional talents as a civilian employee to several railroads, including the LC&C. This was a smart decision financially. The LC&C paid handsomely, providing him with a salary of $8,000 and an additional $2,000 for expenses. Indeed, his annual income was twice that of company president Hayne. At least seven other officers also left the army to join the Charleston to Ohio River project, including Abbot Brisbane, Thomas Drayton (later active in the Charleston & Savannah Railroad), James Gadsden (future president of the LC&C) and James Reed. Captain William Williams, however, continued his military career.[11]

The desire of army engineers to leave the military is understandable. After 1838 the survey and engineering services provided to canal and railroad companies ended. Yet seven years earlier Washington had become less generous, ending payments for the full costs of surveys. The War Department still provided trained engineers, but the private sector needed to pay their expenses. Members of Congress grew to believe that even this assistance was too public-spirited, and so they repealed the legislation. U.S. Senator James Buchanan of Pennsylvania (and future president), for one, thought that investors in canal and railroad companies prospered while the business of the federal government was being neglected. There were also charges that these army surveyors concentrated too much on local projects that produced little in the way of national military benefits. The dramatic impact of the Panic of 1837 further dampened congressional enthusiasm. As the economy worsened, members of Congress who wished to save money, and some who considered the academy itself to be anti-republican and aristocratic, pushed, albeit unsuccessfully, to abolish the school.[12]

The LC&C leadership demanded the highest quality of survey work and provided the necessary financial support. "Too much attention could not possibly be bestowed [on surveys]," reasoned Hayne, "as a hasty and inconsiderate decision in this respect, though it might save present expense, may be followed by the *expenditures of millions,* to overcome difficulties which might at first have been avoided." He underscored the contention that the costs involved were a *"true economy"* (italics in original)."[13]

It is not known how many surveyors the LC&C employed. Major McNeill had requested that there be ten to twelve brigades, "each consisting of three officers, with a sufficient number rod-men, chain carriers, axe-men, &c." And these men needed "to be furnished with the proper instruments, camp equipage, and transportation." The company surely complied.[14]

Once in the field the daily life for railroad engineers and fellow location-party members, whether engaged in military or civilian work, was not always easy. For those involved with the LC&C, the rugged countryside of western North Carolina, with a landscape burdened with craggy outcroppings of rocks, heavily forested slopes and valleys, dense thickets of dog hobble (fetterbush) and rhododendron and the seasonal threat of poisonous plants and snakes and annoying insects, made for a difficult environment. Usually field operatives had to lug about their instruments and their camping equipment and supplies. "Was ordered down to Green River [in North Carolina] to join Mr. Whites party as leveler so I struck off for their camp and the day after my arrival commenced my duty in a little of the roughest country that you ever saw, reckoning," observed a member of the brigade of surveyors. "We could not advance with the minuteness and accuracy necessary more than a quarter of a mile a day as great parts of the ground required to be run over [with survey equipment] four or five times before leaving it."[15]

Yet accounts suggest that this field work produced positive experiences. Survey participant John C. Frémont, later the "Great Pathfinder of the West" and first presidential candidate of the Republican Party, retained pleasant memories. Employed as a civilian assistant to Captain Williams, Fremont wrote in his memoirs: "The survey was a kind of picnic, with work enough to give it zest, and we were all sorry when it was over." John Smedberg, a West Point graduate who also tramped about the wilderness, reiterated Frémont's remarks in a November 1837 letter to a friend in New York state: "We enjoyed ourselves to the upmost in camp, having an excellent opportunity to make ourselves comfortable, as we remained encamped in the same place for two weeks or more, and were allowed a cook and waggoner by the company, the latter of whom had nothing to do but cater for us between the periods of moving. I do not think that I ever passed a pleasanter six weeks in my life than those that we spent on Green River." Added Smedberg: "We had a most jolly time of it, having a party under us of 13 capable hands, and our camp consisting of four tents being pitched right in the midst of a wild uninhabited forest, in one of the prettiest little spots that I ever beheld."[16]

More important than contented surveyors, the extensive field operations, where personnel demonstrated close attention to topography and precise measurements, produced results. Their work collectively supported the flippant remark made by a contemporary West Pointer: "Give an Engineer money and he can go anywhere!" The examination of the mountainous region of the greater Asheville-Hendersonville-Flat Rock area had been painstaking. "Many of the routes have been traversed two or three times." The McNeill survey found that a workable passageway existed at Butt Mountain Gap, located about 2 miles southeast of Flat Rock near the South Carolina border and close to where the Asheville–Greenville turnpike spanned the Green River southeast of Hendersonville (near present-day U.S. Highway 25). As a crossing site it was deemed superior to the valley of the Reedy Patch Creek, east of Hendersonville, a tributary of the French Broad River. The Reedy Patch Gap summit was judged to be higher (2,218 feet) than the comparable point at Butt Mountain Gap (2,168 feet), and it would likely require multiple inclined planes and stationary steam engines. The McNeill team determined that if Butt Mountain Gap was selected, existing (and always improving) steam locomotives could be employed that would negate the need for expensive and labor-intensive inclined planes and their support machinery. The Reedy Patch Gap route, furthermore, would create a somewhat longer line.[17]

Once the mountains had been conquered, the remaining route to the Knoxville vicinity posed no serious problems. The French Broad River had cut a convenient passage through the often rugged terrain. Taking advantage of this natural route, the Buncombe Turnpike, chartered by North Carolina lawmakers in 1824 and completed four years later, extended "from the Saluda Gap, in the county of Buncombe, by way of Asheville and the Warm Springs [later renamed Hot Springs], to the Tennessee line." This primitive but usually passable roadway "brought a stream of travel through Western North Carolina." The turnpike became more than an avenue for human passage; it also served as a practical way to send an assortment of animals from Kentucky and Tennessee to markets in the Carolinas. "Drives at times included horses, mules, cattle, sheep, and even turkeys and ducks, [but] hogs soon came to be far and away the most important item of the traffic." These movements demonstrated the value of the French Broad valley as a commerce corridor.[18]

At the first annual meeting of LC&C stockholders, held in Flat Rock on October 16, 1837, and not far distant from Butt Mountain Gap, the decision was made to accept the McNeill surveys. The railroad would utilize this natural passageway to make its principal mountain crossing. This routing strategy drew enthusiastic comments. "The ascent of the mountains from South Carolina, was expected to be a work of extreme difficulty and expense, but a route has been found which ascends the Alleghany [*sic*] mountains, and crosses at the Butt mountain gap, without a single inclined plane or stationary engine, and with a grade, the highest point of which does not exceed 60 feet to the mile, and that, too, only for 14 miles," said an exuberant Christopher G. Memminger, "and even this grade can, by a slight change in the plan, be reduced to less than 50 feet to the mile."[19]

Those stockholders who assembled at Flat Rock dealt with other important matters. They agreed to have rails terminate at or near Columbia, and they voted to run track to Knoxville before swinging northward through the Cumberland Gap and eastern Kentucky toward the Ohio River.[20]

During the latter part of 1837 and into the following year, the survey corps explored a route to the north. The LC&C received profile maps of three "Experimental Surveys" for the approximately 200 miles between Knoxville and Lexington, revealing that there were several ways to manage this hilly and mountainous country. "It has been ascertained that the Mountains can be passed with locomotive engines, at grades less than had been adopted on other Roads; and that no serious obstacles were presented to the construction of the work on any part of the line." Also it was reported that a "new pass," known as Bill Creek near Wheeler's Gap in Hancock County, Tennessee, "promised to afford a ready passage across the Cumberland Mountains, without the use of inclined planes of stationary engines." The McNeill-supervised surveyors indicated that access to Cincinnati across northern Kentucky could be accomplished by running along the ridge from the Lexington area to Covington or by descending from the ridge north of Lexington and then following the valley of the Licking River to near Newport.[21]

And Louisville could be reached. There was the expectation that the long-struggling and partially built Lexington & Ohio Rail Road (L&ORR) would provide the connection. Although the L&ORR planned to span the nearly 70 miles between Lexington and Louisville, via Frankfort, by 1834

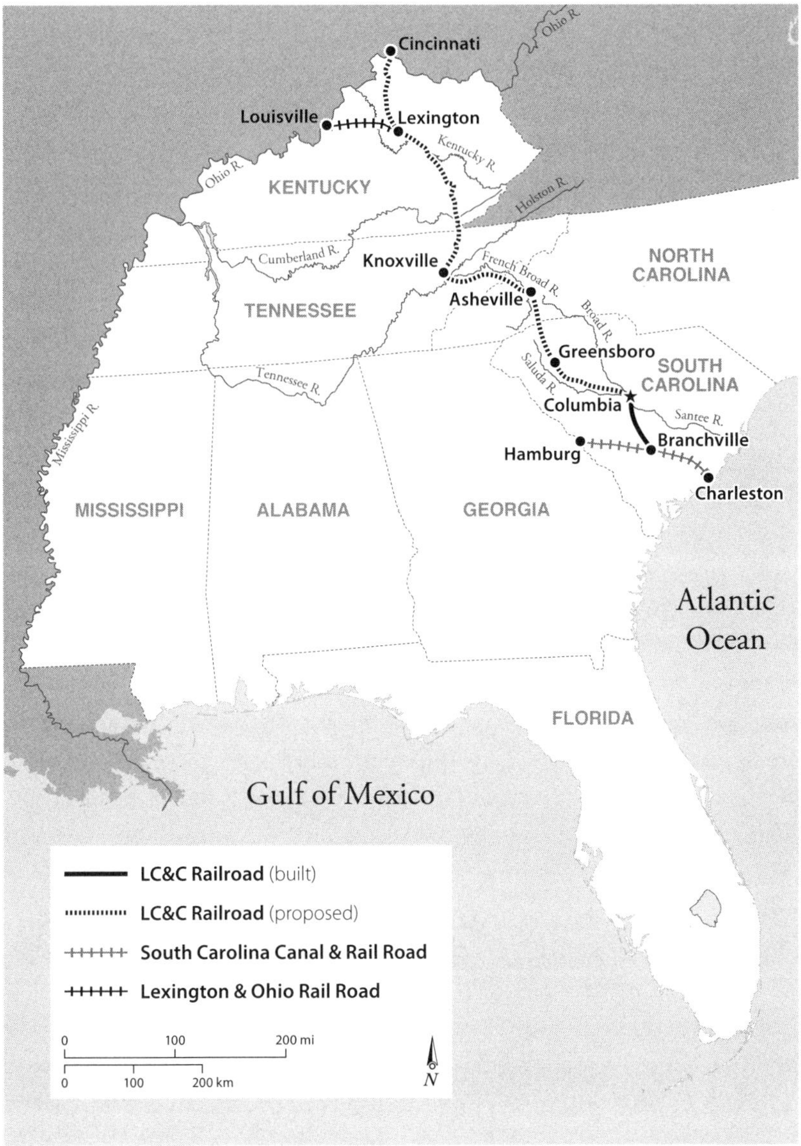

Although the route for the Louisville, Cincinnati & Charleston Rail Road was never precisely determined, this map reveals the most likely path that would have been taken between South Carolina and the Ohio River. Admittedly it is only an approximation.

Created by the Office of Creative Services, Indiana University.

it ran for only about 30 miles between Lexington and the top of the hill east of Frankfort. An inclined plane was needed to reach the Kentucky River and the capital. A year or so later the L&ORR built a disconnected segment, known as the "Portland Railroad." This trackage extended the several miles between downtown Louisville and Portland, Kentucky, situated at the west end of the Louisville and Portland Canal, the first major internal improvement in the Bluegrass State. A few years earlier this steamboat canal had opened, permitting river traffic to bypass the treacherous Falls of the Ohio River and "overcoming the only serious impediment to the free navigation of that great river." The rail spur had caused some Louisvillians to fret about a "rival city," Portland, in their midst. The L&ORR also held charter rights to build beyond Lexington to the Ohio River, to either Maysville or opposite Cincinnati, but the L&ORR had not commissioned surveys to the latter destinations.[22]

But Lexington & Ohio rails were not the only possibility for servicing Louisville. LC&C brass argued that its own line could easily reach the city. "A branch, starting from the main truck before it reaches the Kentucky river," suggested a company publication, "in a direct course from the Crab Orchard, or between that point and the Cumberland mountains, for Louisville, would be perhaps forty miles shorter than the road to Cincinnati [and] would pass over more favorable ground."[23]

It appeared that debate over the most hotly contested aspect of the routing of the LC&C had finally been put to rest. But that was not to be. Just as Georgians objected to a French Broad River route, so, too, did John C. Calhoun, and he made his unhappiness known. Following the Knoxville Convention this Olympian political figure, who lived at Fort Hill Plantation in the Anderson District of Upstate South Carolina and within sight of the Blue Ridge Mountains, lobbied for alternative routes. In no way was Calhoun opposed to the iron horse, only the McNeill survey. "I think with you the rail road system must be greatly extended in the South," he wrote to a Pennsylvania friend in 1833, "but there will probably be a short pause to see how the experiments already made will succeed." Soon railroad technology scored impressive advances, and Calhoun kept abreast of these changes. He also saw the value of a long-distance transmontane road. "I am rejoiced to learn by your letter that a point so important as Cincinnati, is taking so deep an interest in connecting the West, by a rail-road, with the southern Atlantic States – an object which I have long considered the most important in the whole range of internal improvements," he replied to a Cincinnati correspondent in September 1835. "I have no doubt of its practicability at a reasonable cost, and of the immense importance, commercially, politically, and socially."[24]

Following the Knoxville Convention, the preferred route that Calhoun advocated almost literally ran through his backyard, the sprawling Fort Hill Plantation located along the Seneca River – a tributary to the Savannah River – and close to the confluence of Twelve Mile Creek and the Keowee River, streams that formed the Seneca. He foresaw the LC&C extending from its western terminus at Hamburg northward along the river valleys of the Savannah, Seneca, Keowee, and Little Tennessee and then to the Cumberland Gap and beyond.[25]

The geography of this region had long fascinated Calhoun. When he served as secretary of war, he ordered army engineers to survey the Savannah and Tennessee Rivers and requested that they draw detailed maps. "In this map of Tennessee river [it] was laid down with all its tortuous windings through the mountains overhanging its banks, from the Blue

This frequently reproduced portrait of a youthful John C. Calhoun correctly portrays a determined politician and individual.

Courtesy of Clemson University Archives.

Ridge to its egress," a Knoxville resident remembered decades later. "A copy of this map was exhibited for several years here in Knoxville." And from his plantation, according to his biographer Charles M. Wiltse, "Calhoun often studied the southeastern rim of the Appalachian rampart, and from the peculiar formation of the mountains just a compass point west of north he judged there must be a passage through the ridge."[26]

But Calhoun did more than have army personnel examine his home locale and make occasional views of the Blue Ridge mountains with his "glass"; he wanted to explore for himself what he believed to be the potentially ideal route for the LC&C or, for that matter, any other railroad. He was troubled that the Knoxville Convention had opted for the French Broad route without a dissenting vote. Furthermore Calhoun was not about to be merely an armchair advocate. Supposedly Calhoun had learned of an acceptable mountain passage from area residents who were familiar with the long-distance trails made by the Cherokees, the dominant Indian tribe. He was surely familiar with Robert Mills's belief, publicized in the 1820s, that a transmontane canal could be built through this general region, in this case connecting the Tugaloo and Hiwassee Rivers and thus forging that critical link between the Savannah and Tennessee streams. During the summer of 1836 it was also reported that J. Edgar Thomson, the Georgia Rail Road chief engineer, contemplated a rail line from Athens to Knoxville through the Rabun Gap and along the Little Tennessee River. In September 1836, two months after the Knoxville meeting, Calhoun decided to check out a pathway to the north and northwest of his plantation home. This he did. But he did not go alone, being joined by Colonel James Gadsden, a friend from his tenure at the War Department who had served as army adjutant general, and Colonel William Sloan, a Fort Hill neighbor.[27]

Calhoun did more than explore; he penned a multipage report, written at Fort Hill on September 22, 1836. He quickly delivered his commentary to Frederick Symmes, editor of the nearby *Pendleton Messenger,* who also represented the Anderson District in the state legislature. The intrepid Calhoun offered a description of his travels and findings that followed nine days of being "incessantly engaged." The route he suggested bypassed Rabun Gap somewhat to the southwest, and ran through what he called the Carolina Gap, located near present-day Cashiers, North Carolina. Calhoun told his friend Symmes, in part, "We commenced our examination near his residence [James McKinney of the Pickens District], and extended it to the gap in the mountains, in which the White Water, one of the Western branches of the Keowee, takes its source, and thence down the Tuckasiege [*sic*], which rises on the Western side of the same gap, to which it joins Little Tennessee in Macon County [later Swain County, North Carolina]; the distance about 45 miles by estimation." He explained that his party did not push beyond the Tuckasegee River "as the survey of Capt. [Herman] Batche [Bache] under the orders of the War Department gives ample information in relation to Little Tennessee from the junction of the Tuckasiege [*sic*] to the head of steamboat navigation on that river. It is sufficient to say, that there is no serious difficulty below." Calhoun added, "On our return, we examined the parts of the route that required further attention, and extended the examination from where we first commenced, across the Keowee River along the old [Cherokee] Indian path. From thence to where the route would strike the dividing ridge between the waters of Saluda and Savannah, about 8 or 10 miles below Pickensville [later Easley, Pickens County], there can be no difficulty, as there can be none from that point to Charleston." Calhoun did not fuss about the projected rail route north of Knoxville, but he suggested that a railroad should also be built from Knoxville through Crab Orchard Gap, Tennessee, an opening in the Crab Orchard Mountains, a subrange of the Cumberlands, northwestward to the Cumberland River, allowing for a connection to Nashville and other points along that navigable stream.[28]

Calhoun correctly anticipated that newspapers in South Carolina and elsewhere would reprint his letter to the *Pendleton Messenger*. This weekly organ, albeit published in a remote upstate village, served as the conduit for some of his most important position statements. Calhoun also shared his positive findings with others, including several influential planters. In a letter to his brother-in-law Colonel James Edward Colhoun (an alternative spelling of the Calhoun family name), who owned Midway and Millwood plantations in the Abbeville District along the suggested Carolina Gap route, Calhoun reported the results of his exploration party as being "eminently favourable; far more than I anticipated. It has a decided preference over all other routes and nothing but suitable efforts are required to ensure its success." In another communication with his brother-in-law, Calhoun opined that if the LC&C management embraced his routing, "I feel confident that $6 million by the Carolina Gap will carry it [LC&C] from Charleston to the Ohio, such as the great facility of the route." He also believed that the French Board River route had been a sop to North Carolinians, being a quid pro quo arrangement to get support for the railroad from the Tar Heel State.[29]

What Calhoun mentioned to neither Symmes nor Colhoun was that a railroad built through the Carolina Gap, via his homestead, would be personally beneficial. If such a line opened, the Fort Hill Plantation could send cotton reliably to merchant-brokers in Charleston; after all, steamboat service on the upper reaches of the Savannah-Seneca river system was erratic at best. Supplies and other items for family and plantation needs could also be conveniently received by rail. Since Calhoun traveled regularly and often experienced difficulties with stagecoaches over the miserable roads, access to dependable passenger train service would enhance his quality of life. He remembered the unusually wet winter of 1832–1833 that had made a quagmire of roads through much of the region. Perhaps Calhoun sensed that as a member of the U.S. Senate he might receive complimentary rail travel; after all, beginning in 1844 he obtained a free lifetime "frank," or pass, for trains on the South Carolina Railroad. As with all railroads, at least initially, land prices along and near the right-of-way rose, even soared. In one case, Eastin Morris, president of the La Grange & Memphis Rail Road, wrote in 1839 that "there is not a track of land on the whole line that has not advanced in value from 25 to 100 per cent. in consequence of the location of the Road through it." Calhoun was hardly adverse to having the value of his real-estate holdings increase. Moreover, he and his son-in-law, Thomas Green Clemson, diplomat and scientist, were invested in a gold mining venture located in Lumpkin County, Georgia, site of America's first great mineral rush. A railroad that would run about a 100 miles from their O'Barr Mine outside Dahlonega would make that property somewhat more convenient and potentially more profitable. And who knew; a branch line might eventually connect the mining region with his home neighborhood. Calhoun and Clemson agreed that local transport throughout most of South Carolina and Georgia was abysmal, whether for personal travel or freight shipments. A contemporary described a trip to the Dahlonega mining district as being in "a clumsy stage, rumbling and jolting over intolerable roads."[30]

When it came to potential railroad routes, Calhoun revealed some flexibility. Although he singled out Captain Williams, Major McNeill's principal associate, for harsh and unfair criticism – "I have no confidence in his impartiality & but little in his judgement" – the established credibility of McNeill may have caused his intense enthusiasm for the Carolina Gap option to wane. The major argued that the French Broad valley was far superior to what Calhoun had proposed, and he showed no interest, either, for a railroad through Rabun Gap. Each was "manifestly impractical." Later, as McNeill told state officials:

> Several routes surveyed for our Rail Road, connecting the Eastern and Western routes, *through the Carolinas,* are distinguished over all others, by the great ease with which it enables us, from the Eastern or Southern base of the great chain of mountains so to distribute the ascent as gradually to attain the very summit or the Allegheny, or Blue Ridge, at inclinations far within the limits of the advantageous application of locomotive engines, (and without the intervention of a single *inclined* requiring stationary power), and peculiarly are they so by the extraordinary facility with which the descent Westward is effected from the summit of the Great Allegheny Range [italics in original].

Nevertheless, Calhoun continued to oppose the French Broad Valley alternative. "The more I reflect the more I am convinced," he told Colonel Colhoun in December 1838, "any route that overlooks this important advantage must fail[,] that the success of the road will depend on the direction, and that on striking steam navigation on the intermediate streams between the Blue ridge and the Ohio at the nearest and most favourable point."[31]

Hayne rejected Calhoun's survey suggestions, and for good reasons. The LC&C activist trusted McNeill and his experienced associates, and he firmly believed that the valley of the French Broad River was "unexampled in the topography of the world." Hayne, too, did some personal exploring of his own. The Calhoun findings prompted him to check out these alternative routes, and he concluded that they were impractical. Calhoun's scornful response: Hayne had been "misled by the guide."[32]

Construction costs also influenced Calhoun's reasoning. Even earlier he had stated privately that the success of the LC&C involved locating suitable connections with navigable Southern rivers, namely "striking steam navigation on the intermediate streams between the Blue Ridge and the Ohio at the nearest and most favorable parts." As he contended, "Steam navigation on the western waters is many times cheaper than on railroads, and of course the Tennessee and Cumberland Rivers, if struck where navigable for steam, would be the best and cheapest extension of the railroad." Calhoun closed with his oft-repeated remark: "Any route that overlooks this important advantage must fail."[33]

The sharp differences in routing philosophies led the South Carolina senator to sever his ties with the LC&C. In time Calhoun dismissed *any* route that would run directly to Cincinnati and Louisville. Instead he expressed his desire for an *all-southern* railroad to the West. In 1841 Calhoun explained his sectionalist thoughts to John P. King, president of the Georgia Rail Road and prominent politician from Augusta. The South Carolinian thought that it was essential to establish direct trade between the "staple States" and that "it could not be done unless by opening the connection between Charleston and the valley of Mississippi." He eagerly endorsed iron rails running west from Hamburg through Georgia, Alabama, and Tennessee to the Mississippi River at Memphis. In achieving this goal the line would likely use the completed Tuscumbia, Courtland & Decatur Rail Road (TC&DRR). Such a rail artery would bind the South economically and socially, two outcomes that pleased Calhoun.[34]

The importance of the TC&DRR was rightly recognized. This pioneer road, which had been built to contemporary standards, connected the Tennessee River at Tuscumbia Landing with the towns of its corporate name. When it opened in late 1834 for freight and passenger operations, this 45-mile road offered a valuable bypass to the treacherous Muscle Shoals of the Tennessee, and it was situated on a direct path to Memphis.[35]

Calhoun (and others, too) believed that the Alabama pike could be easily connected to the emerging rail projects in Georgia. In 1833 Georgia investors had organized the Central Rail Road & Canal Company of Georgia (Central of Georgia) and two years later reorganized their firm as the Central Rail Road & Banking Company of Georgia. The goal was to tie Savannah with Macon, but not until 1843 did service begin between these two cities, a distance of 191 miles. Later the Central of Georgia prospered by connecting with two other early carriers, the Macon & Western and the South Western railroads, properties that the Central of Georgia came to control. And an affiliate spiked down 54 miles of rails between Millen, located on its main line, and Augusta. Before the Civil War an observer called the Central of Georgia the "best managed road in the world." Another contemporary project, albeit one that was more attractive from Calhoun's perspective, was the fledgling Georgia Rail Road, also chartered in 1833 and likewise permitted to operate a railroad bank. Backers of this Central of Georgia rival planned to build west from the Savannah River at Augusta. But a physical connection would not be immediately forged with the SCC&RRCO at Hamburg, permitting freight traffic diversions to Charleston. Not until 1853 did that vital bridge open. Still, each road shared the Southern gauge of 5 feet. The immediate objectives for the Georgia Rail Road were reaching Athens, the "Classical City," home of the state university and a budding manufacturing center, and to extend a branch to Madison, Georgia. This Peach State company also contemplated a 211-mile line between Athens and Knoxville and a somewhat shorter, albeit more expensive, trackage between Athens and the proposed Hiwassee Rail Road, a Tennessee company that hoped to build from Knoxville southwesterly to the Georgia border. But not until 1845 was the 173-mile Georgia Rail Road completed. In the interim the company pushed the Madison extension to White Hall (now part of Atlanta) and proceeded to the proposed junction with the state-owned Western & Atlantic Rail Road at Marthasville (Atlanta), a village that then consisted of five dwellings and "little else except pretension." But it did not take that long before Atlanta or "Terminus" emerged "from the shadows of the forest and leaped into prominence as a [railroad] focal point."[36]

The west-of-Hamburg strategy garnered only lukewarm support in South Carolina. Leaders in business circles considered a Memphis, via Georgia and Alabama, rail network potentially detrimental to their pocketbooks. Traffic from along that route would be susceptible to diversion by rail or water to Savannah, Mobile, Alabama, and possibly elsewhere. Perhaps the most vocal advocate for the rail artery to Memphis besides Calhoun was Colonel Gadsden. Ironically, he had once embraced the French Broad River route, having then stated, "That from actual examination of the gaps of the Saluda Mountains, the railroad may be made to cross the chain with more facility than was first imagined." But his closeness to Calhoun and the growing financial problems faced by the LC&C prompted a reconsideration. At the time, though, Gadsden was not a powerful opinion maker in the Palmetto State; he posed no real threat to Hayne and those who backed the McNeill survey.[37]

Calhoun also advocated for more regional railroads. He wanted iron rails to extend from the proposed Memphis line and other trackage in Georgia to Mobile and the "Gulph of Mexico." As he wrote in 1844, he favored another railroad that would link the TC&DRR not only with Memphis but "with the Cumberland [River] at Nashville." Added the South Carolinian, "The completion of the whole, I regard as of the utmost importance in every view; commercial, political and social. It will effect a revolution in the trade of the Great Valleys of the West." He continued to agitate for "Southern Rail Roads" and played a pivotal role in a railroad convention held in Memphis in 1845. As body president, Calhoun told fellow delegates that he wished to unite the South and West but *not* with the North, specifically those states and territories of the Old Northwest and the upper Mississippi River valley. Not surprisingly Calhoun earlier had backed a rail connection from the SCC&RRCO northward to the Abbeville and Anderson Districts and approved of additional trackage in his native state. "A branch will probably be made to Columbia to gratify the interests in that quarter," he opined in late 1837, "to which there can be no great objection."[38]

The developing network of southern railroads that Calhoun envisioned slowly emerged. In early 1858 key trackage, flying the banner of the Memphis & Charleston Rail Road, which had acquired the TC&DRR, at last opened between Memphis and Chattanooga when crews finished their work outside the Tennessee city. Service then became possible to Atlanta by the connecting Western & Atlantic Rail Road. After May 1, 1858, through rail travel became possible between Memphis and Charleston, but Calhoun did not witness these accomplishments, having died eight years earlier.[39]

FINANCING

As critical as establishing a practical route was financing. More precise cost estimates suggested that the price tag for Charleston to Cincinnati or Charleston to Lexington railroad would be about $11 to $12 million ($226.6 to $247 million in 2012 dollars), excluding locomotives, freight and passenger equipment, depots, wood and water stations, and other infrastructure. Those who opposed the railroad, including tavern and stagecoach owners, individuals removed from the survey or who sought an alternate routing, and staunch fiscal conservatives, all contended that the railroad would be too costly, and exploited that perceived weakness to thwart proponents. Andrew Jackson, who personally despised Robert Hayne and some other proponents of the road, announced, according to the *Knoxville Register,* "that it will require fifty millions of dollars to construct the railroad." This was a gross exaggeration, although some in the know believed that the final construction cost would approach $19 million ($391 million in 2012 dollars). The former U.S. president, in his paranoid fashion, went on to say that "it is all a scheme of nullifiers to get into power." And there were other "men in high places," whom a Georgia newspaper editor identified in 1837, who found the status quo in transportation acceptable. Still, this pro-railroad journalist was optimistic: "*Opposition* however fortunately cannot *prevent* the success of such works as the *New-York and Erie,* the *Baltimore and Ohio,* the *James River and Kanawha,* the

Charleston and Cincinnati [LC&C], and the *Georgia, Western and Atlantic* Improvements" (italics in original). He closed with this argument (and the sentiment of many others): "The PEOPLE require them and they will be accomplished in due time" (capitalization in original). And there were individuals who remained unconvinced that railroads were superior to canals. This minority, albeit at times vocal, was repeatedly criticized as antimodern. "Of the superiority of railroads as a means of communication, we had conceived that there was no doubt. The old and ill founded prejudices in favor of Canals are yet entertained by many who should know better," chided the *American Railroad Journal*.[40]

Following the Knoxville Convention, the LC&C supporters were confident about achieving their "magnificent" project. Yet they realized that the undertaking would be expensive and fraught with financial difficulties. Nevertheless, they believed that funding could be arranged, notwithstanding that the underdeveloped nation suffered from limited investment capital. Also there really was no warning of the impending Panic of 1837. Nor was there an expectation of what that sharp downturn would bring, although some businessmen and agriculturalists worried about an inflationary wage spiral that had begun toward the end of 1836. A manic prosperity existed; ebullience and optimism reigned. Land prices rose, and foreign demand for American agricultural products grew, with cotton advancing from six to eight cents per pound in 1833 to from fifteen to twenty cents per pound in 1836. Domestic banking prospered as the money supply expanded and credit restraints eased. This new age of "free banking" created a financial environment that led to a proliferation of frequently dubious state and private banks, allowing the number of these institutions to grow from approximately 300 in 1820 to about 1,000 in 1840. Furthermore, proponents anticipated that the federal government, buoyed by elimination of the national debt in 1834 and a growing treasury surplus, would extend loans to the states under terms of the Surplus Revenue Act passed in June 1836. The thinking prevailed that these funds would not have to be repaid and that the distribution policy would continue indefinitely. As James Clark, the Whig Party pro-business governor of Kentucky, told state lawmakers, "It is evident that the intention of Congress was to make a permanent distribution rather than a temporary loan to the States."[41]

There were other positive possibilities. It seemed probable that adjoining landowners would donate property for the right-of-way or sell cheaply. Perhaps they could be compensated through complimentary train travel. Similarly, communities would surely provide real estate for stations, yards, and other facilities. Promoters of the LC&C knew that real-estate contributions to the SCC&RRCO had been generous and cost-saving. It was also widely recalled that the Charleston to Hamburg line had successfully financed its long-distance construction between 1830 and 1833, and that recently, in February 1836, the emerging Georgia Rail Road scored brilliantly with the quick sale of its securities after opening its subscription books. These shares subsequently sold at a premium if they could be found at all. Somewhat earlier, newspapers nationwide had made much of the frenzy to invest in the Utica & Schenectady Rail-Road. When that company made public its subscription books, shares were immediately oversubscribed.[42]

The economies associated with slavery potentially offered much. The LC&C would slice through four slaveholding states, and the company could either buy slaves or lease them from their masters. Early on it became apparent that employment of slaves in railroad building projects reduced construction costs and the later expenses associated with operations and maintenance. Already the money differential had become clear. In the mid-1830s the SCC&RRCO paid about $18,000 per mile to build its trans-state line, while the price tag for the Baltimore & Ohio to construct its Baltimore to Washington, D.C., extension exceeded $53,000 per mile; slave versus free labor contributed to the sizable dissimilarities in expenditures. "In the slave-holding states," observed Hayne, "we can command slave labor to any amount at reasonable prices." Already the peculiar institution had become fused with railroad development. Any objections went unrecorded. After all, contemporary science taught that blacks were intrinsically inferior to whites, a belief that supported slavery.[43]

The heart the LC&C financing strategy involved stock sales to individuals and governments. As a mandate of its corporate charter the company called for the issuance of $4 million of securities to take place beginning in mid-October 1836. Therefore 40,000 shares, selling for $100 each, would need to be subscribed to as a requisite for the formal organization. But the full amount of any stock sale did not have to be paid immediately, a common practice of antebellum railroads. In other words shares were floated on the installment plan. Only $5 at the time of the initial commitment was expected. These subscription books became available to potential investors at various places between Charleston and Cincinnati, including Columbia and Knoxville.[44]

Initially the leadership of the LC&C opted for common stock and not corporate bonds. After the Civil War the latter became popular as the primary way to finance railroad construction, but in the 1830s railroads, including those in the South, often took the stock approach. This was hardly a foolish decision. Relying on the sale of shares would eliminate interest payments on debt and would guarantee stockholder control. Also, domestic investment banking houses were just developing, and the financial system remained somewhat primitive. Furthermore, European money men, especially those in the leading financial centers of London and Amsterdam, expressed growing reservations about bonds issued by some American public bodies and individual companies, particularly for canal construction and improvements. These foreign capitalists, nevertheless, continued to endorse certain projects, being eager to accept Massachusetts, New York, and Maryland state paper; in fact, they generally favored government issues. Even during the financial setbacks caused by the Panic of 1837, the Dutch house of Daniel Crommelin and Sons gladly promoted the sale of $200,000 of 3-percent State of Maryland bonds to aid the Baltimore & Susquehanna Rail Road. Yet some financiers, usually those associated with London houses, expressed an unwillingness to purchase securities of the "*Southern* or *Slave* States" (italics in original). This tendency prompted an industry trade writer to comment correctly: "The question of slavery has nothing to do necessarily, with the value of railroad securities, nor the productiveness or management of these works." The issue of the peculiar institution really did not stymie the money flow to any one state. By the 1850s more than 70 percent of all foreign investments had been placed in public securities, being heavily oriented toward state debts. Europeans' big interest in American railroads, however, developed nearly two decades after the Knoxville Railroad Convention. The massive federal land grant to the Illinois Central Railroad in 1850 convinced a range of non-American investors that the debt of this company was secure. And this feeling grew for many operating and projected railroads.[45]

If the LC&C was to become a functioning railroad, shares must be taken. Supporters turned to moral suasion to attract investors. "Let SUBSCRIPTION be the order of the day," proclaimed the editor of the *Charleston Courier,* and he was not alone in his quest for financial support (capitalization in original). In Charleston backers canvassed the city to made certain "that no citizen should omit to enroll his name on the list of the supporters of this noble enterprise; if he can do no more, even for a single share." No one could deny that the power elite in Charleston controlled the city (and the state for that matter); these were men who commanded great economic, political, and social power.[46]

After the subscription books had closed, representatives of the LC&C gathered in Knoxville in early November. The results were encouraging. South Carolina led the way in an impressive fashion, hardly a surprise to observers, committing to 32,336.5 shares. Next came Tennessee with 3,554 shares, followed by Kentucky with 1,871 shares, North Carolina with 1,026 shares, and Ohio with a distant 122 shares. That meant a shortfall of 2,090.5 shares. Fortunately a white knight, who had already invested heavily in the LC&C, came forward. Purportedly the wealthiest man in South

Carolina, Wade Hampton II, who had made a fortune from land speculation in Mississippi, sugar production in Louisiana, and cotton raising in South Carolina and who also had married a rich wife, subscribed to the remaining shares. In his hometown of Columbia he made a cash payment of $10,452.50. Said the *Charleston Courier:* "The glory of the enterprise belongs to South Carolina and South Carolinians."[47]

The stock picture revealed that South Carolina and Tennessee were anxious to have the LC&C and that Ohio showed little interest with that paltry commitment from its residents, most of whom hailed from Cincinnati. One likely explanation for what was largely token support was that so many denizens of the Queen City remained oriented toward river commerce. Some of its leading citizens had made substantial investments in river vessels and bankside warehouses and related facilities. Construction of steamboats steadily increased, and by 1837 output rivaled Pittsburgh, the premier boat-building center on the Ohio River. Through various financial investments Cincinnatians also had supported local turnpikes and canals, taking delight in the extension of the Miami Canal from Dayton northward to the Wabash and Erie Canal and thereby gaining access to Lake Erie. They also sought better transport connections to southeastern Indiana through the Cincinnati and Whitewater Canal, a private corporation that received strong backing from Cincinnati investors and also municipal largess.[48]

Still the realistic expectation of the LC&C having $4 million in its coffers and a functioning charter did not resolve financial matters. At least another $7 million was needed, and probably much more. Led by the indefatigable Hayne, the company pushed for major commitments from the states, and it did so with some success. These financial assurances reflected that earlier commitment by individuals to support the railroad; lawmakers in South Carolina earmarked $1 million, and their counterparts in Tennessee committed $650,000. This willingness to participate in the financing was in marked contrast to what happened in some other states. Historian Stephen Salsbury shows that Massachusetts legislators "considered canals and railroads too novel, too untried and financially too risky to merit aid." Later the Bay State invested in railroad securities, but only after the several carriers demonstrated that they were practical and profitable. In the South, however, according to historian Aaron Marrs, more than half of the amount invested in capital stock in the region came from public treasuries. "States proved to be a critical solution to the problem of railroad financing in the South."[49]

Another money-raising strategy emerged that was designed to make the LC&C a reality: creation of a state-chartered railroad bank. "We consider the establishment of the RAILROAD BANK, as *the bond* which will serve to hold the Company together," argued Hayne, "and afford a certain resource in every time of need, and therefore as essential to the success of our great work" (capitalization and italics in original).[50]

Immediately opposition to a railroad bank erupted. George McDuffie, the South Carolina governor, told legislators that it "would be a measure pregnant with danger to our general system of credit and currency, and in all respects inexpedient." The governor and his allies, including Calhoun, worried that the flourishing Bank of the State of South Carolina, which traced its operations back to 1812 and served as the state's depository and fiscal agent, might somehow be injured by a railroad-banking affiliate. That did not stop Hayne and his compatriots from lobbying hard for this ancillary corporation, successfully seeing a measure passed by the legislature that Governor McDuffie agreed to sign. Since the governor was little more than a ceremonial figurehead, McDuffie's support (or lack of it) was largely moot.[51]

These advocates for a railroad bank held great expectations for the benefits that this financial institution could provide. They realized that the Georgia Rail Road reaped the rewards of a bank, so much so that for years its notes had become accepted currency in Athens, Augusta, and elsewhere. Georgians considered this paper to be safe, likely more so than the currency issued by most banks. There were numerous examples of additional railroad banks. In Mississippi alone ten of these institutions had been created between 1833 and 1837, including the Grand Gulf & Banking Company and the Hernando Rail Road & Banking Company, albeit with mixed success. Even the newly formed Republic of Texas granted a charter in 1837 to the Texas Railroad & Banking Company for a railroad to connect the Sabine River and the Rio Grande. And the Erie & Kalamazoo Rail Road Bank, one of five chartered by Michigan lawmakers, made possible construction of the first common-carrier railroad in the Old Northwest, a 33-mile line between Toledo and Adrian that began operations in 1836. Private canal companies had also used their own banks effectively. In the 1820s a charter with banking privileges from the states of New York and Pennsylvania had supported what became the profitable anthracite-hauling Delaware and Hudson Canal. Backers of the LC&C held the realistic expectation that an affiliated bank would encourage private subscriptions to railroad stock, creating a premium price for its shares. They also anticipated that dividends on bank stock would generate funds for construction and would reconcile stockholders to delays in receiving returns on their railroad investments.[52]

What became the South-western Rail-Road Bank involved a complex relationship with the LC&C. First of all, no person who had not subscribed to railroad stock could invest in the bank, but every railroad shareholder would be eligible to take bank securities that were equal to the amount of his original investment. Yet the directorates and the stock of the two institutions were kept separate. Moreover, the LC&C was not liable for the debts of the bank and the bank was not liable for the debts of the railroad. In order to launch the South-western Rail-Road Bank, three of the four states that had chartered the LC&C needed to participate, and collectively $8 million of the stock in the railroad company had to be subscribed.[53]

The bank project got off to an encouraging start. South Carolina lawmakers authorized a subscription of $1 million, but more was needed. At the top of the "to do" list for the LC&C leadership was obtaining financial participation from those states outside South Carolina (Kentucky, North Carolina, and Tennessee) that the railroad would serve.[54]

Shortly after Christmas 1836 work began in North Carolina. The LC&C dispatched Christopher Gustavus Memminger, a Knoxville Rail-road Convention delegate and later secretary of the treasury for the Confederate States of America. This "Special Agent from South Carolina" went to Raleigh to promote this vital financial institution. The smart and articulate Memminger was armed with the reasoned arguments. As he told the governor, the bank would not disrupt the state's existing financial operations, and he stressed the importance of the railroad project, never mincing his words. "Without your aid this scheme utterly fails. If you refuse the demand we now make, the fate of our Internal Improvement is sealed. It will, then, be in vain to call upon the people again to unite their energies for future enterprises."[55]

Soon an authorization bill came before lawmakers, and Memminger remained active in Raleigh. In a speech delivered before the senate on January 2, 1837, he repeated reasons why the bank bill was essential for the railroad and why it would benefit the Tar Heel State. "The question now to be decided is between the grant of Banking privileges and the abandonment of an enterprise the most magnificent which the South has ever conceived, and which involves the destiny our country for many succeeding years."[56]

Memminger and other proponents of the railroad and bank should not have been shocked that opposition emerged in North Carolina's legislative halls. After all, the railroad, using the French Broad River route, would serve only a small portion of the state, albeit an area that suffered from acute isolation. North Carolinians, though, contemplated building a trans-state railroad, most probably linking Wilmington with Raleigh and other locations further west. In reality the LC&C would hardly favor Wilmington or some other North Carolina port, but rather Charleston. There was also the matter of the bank itself: it might weaken the established financial system. A worrisome feature for some was the requirement that the state treasurer would have to accept railroad bank notes for payment of any public debt. Although favoring the LC&C, other lawmakers expressed the feeling that the bank was an "artificial" prop. "A railroad is one thing, and a bank is another, and it cannot follow that because I am friendly to the road I must vote for the bank."[57]

Notwithstanding arguments against chartering the railroad bank, North Carolina lawmakers approved the measure on January 29, 1837. Soon the newly elected governor, Edward Bishop Dudley, a pro-business Whig, added his name, and smiles brightened the faces of LC&C supporters.[58]

Tennessee became the second focal point for ensuring the success of the South-western Rail-Road Bank. In October 1837 Robert Hayne traveled to Nashville to lobby lawmakers for banking privileges and financial participation. The respected South Carolinian found a receptive audience. Not only was he feted at a community banquet, but Volunteer State legislators invited him to speak before a joint legislative session. Hayne's oratorical skills and his cogent arguments resulted shortly in the bank winning the right to operate in the state and a subscription promise of $650,000. Apparently those gathered liked that the LC&C would provide security for the bank notes and that subscriptions to railroad and bank stock were rapidly mounting. The venture would hardly become another "wildcat" banking institution. Tennesseans mostly concurred. Later that year a public meeting of civic boosters took place in Knoxville, and these men warmly backed their lawmakers' actions, "evincing a laudable determination of our Legislature to foster a general and liberal system of internal improvements." At last the bank had met the requirement of being franchised in three of the four states along its projected route.[59]

Then there was Kentucky. Again the Bluegrass State became that thorn in the side of the LC&C. Railroad advocates believed that support from the state was essential. Even though Kentucky had earlier failed to commit to LC&C shares, the case for banking privileges, nevertheless, would be made in Frankfort. In late 1837 the company set the stage by producing a pamphlet that once more outlined the nature and advantages of a railroad bank. And the opportunity was not missed to explain why this railroad was so badly needed.

> The State of South Carolina has merely responded to the earnest appeal which called upon her, "by every consideration of patriotism and duty, *to act an example,* to her young sisters," by coming forward in a liberal spirit, to further an enterprise which was intended *to break down the mountain barriers* which now separate two entire sections of our common country, making their inhabitants strangers to each other; to throw open to the south the commerce of the great west, and to open to the west, by the shortest, cheapest, and most convenient route, an unrestricted intercourse with all the world [italics in original].

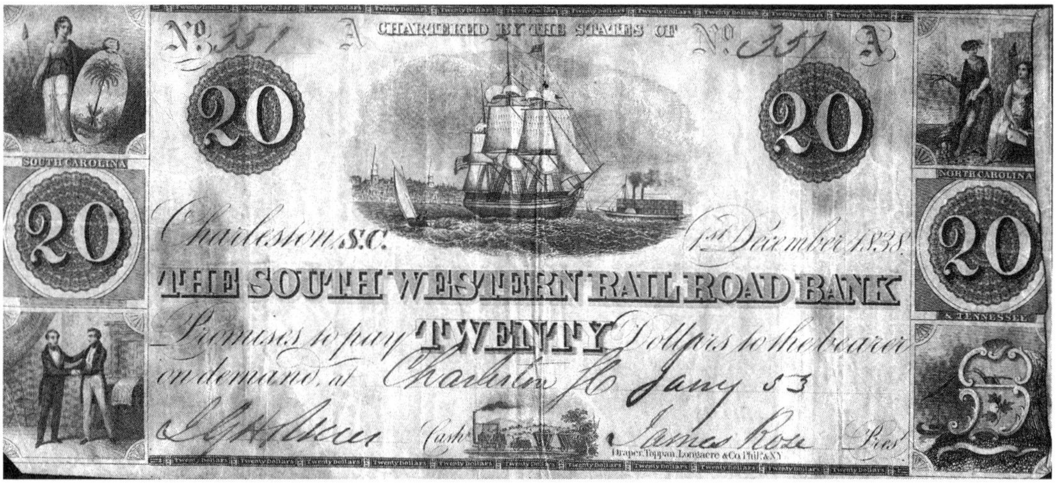

This $20.00 note from the South Western Rail Road Bank, which dates from December 1838, circulated widely following the establishment of this carefully structured financial institution.

Author's collection.

Undeniably it was in the best interests of Kentuckians to participate in creation of this transportation artery, including the railroad bank. "There is no state in the union which needs a free and direct intercourse with the Atlantic, through the southern states, in a greater degree than the State of Kentucky. All her productions find their best, and almost their only market, in the cotton growing regions of the south."[60]

The formal bank application followed in early 1838. But unlike the legislative outcomes in North Carolina and Tennessee, the bank bill failed, albeit by only six votes. Notwithstanding that Louisville would be connected to the LC&C by the independent Lexington and Ohio, feelings remained strong that the city did not want to lose trade advantages to Cincinnati. Residents in western Kentucky also expressed limited interest, being oriented toward river commerce. The Cumberland and Tennessee Rivers flowed through their home region, and they enjoyed access to that active Ohio-Mississippi waterway system. And there was this perception: one opposition politician contended that the bank would be a tool of South Carolinians, using the words "expanding and grasping views of South Carolina."[61]

Although the disappointment in Kentucky meant another legislative attempt, the South-western Rail-Road Bank was a reality, and backers of bank and railroad were sanguine about the future. In spite of events in Kentucky and failed efforts to gain more than token support in Ohio, stock subscriptions in the LC&C neared $6 million. Still $8 million was needed to institute bank operations. Yet that goal seemed in reach, being based on the recent purchase of South-Carolina Canal and Rail-Road Company through an imaginative stock transaction.[62]

Earlier, in 1837, LC&C shareholders had decided they should take control of the Charleston and Hamburg line. Even before that October meeting, the two boards of directors had hammered out the acquisition details. The LC&C would pay a generous $2.4 million for the physical plant, equipment, and franchises. It would execute the takeover of the 20,000 outstanding shares of the SCC&RRCO this way: one-third in cash and the remaining balance equally divided during the following two years and with interest payable from the date of the formal transfer. The LC&C would assume the debt of the SCC&RRCO and acquire "all of our rights," namely its construction franchises. There was more. SCC&RRCO shareholders would *buy* $2 million in LC&C securities, with the first installment to be deducted from the purchase money. Not only would this be a "wise investment in the future" for SCC&RRCO investors, but they would qualify to become shareholders in the South-western Rail-Road Bank. On December 28, 1837, the agreement was made, and implementation followed. The LC&C took control of 19,217 shares, but for the remaining stock "other proprietors have not refused to sell, but accidental circumstance have prevented the transfer."[63]

The decision to unite (but not formally merge) the LC&C and SCC&RRCO made sense; in fact, it was a shrewd move. With the commitment by SCC&RRCO investors to LC&C shares, the railroad now had subscribed stock that totaled $7,950,000, and just $50,000 was needed to sanction the bank. Charleston town fathers kindly made up the difference, and the bank charter was finalized. With control of the SCC&RRCO there would be no need to construct another line from Charleston, and the acquisition positioned the LC&C to take advantage of the Georgia Rail Road that in time would connect Augusta with the emerging rail hub of Atlanta. With the SCC&RRCO in tow, the LC&C would have an immediate source of income, being aided by the expanding freight and passenger revenues of a functioning railroad.[64]

A week before the SCC&RRCO purchase, South Carolina lawmakers, prodded by the determined Haynes, enhanced the financial health of the LC&C when they made a significant commitment. The legislature pledged the credit of the state to secure funds borrowed by the railroad to a maximum of $2 million, provided the interest did not exceed 5 percent. However, the $2 million guarantee would not be immediately forthcoming; the first million would be available only when $500,000 had been paid in on company stock, and the second million would be certified when $1 million had been collected. Without question the Palmetto State offered generous support and strengthened the railroad's ability to sell debt. It would be in the later part of 1838 that a loan for $2 million would be secured in London and at an acceptable rate of interest – 5 percent – for twenty-six years. "Of this sum half a million of dollars have been ordered to Charleston in *specie,* to enable us to put our Bank in operation under the most favorable circumstances" (italics in original).[65]

Taken as a whole, the LC&C developed realistic financial strategies. Its supporters surely took pride when their South-western Rail-Road Bank gained praise from other railroad promoters. Directors of the La Grange & Memphis Rail Road, which planned to build from Memphis toward Tuscumbia, Alabama, lauded the approach in their semiannual report, issued in July 1839. "It is difficult to conceive the plan of the Bank less exceptionable, or better calculated, with judicious management, to secure public confidence. It would have an independent action of the Rail-road Company, and in every respect be conducted as banking institutions generally are, except that the Railroad Company would guarantee the redemption of the issues of the Bank." More positive commentary followed: "We are aware that Railroad Banks, or Banks connected with works of Internal Improvement, have frequently been unsuccessful, but it should be borne in mind that in every instance of failure, the charters were defective. They were permitted to base their issues upon the credit of the stockholders, instead of a metallic capital and actual road formation combined."[66]

TO COLUMBIA

A real, physical railroad appeared to be in the immediate offing for the LC&C. (The SCC&RRCO corporation remained.) By juggling finances, which included short-term loans from Charleston banks, a call for stockholders to pay their second $5 installment, and the sale in London of state-backed bonds, the leadership believed that construction could begin shortly on the approximately 65 miles of line between the main stem at Branchville and Columbia. Earlier, albeit "crude," surveys existed, but a suitable route could undoubtedly be found.[67]

It was a good decision to build a connecting segment. "As a general principle, it is deemed wise and prudent to progress step by step from the sea coast towards the interior, and not to attempt simultaneously the construction of detached and independent sections, which would be comparatively useless until the whole is completed." Most railroads embraced such a strategy, although a notable exception occurred early in the twentieth century when the Chicago, Milwaukee & St. Paul Railway built its Pacific Coast extension between South Dakota and Washington State in a series of segments.[68]

Residents of Columbia and other localities along the anticipated line to a Branchville connection anxiously awaited the iron horse. Columbians believed that money invested in a railroad, rather than more resources spent on river and road improvements, was an imperative: "indispensably necessary, not merely to the prosperity of Columbia, but to save it from

decay and ruin." In 1834 Capital City citizens had organized the Columbia Rail Road Company, but their project stalled, partly because of financing and the need for at least one inclined plane since the projected line ran "through a very difficult country." Two years later the SCC&RRCO took charge and made its own cursory exploration. Then in the early months of 1838 the LC&C orchestrated a detailed appraisal. Field personnel found that a practical and affordable (perhaps $1.5 million) line could be built from Branchville northward to Orangeburgh (Orangeburg), seat of the Orangeburgh (Orangeburg) District, wind through the hilly terrain to the Congaree River near the mouth of the Wateree River, and extend northwestward to Columbia. "This route was preferable to the one recommended in 1834 in that it avoided the necessity of an inclined plane and passed through a much less barren country."[69]

In 1838 the dream began to be realized when the LC&C started to award grading contracts. Unlike much of the original SCC&RRCO, the right-of-way would not be constructed "on stilts," but rather on what had become the accepted standard for supporting a track structure, namely a graded "embankment." Differing from the initial Charleston to Hamburg stem, the extension would use "heavy iron rail" (40 to 50 pounds per yard) and not light strap rail (usually 15 pounds per yard) with all of its faults. Solid rails – by now the popular T-shape design – did not separate and curl backward, causing the loosened metal rails – "snake heads" – occasionally to penetrate the floor of a car as it passed or even to derail the train. Furthermore the old wooden rails with their iron strapping could not sustain heavier loads and increased traffic moving at faster speeds. Already most of the Charleston to Hamburg line sported replacement iron T rails. (The company avoided the U rail. While superior to strap rail, it was inferior to T rail, although on some early roads U, or "trough," rail served as a transition between the two.)[70]

At first the plan for the Columbia extension called for a "double railway," but the cost of dual tracking, including a wider roadbed, led to the decision for only a single track. In fact, the LC&C leadership already had made the same decision for the future road from Columbia northwestward. In both cases, though, workers would install the appropriate number of passing sidings. As William Gibbs McNeill, the company's chief engineer, explained to the directors: "I think generally speaking, dual tracks are not indispensable to the *accommodation* of trade" (italics in original). If traffic volume warranted double tracking, the expensive and time-consuming upgrade could be made.[71]

With these positive signs Columbians were not about to miss an opportunity for a great celebration. Throughout the Railway Age it became commonplace for a community to welcome the start or completion (or both) of a railroad project with a big "blow out." On July 4, 1828, the harbinger for such festivities had taken place in Baltimore, Maryland. A grand parade, which featured fire companies, fraternal orders, and schoolchildren, booming cannons and pealing church bells, lengthy orations, and food and drink for guests, commemorated the laying of the cornerstone for the Baltimore & Ohio Railroad. It was at this historic occasion that Charles Carroll of Carrollton, Maryland, last surviving signer of the Declaration of Independence, turned the first spade of earth. As has been frequently quoted, he said, "I consider this among the most important acts in my life, second only to my signing of the Declaration of Independence, if even it be second to that."[72]

Just as thousands flocked to the Maryland city, crowds journeyed to the South Carolina capital in March 1838. As with Baltimoreans, Columbians turned out in droves, numbering in the thousands. There was the parade that in midmorning proceeded from the state house to the ceremonial site. This lengthy procession included the governor, lawmakers, judges, clergymen, railroad officials and prominent stockholders, military personnel, "citizen Calvary," and faculty and students from South Carolina College (now University of South Carolina). Once parade participants reached their destination, an invocation took place, and according to the *Columbia Times,* "the President of the Company, Robert Y. Haynes, Esq., addressed the meeting in an appropriate and patriotic speech prepared for the occasion. After the address the President set the example of throwing up a shovel full of ground, which was followed by all who were near enough to partake of that honor." The newspaper added: "The assemblage was altogether the largest one we have ever witnessed on any

About the time that the Columbia line opened, the William Norris Works of Philadelphia was producing an attractive, state-of-the-art steam locomotive. This machine, sans cab, featured a 4-2-0 wheel arrangement with a four-wheel swiveling truck under its tall stack, a type popular between 1835 and 1842. This engine weighed approximately ten tons, was designed for freight and passenger service, and portrayed the straightforward and well-proportioned design developed by early American builders. When the Baltimore & Ohio Railroad hosted the Fair of the Iron Horse outside Baltimore in 1927, it displayed this working replica of the *Lafayette,* which had entered service in 1838. The B&O, however, called the locomotive the *William Galloway,* wanting to honor company vice president W. C. Galloway for his work on the centennial celebration.

Courtesy of Baltimore & Ohio Railroad Historical Society Archives.

occasion in Columbia, and comprised all the beauty, patriotism, talent and wealth of the surrounding country." For invited dignitaries an array of food and beverages brought this special day to a close.[73]

The LC&C expected that within two years or so residents of Columbia, Orangeburgh, and other places along the extension could once again hold a railroad celebration. This time it would be to welcome the iron horse. But that was not to be. Not until September 1839 was the final survey completed, and then limited funds made only the 18-mile Branchville to Orangeburgh section possible. Management had hoped that the entire length could be finished by the end of 1840, yet by August only the Orangeburgh portion had opened. But these residents were delighted, having lobbied the SCC&RRCO for rail service since 1835. Toward the end of 1841 service had been established to Lewisburg (renamed St. Matthews in 1878), 13 miles north of Orangeburgh. In the Lewisburg vicinity the right-of-way required extensive excavation. It took gangs of slaves and white laborers, using picks, shovels, wheelbarrows, and mule carts, months to prepare a single long, deep cut, approximately 2,700 feet in length and 100 feet wide, through a mixture of dense clay and sand. The first passenger train would not steam into Columbia until June 20, 1842, and the first freight train arrived about a week later. These movements (and ones in the immediate future) were technically operated by the SCC&RRCO; a complete corporate merger still remained to be formalized.[74]

No wonder Columbians felt the need to host another celebration. They had waited more than four years from the time of that festive commencement ceremony to get their railroad. So on June 28, 1842, Capital City residents, joined by a throng of visitors, many hailing from Charleston and the Low Country, took another holiday. A military parade and speeches took place, and "in the evening many social private parties were given." A crowd estimated at between four and five thousand made this a memorable day.[75]

Residents of the district-seat town of Camden, a trade center that predated the American Revolution, however, likely did not share the jubilation felt by Columbians and others who benefited from this newly opened line. "The trade of Camden is jeopardized," warned the *Camden Journal*. This concern prompted a town meeting to discuss how a railroad might be financed between Camden and a connection with the Columbia extension, a gathering that led to the naming of representatives to examine construction possibilities with the LC&C. In time Camdenites subscribed $200,000 for building this 38-mile branch. With the line opened in sections north along the east side of the Wateree River, the iron horse at last arrived in this central South Carolina community in October 1848. "We trust the completion of this work ushers in a prosperous era in the history of our town," said a Camden newspaper. "Its commercial business must be increased, and our up country and North Carolina friends will find it the most advantageous market both for buying and selling this side of Charleston."[76]

Before the Columbia trackage had been completed, LC&C officials had taken pride that through control of the Hamburg line the company was "now in possession of all the Railroad enterprises within the limits of South Carolina, enjoying the peculiar advantages of being able to give *unity* and *harmony* of movement to the travel and transportation of the community" (italics in original). The future outwardly looked bright, with "under construction a road, a portion of which has been finished, to Columbia, penetrating the interior and one of the richest portions of the State of South Carolina, and demonstrating, in its future projected extension beyond that place, on the vallies of the upper Tennessee and of the Ohio rivers."[77]

Traffic on the Columbia line looked promising. In addition to a daily-except-Sunday round-trip passenger-mail train between Branchville and Columbia, a daily-except-Sunday "accommodation" freight also carried fare payers and the U.S. mail. The bulk of the revenue came from seasonal shipments of cotton, but trains also handled a range of other cargoes, including an array of agricultural products – animal skins, feathers, grain, roots, wax, and wool – an assortment of manufactured goods and forest and quarry products. Even before rails reached the Capital City, net income approached $4,000 for the calendar year 1841, a positive sign during these years of struggle for state, regional, and national economies.[78]

There was a financial disappointment. The cost of the Columbia extension exceeded early estimates. In November 1842 stockholders learned that the price tag had reached $2.27 million. The construction total was $1.87 million, and the remaining amount covered engineering work, interest on borrowed money, and other items, including land purchases.[79]

To worsen the financial picture, hard times had fully descended upon the country by the time rails reached Columbia. The words spoken by William Myers, intendant (mayor) of Columbia, at the June 1842 celebration rang true: "The struggle is now over, and the triumphant consummation of this important object, in the midst of the most disastrous financial crisis which the last half century has witnessed, wholly unaided from abroad, reflects the highest honor on all concerned in its construction, and vindicates the character of our people for enterprise and perseverance." Much had changed in the financial world between 1838 and 1842, and that affected railroad promotion and construction. The LC&C was not immune to the negative repercussions of the nation's worst and most enduring depression to date.[80]

5 Crisis and Contraction

PANIC OF 1837

Throughout the nineteenth century Americans lived through repeated financial panics. Serious economic dislocations began in 1819 and occurred again in 1837, 1857, 1873, and 1893. Economist John Kenneth Galbraith mused that the intervals between these major panics corresponded "roughly with the time it took people to forget the last disaster." As the national economy matured, with expanding industrialization and urbanization, the potency of financial downswings increased. The final large-scale economic disruption of the century, triggered by the Wall Street panic of May 1893, spawned five troubled years and caused the worst depression in American history, exceeding the intensity of the Great Depression of the 1930s and the recent Great Recession of 2008.[1]

Although the relatively short-lived Panic of 1819 shook the business community, the Panic of 1837 affected more people and was more widely felt. It became, sadly for Americans, the "First Great Depression." Earlier some fatalists had called the Great New York Fire in December 1835, which consumed the New York Stock Exchange and most buildings around Wall Street, an omen of impending economic doom. In their minds it was a sign from Providence. When disaster struck two years later, some Americans feared that depression would never lift, believing religious millennialists who claimed that end-times were near. Even a secular Philip Hone, former mayor of New York City and inveterate diary keeper, held similar thoughts. "Where will it end?" he asked. The answer he thought: "In ruin, revolution, perhaps civil war." On April 1, 1837, the *New York Herald* described the growing economic calamity this way: "Wall street [*sic*], and its business neighborhood, from river to river, has been for a week in a terrible convulsion. The banks – the merchants – the brokers – the speculators, have been rolling onward together in the undistinguishable mass, down the stream of bankruptcy and ruin."[2]

Multiple factors led to these painful events. One cause was destruction of the Second Bank of the United States – "Mr. Biddle's bank" – by President Andrew Jackson and his anti-bank allies. The refusal on the part of Jacksonians to recharter this well-managed institution with its twenty-eight branches eliminated the only real brake on the banking system. The result was a dramatic increase in the number of state and local banks whose loans and notes, especially in the West and South, expanded in a reckless fashion. After his reelection in 1832 "Old Hickory" ordered federal funds to be deposited in "pet" banks, believing incorrectly that these institutions would be safer than the expiring "monster." This foolish action further fostered instability and led to extensive banking fraud and mismanagement. Also contributing to the coming of hard times was the controversial Specie Circular that Jackson issued on July 11, 1836. The federal government now required gold and silver coins – "specie" – and not bank notes in payment for public lands. Soon sales plummeted. Speculators, the largest purchasers, used paper money, drawn on local banks, to buy land, and this turn of events drastically reduced a principal source of income for Washington. Yet the president and his supporters believed that "hard money" would protect the national economy. This policy, however, drained precious metals from the East, tightened the money supply, and promoted a general uneasiness in financial centers. Actions taken by the Bank of England added to the mix of negative factors. This powerful London institution reduced its willingness to extend credit abroad, reacting to Jackson's Specie Circular, years of global speculation, and considerable economic stress brought about by poor grain harvests throughout Britain. By 1839 credit in America had become more stringent and the money supply limited, hardly helped by a 30 percent decrease in the capital of domestic banks between 1836 and 1843. These troubling events led to the collapse of world prices for cotton, America's leading export earner and economic engine. For Southerners, especially, the miserable cotton market revealed the danger of relying so heavily on one commodity.[3]

Throughout the country doubt and hesitation in business matters spread steadily, and confusion and retrenchment followed. Jobs disappeared, land values sank, and deflation spiked. In May 1837 Clarissa Gest wrote to her brother about conditions in her home city of Cincinnati, Ohio, mentioning "several failures among our speculating men" and believing "more, perhaps are expected." She noted, too, that "Our papers say little else but hard times and worse coming. Two or three shipbuilders have given up; and several foundries, last week, discharged workmen to the number, it is thought, of 200 or more." She ended her letter by saying, "No money can be got to defray expenses." In February 1840, nearly three years later, conditions had dramatically worsened. Explained Gest, "Times are very hard. We can scarcely get any money, and all are oppressed, seemingly. The poor are suffering terribly, many without food for a day or two at a time, and no employment, with a reduction of wages to those in employ." The effects of this catastrophic business contraction were felt by all classes, causing a sense of helplessness to permeate society. "We might as well attempt to arrest the setting sun! or put down the rising cloud! as to attempt to dispel the darkness and gloom of the present day," opined a South Carolinian, who commented on the state of economic affairs as hard times deepened. The president of the Petersburg Rail Road described conditions simply as "these days of gloom and distrust." Along with other businesses, the Louisville, Cincinnati & Charleston Rail Road (LC&C) felt the sting of a deep and widespread depression.[4]

As always Robert Hayne labored for the cause. He willingly journeyed great distances and endured the hardships of travel to make the transmontane railroad project better known and appreciated. In February 1839 he attended a lavish dinner at the Southern Exchange building hosted by the City of Natchez, Mississippi. The occasion was to celebrate construction of the Mississippi Rail Road. This a 140-mile line was projected to extend from the Mississippi River at Natchez through Jackson to Canton; later that year it completed its first 25 miles. More than two hundred guests applauded Hayne's after-dinner toast to the Magnolia State project, "which thrilled the audience for the space of half an hour." In return Hayne and his home state were warmly honored: "South Carolina – Our elder sister of the South: we hail with pride and pleasure the distinguished individual who represents her on this occasion; the living personification of her chivalry, her talents and her enterprise."[5]

Hayne was surely a happy man at the Natchez banquet, but that feeling was fleeting. Despair consumed stockholders of the LC&C when they gathered in Asheville, North Carolina, on September 16, 1839. In his presidential report Hayne reflected the shift from brash optimism that followed the Knoxville Railroad Convention to profound pessimism. "The late and present commercial embarrassments of the country, which have shaken the foundations of credit and rendered unstable the commercial transactions of the world – these and a multitude of lesser evils have thrown obstacles in our way almost insurmountable."[6]

Haynes and those associated with the LC&C knew that it would be foolish to demand payments on stock subscriptions and that funding sources would be difficult, if not impossible, to find. Most stock subscribers were in no position to contribute more money to the railroad's coffers. Charlestonians, many of whom were major investors, continued to experience the negative effects of a conflagration in their city that in April 1838 had destroyed nearly $3 million worth of property. Hard times, it was understood, had caused popular sentiment to turn against government support for internal improvements and related betterments. And domestic and foreign financial markets stood in a state of disarray.[7]

Yet throughout this time Hayne remained determined to turn dream into reality. "I am rendering the highest public service in my power. I shall enter upon this duty with the firm resolutions to secure success, if success be practicable; and at all events to make such efforts as shall relieve myself, as well as the people of this city [Charleston] and State, from any imputations, should the work be destined to fail." While Hayne showed grit, his words were hardly reassuring.[8]

Soon the LC&C confronted another grave problem. Shortly after the Asheville assembly the tall, fair-haired, and relatively young Hayne died. He had been stricken by a "bilious fever" on his trip from Charleston to Asheville, yet he had struggled valiantly to conduct the stockholders' meeting. On September 25, 1839, five days after adjournment, this forty-eight-year-old workhorse expired in his room at Asheville's Eagle Hotel due to his illness and "under the load of his responsibilities." The funeral, held in Charleston, drew an outpouring of mourners, but eulogies presented at St. Michael's Church focused on Hayne's career in the U.S. Senate and his prominent role in the nullification crisis rather than his work as a tireless railroad advocate. Similar commentary occurred at a well-attended public commemoration held later in the city. Those who publically praised his life may have wanted to forget the immediate plight of the LC&C.[9]

Nevertheless, contemporaries considered Robert Hayne to be the personification of the LC&C. He was, in the words of an associate, "Mr. Louisville, Cincinnati & Charleston Rail-Road, Esq." Others referred to the railroad as "Hayne's magnificent dream." This point of view was not without merit. The observation by Ralph Waldo Emerson that "an institution is the lengthened shadow of one man" seems fitting. If Emerson had lived in the South prior to Hayne's death, he could have had the LC&C in mind as the institution and Hayne as the man.[10]

Even years after Hayne's passing, knowledgeable people understood his contribution to early railroad development. In reflecting on the project more than a decade after the Knoxville Railroad Convention, James Gadsden, then president of the South Carolina Rail Road, successor company of the LC&C, and sometimes Hayne adversary, ruminated about Hayne before an assemblage of internal improvement enthusiasts. Gadsden called the late South Carolinian "gifted" and argued in a flowery fashion that his "persuasive eloquence" in promotion

> awakened the public attention to the vast importance of bringing into more intimate intercommunication the new and enterprising States of the West, with the older sisters of the Atlantic – a connection, which, by frequent

> intercourse, was to break down the prejudices of ignorance, harmonize disagreements in opinion, and stimulate all those friendly relations, which, in making us feel as *one people* were to prove the surest guarantees of the perpetuation of a Union based on equality of rights and the reciprocation of interests [italics in original].

Much later, in 1883, this same spirit was reflected at the centennial observances for the incorporation of the City of Charleston. At that time local dignitaries unveiled a marble bust of Hayne. The inscription on the pedestal contained these words: "His last public service was his effort to open direct railroad communication with the vast interior of our continent." Early in the twentieth century historian Ulrich B. Phillips agreed on the importance of the LC&C president, but exaggerated the impact of his death: "Hayne died in 1839; and with him died the company's dreams." Likewise as Samuel Melanchthon Derrick wrote in his 1930 history of the South Carolina Rail Road, "By his death, the company had lost its chief asset. He has been the moving spirit of the enterprise from its inception." Both scholars merely reiterated the commentary of the October 24, 1839, issue of the *Charleston (S.C.) Courier:* Hayne's death was "the greatest calamity which could have happened to the company."[11]

About the same time came the death of another principal of the LC&C project, including the Knoxville Railroad Convention, Colonel Abram Blanding. This graduate of Yale College and prominent South Carolina lawyer and banker died in Charleston four days before Hayne, being a victim of the "fearful yellow fever scourge." At the time of his passing this talented sixty-three-year-old public servant was skillfully discharging his duties as president of the South-western Rail-Road Bank and providing financial advice to Hayne and others in the railroad. The LC&C may not have been totally rudderless, but this double calamity in leadership had a troubling effect.[12]

Likely both Hayne and Blanding would have rolled over in their freshly dug graves had they known that less dedicated, at times hostile, forces assumed control of the Charleston to Ohio River project. Although a sympathetic Mitchell King, Charleston lawyer, judge, and wealthy landowner, soon took charge temporarily following the December 1839 board meeting, John C. Calhoun and James Gadsden gained influence. Then in September 1840 Gadsden won election to the LC&C presidency. Both men had their eyes on a chain of railroads westward to Memphis or New Orleans and not to Cincinnati or Louisville. It would be Gadsden, as U.S. minister to Mexico in 1853, who achieved lasting fame by negotiating the purchase of about 30,000 square miles of land in northernmost Mexico for a modest $15 million. A year later both governments ratified what became known as the Gadsden Purchase, but the bargain price tag dropped further to only $10 million. While this last territorial acquisition to the continental United States was arguably in the public interest, Gadsden, Secretary of War Jefferson Davis, and other Southerners expected the acquired area in present-day New Mexico and Arizona to be suited for a low-grade transcontinental railroad between the Lower South, Texas, and California. Such a line would strengthen regional economies and promote the expansion of slavery.[13]

RETRENCHMENT

The latter part of 1839 became the tipping point for the LC&C. Its leaders, its supporters, and the public came to believe that for the immediate future the anticipated transmontane rail link between the Atlantic Ocean and the Ohio River was doomed. Hard times showed no signs of abating; depressed conditions actually worsened, and available financial resources diminished. As one newspaper surmised, "the probability of the Louisville, Charleston, and Cincinnati [*sic*] road being farther than Columbia, S.C. appears to be fast fading away."[14]

What should the LC&C do? In the wake of economic downturns it became customary for railroads to embrace retrenchment policies. Similarly for either "paper" or largely unbuilt railroads, it nearly always meant either delays in executing their construction plans or total collapse. During the late 1830s and early 1840s the actions of the LC&C reflected what became an established industry response to hard times.

The LC&C leadership decided it best to commit available funds to the Columbia extension. The length was hardly as daunting as the goal of the Ohio River, although there would be construction challenges. Yet before work could commence, some decisive actions were thought to be mandatory. At the annual stockholders meeting held in Columbia in early December 1839 money manager Christopher Gustavus Memminger, described as "able and unrelenting," offered ways to cope with the immediate economic crisis. He suggested canceling much of the large order for iron rails that the company had made to English suppliers, discharging surveyors who were in the field beyond Columbia, and reducing the size of the remaining survey and engineering staffs. Memminger also proposed cutting managerial personnel and slashing salaries for officers. As for the latter, critics had blasted the company for permitting unrealistically high rates of pay. Stockholders endorsed these economies.[15]

Although some individuals who were associated with the LC&C held out little hope for a railroad between Columbia, Knoxville, and points north, President King sounded a note of optimism at the 1839 meeting. "The present depression will pass away," he told investors. "The pressure for money cannot continue. Let the stockholders meet the present difficulties with firmness and perseverance and we confidently trust that our greater enterprise will be finally crowned with success." Some of this sanguineness surely involved the positive revenues earned by the Charleston to Hamburg line, with its monopoly status, and the recent repairs that "had made the road nearly equal to new." An efficiently functioning railroad meant higher profitability and lower operating costs. The sentiment was also expressed for a long-term, step-by-step construction policy. Greenville businessman Vardry McBee recommended first constructing to Columbia, next extending into the Upstate, and finally building along the survey to Knoxville and beyond.[16]

But not long after King pronounced the inevitability of rail service between the Atlantic Ocean and the Ohio River, events, at least for the near term, suggested a different scenario. In 1840 the immediate prospects for the transmontane road were nil. This state of affairs pleased John C. Calhoun. "Thus ends the humbug with a debt of several millions on the state, great loss to those concerned, and the loss of credit and mortification to the projectors," wrote Robert Hayne's arch-nemesis in September 1840. "If I could triumph, when state and friends have suffered, what a triumph I would have." Lawmakers in South Carolina quickly voted to amend the railroad charter to permit financial supporters from North Carolina and Tennessee to release their shares to the company and receive back the amount of their subscriptions. The costs of the completed survey work in the two states, however, would be deducted from the value of each share, specifically $3.60 for North Carolina investors and $2.50 for those from Tennessee. While some shareholders expressed disappointment, no audible outbursts resulted. The Tennessee legislature did appoint Dr. J. G. M. Ramsey, the unflagging internal improvement advocate from Knoxville, to represent the state's interests in the stock divestiture. Residents of Kentucky were unaffected. "The interest of the Kentucky stockholders was withdrawn from the company at a very early date." South Carolina politicians decided that the charter would be limited to the Palmetto State and the document would substantially reduce the number of directors. All agreed that there was no longer need to have representatives from beyond its borders. However, there would not be any legal or political hurdles to have the LC&C serve Columbia and intermediate points to a junction at Branchville.[17]

Toward the end of the 1830s, when word spread of the likely collapse of work on the LC&C beyond Columbia, officials of the languishing Hiwassee Rail Road proposed to link the two roads. Organized in 1836, six months before the Knoxville Railroad Convention, and spearheaded by farmers and merchants in southeastern Tennessee, the Hiwassee was projected from Knoxville (and interchange with the LC&C) southward "through the Hiwassee [River] District to a point on the Southern boundary of Tennessee, to be designated by the Commissioners hereinafter mentioned as the most practical route to intersect the contemplated railroad from Augusta to Memphis." Backers bragged that their road "will be the most grand and important link in all the railroads of the United States." Initially this meant joining an anticipated extension of the Georgia Rail Road & Banking Company. But plans changed. As the company explained its intentions to Tennessee officials in November 1839, the Hiwassee would be "a Rail Road having its northern terminus Knoxville, and connecting at the Southern boundary line of the state, a distance of 98½ miles with the Western and Atlantic Rail Road of Georgia, and forming continuously with the improvements of that state an unbroken chain of Rail Roads from the heart of East Tennessee to Charleston and Savannah on the Atlantic." At that time the Western & Atlantic, backed by Georgia state largess, was building northward from Atlanta to the Tennessee River at Chattanooga. With its completion Georgia could claim to be the first of the South Atlantic states to have opened a railroad connection with a transmontane waterway. Even with the likelihood of uniting with this publically sponsored line, the ongoing depression, with the difficulty of securing capital, made the Hiwassee a moribund undertaking.[18]

Yet merger (or union of some sort) with the LC&C could change everything. Hiwassee officials thought that their salvation lay with some type of coupling between the two companies. And they considered the South-western Rail-Road Bank to be an especially attractive institution. As the president on several occasions told his board of directors, this well-grounded financial agency could attract investors to the Hiwassee. Fortunately its Tennessee charter did not prevent it from connecting with the seemingly stymied South Carolina project. The tie-in would be made at the Hamburg railhead rather than along the proposed Butt Mountain Gap–French Broad River survey. Consolidation was perhaps a good idea, but preliminary talks went nowhere.[19]

Hard times continued for the LC&C. The financial picture revealed that in the near future only a Columbia construction objective was feasible. The LC&C faced a considerable level of debt, having invested $2.4 million in the South-Carolina Canal & Rail-Road Company (SCC&RRCO) of which $1.6 million would come due on January 1, 1839, and the remaining amount a year later. There were also those obligations for maintaining the SCC&RRCO and expenses associated with the Columbia construction. Collectively this meant that more than $4 million was needed. Although the LC&C had access to a $2 million loan obtained in England, secured by the credit of South Carolina, only half was immediately available. These funds, together with $150,000 on hand that had been generated by paid-in subscriptions, gave the company a working capital of $1,150,000. Then there was the debt of $350,000 to banks in Charleston, money that had been borrowed to buy SCC&RRCO stock. After more financial juggling, which involved additional loans and subscription demands on shareholders, the LC&C by the close of 1839 had approximately $650,000 available, hardly enough to build and equip a long-distance line.[20]

While the general state of economic affairs created concerns for those associated with the LC&C, hope for a better future did not vanish. Income that might be generated by the Charleston to Hamburg property and the South-western Rail-Road Bank offered encouragement, although the "cotton crisis" of 1839–1840 adversely affected both operations. Gross earnings for the railroad stood at $388,927 in 1840, dropped slightly the following year, but rose to $408,705 with the opening of the Columbia branch in 1842. Two years later that figure stood at $532,870, producing a net income of $71,523. As early as 1840 a positive trend for the railroad had begun; the economy was on the mend and the company had developed acceptable operational procedures and had overcome technical shortcomings. For that year the annual report noted that "the accounts continue to show the pleasing fact of an *increase* of *income,* while the expenses *continue* to *decrease*" (italics in original). Unlike many other financial institutions in the South during the panic period, the bank remained solvent, and by the mid-1840s it showed profitability and growth potential. Fortunately, state lawmakers remained generally willing to offer assistance to railroad projects, continuing to realize the importance of rapid, reliable transport.[21]

By the 1840s the forward thinking of the Knoxville Railroad Convention seemed to have taken hold in American and regional thought. In 1842 a writer for the Carrollton, Georgia, newspaper discussed what he cleverly called "Insane Projects." He observed this about canals: "When De Witt Clinton struck out in conjunction with an humble engineer, the grand plan of connecting the great lakes of the north, with the waters of the seaboard, he was ridiculed as a fanciful theorist, who had lost the balance wheel of his judgment." But that opinion changed dramatically. "The Erie canal was however completed, and the mere tolls of the last year amounted to *two millions and thirty thousand dollars,* sufficient to pay off the entire interest of the State debt of twenty millions, and leave a surplus of over a million for incidental expenditures, to say nothing of the incalculable benefit this work has been to western New York, and the western States" (italics in original). Then there were those impressive railroad triumphs. "When the plan was first proposed of uniting the city of Boston, with the pier heads of St. Louis in Missouri, it was laughed at as the absurdity of a dreamer; and when General [Henry] Dearborn spoke of tunnelling the Housatanic mountain, to get to Albany, they thought him almost qualified for a cell in the McLean Asylum. But the mountains have been crossed [by the Western Rail Road of Massachusetts], Albany has been reached." What did these events mean?

> The rewards of genius lie in the future; the generation which surrounds such men seldom appreciate or understand their value, and yet, but for these men, who throw themselves forward into coming ages, and disclose the vista of human improvement, society would stand still, or revolve like that of China, in a perpetual circle without advancing in arts, in knowledge, in government, or religion, speculation produces theory – theory of experiment – experiment, result; and these results giving impetus to mind, carry forward society to the threshold of new projects, which in turn are denounced as visionary and insane.

Hayne and his cohorts would have endorsed this provocative commentary.[22]

Next in the always changing South Carolina Rail Road scene came the formal merger of the LC&C with the SCC&RRCO. The event did not occur overnight; negotiations and legislative actions extended over a three-year period. Even though the LC&C had earlier taken financial control of the SCC&RRCO., two separate corporations remained. In November 1842 representatives of both railroads petitioned the South Carolina legislature for an official union. When the body convened in December, their request was granted, but legally the merger was not perfected until an act passed the following year. Now the entire railroad flew the corporate banner of the South Carolina Rail Road Company (SCRR), a name that reflected reality.[23]

INTRASTATE RAILROADS

In the wake of the stymied LC&C railroad, advocates in South Carolina concentrated on intrastate projects, and they did so with considerable success. Contraction led to enhanced transportation opportunities for South Carolinians and demonstrated the continued determination of Charlestonians to advance their economic interests. While residents appeared resigned (but not necessarily antagonistic) to the construction that was ongoing or proposed in neighboring states, principally Georgia, which included roads with an interstate orientation, merchants and other businessmen, most of all, eagerly embraced the iron horse and wished to expand its domain. Few if any South Carolinians challenged the belief that railroads were engines of progress and that they should be allowed to work their wonders. As early as 1851, citizens could take pride in the editorial statement made by the *American Railroad Journal* that "when her [South Carolina] area [size of state], and the extent of her railroads are taken into consideration, she occupies a very respectable position as a railroad State."[24]

An expanded intrastate rail network offered an attractive possibility. What if one or possibly more of these localized carriers could become a springboard to points in Tennessee, Kentucky, or beyond? A solid railroad foundation might be laid that ultimately would achieve the goals of the Knoxville Railroad Convention. Early in the twentieth century a Southern Railway official made this astute observation: "It was as if the State was putting out from her capital three antennae [Greenville & Columbia, Spartanburg & Union, and Charlotte & South Carolina railroads] in the hope that one of them might grapple with the ardently desired western railroad connection and so secure the vast seaboard commerce of the company beyond the mountains for the State of South Carolina."[25]

In the 1850s the last great short-staple cotton boom and a "whiggish" pro-development political milieu aided efforts to have the Palmetto countryside cross-hatched by local lines. Not only were economic conditions improving, but state coffers had received more than $1 million from the federal government, the result of that controversial, albeit highly anticipated, surplus distribution. Public officials were willing to back railroad endeavors through a revolving fund. This financing would come from state stock investments in the South Carolina Rail Road and the Southwestern Rail-Road Bank that then could be exchanged for securities in these newly formed railroad companies. Municipalities, too, opened their pocketbooks, the most generous being Charleston. Between 1848 and 1856 this city, modest in size yet one of the two largest in the South Atlantic region, made a staggering investment in statewide railroad ventures, amounting to nearly $2 million ($50 million in 2012 dollars).[26]

With the return of a healthier economic climate by the latter half of the 1840s and continuing into the following decade, a number of railroad schemes materialized in South Carolina and wove together far-flung communities throughout the state. In some ways the project that most closely resembled the LC&C involved building more than 100 miles of track from Columbia to Greenville, a developing Upstate courthouse town and trade center. In 1845 the legislature granted organizers of the Greenville & Columbia Rail Road Company (G&C) an authorized capitalization of $1 million and the right to connect the two places in its corporate name. It also allowed the company to "unite with and become part of the South Carolina Railroad Company," considering the project as part of an integrated state rail network. Most of the initial funding came from a combination of Charleston, Columbia, and moneyed on-line investors. Later state and local governments made large purchases of stock that allowed promoters to sustain construction and to take advantage of attractive prices for foreign-manufactured rail. In time the state's commitment to the G&C was hardly inconsequential, standing at $293,275 by 1851 and reaching nearly $350,000 three years later. Comparable investments came from the municipalities of Columbia and Charleston, the former contributing $250,000 and the latter $100,000.[27]

Building the G&C did not take place with haste. Just as determining the route of the LC&C between South Carolina and the Ohio River had involved multiple surveys and conflicts, the past repeated itself, albeit on a much smaller scale, with the location of this freshly launched railroad. Because of competing forces to the north and west of Columbia, the line as finally fixed could hardly claim "air-line" status, at times running for miles on an east-west rather than a north-south axis. Greenville leaders, led by Vardry McBee, who personally invested heavily in the project, demanded a direct route. These men thought the line should extend from their community along a ridge east of the Saluda River through the courthouse settlement of Laurens toward Columbia. But the demand by a combination of powerful economic and political interests for a railroad trumped a more logical routing strategy, at least from the perspective of Greenville and Laurens residents. After all, cotton planters, merchants, and others needed improved transportation to meet the competition of the still newer cotton lands of the Old Southwest. They could not rely on the area's relatively shallow, although at times navigationally enhanced, streams, including the upper Savannah River system. Nor could the planters and businessmen depend on roads, even with improvements, since they generally retained their "dreary" status. Once again the influential and aggressive John C. Calhoun entered the fray, demanding that the G&C at least reach Anderson, less than 20 miles from his Fort Hill Plantation.[28]

Locational discords nearly sabotaged the Greenville & Columbia, but they did not prevent completion of the mandatory field work. As the result of surveys supervised in 1847 and 1848 by William Spencer Brown, a West Point graduate and an experienced canal and railroad civil engineer, a practical route was determined between Columbia and Anderson through Newberry and Greenwood. Then during the following year additional changes occurred, and a route into Greenville was established. Pushed by Greenville interests, who earlier had received a charter for a Greenville Rail Road Company that would miss Anderson and Greenwood, a compromise was reached. Anderson would be served by a 10-mile appendage to be extended westward from what would be the main line at Belton. Brown also oversaw the location of a 12-mile branch that would connect the Hodges station, north of Greenwood, with Abbeville. Collectively this resulted in trackage that exceeded considerably the original projected length, but benefited the centers of population and economic activities, being a true "courthouse" route: Abbeville, Anderson, Greenville, Greenwood, and Newberry. Yet before the arrival of the steam cars these seats of district (county) government were somnolent villages that came to life only on sales day once or twice a month or when district courts were in session.[29]

As with the extended time that it took for the LC&C to open its Columbia line, construction of the G&C began in 1849 and continued for another four years. By the end of 1849 only a few miles outside the Capital City had been readied, yet a celebration of sorts took place. Officials decided to use their sole locomotive, the American-type (4-4-0) *Abbeville,* to pull a short train of borrowed equipment, hoping to impress investors and politicians and to instill public confidence in their endeavor. Unfortunately, a combination of financial, material, bridging, and flooding problems led to extensive delays. It was not until March 1851 that the G&C established service between Columbia and Newberry, a distance of 40 miles. Sixteen months later rails reached Greenwood, and by the spring of the 1853 crews had completed the 110 miles to Honea Path, 8 miles south of Belton. Next, service began to Anderson, and finally on December 9, 1853, the iron horse made its magisterial entry into Greenville, 144 miles from milepost 0 in Columbia. The track gauge of the G&C – 5 feet between the rails – provided compatibility with the South Carolina Rail Road.[30]

The price tag for the G&C was comparatively low; in fact, the *American Railroad Journal* marveled at its cheapness. By 1854 construction and equipment expenditures had amounted to about $2 million. The average cost per mile was only $13,400, far less than most contemporary railroads. In practices resembling those of other roads in the South, the company embraced flimsy construction standards, building a "crude, zigzag, hill-and-dale road-bed" and installing inexpensive strap iron for much of its length. That rail policy resulted in the pressing need for much more satisfactory (and expensive) iron T rail.[31]

The excitement of reaching Greenville triggered discussions for expansion. The object would be Asheville or further, taking the course of the projected LC&C along the French Broad River valley westward into East Tennessee. In late December 1853 the corporate charter of the G&C was amended to allow for such an extension: "To build and construct a railroad from Greenville, the present head of this road, upon the most practical route to the line between this State and North Carolina in the direction of Asheville." This plan, however, remained a paper proposition.[32]

Until heavily damaged during the Civil War the G&C regularly generated a small profit, but debt and maintenance costs prevented dividend payments. As with so many railroads in the South, the one-crop farms and plantations and scattered villages and small towns produced less year-round freight than did the more diversified economies found in the North, with its greater number of cities and businesses and denser population. Management did its best to exploit the road's monopolistic position as a local road. Within reason the G&C and similar lines could employ a higher, noncompetitive rate structure for both their freight and passenger services.[33]

As with virtually all railroad construction, including the G&C, reliable transportation produced its positive developmental impact. Land prices rose and business activities increased. Residents gained options, not only for personal travel and for the shipment of goods but for trade generally. Commercial travelers sprang into action, carrying their sample cases and order books to retailers. Then there were those denizens of Charleston and the Low Country who wished to escape the oppressive heat and humidity of summer. Even before the line opened, the *Charleston Mercury* expected that "our citizens who propose leaving Charleston during the summer months will take this [railroad], leading to our own mountain region than which no more delightful summer climate can be found anywhere." "Train-time" at the Greenville station and elsewhere along the G&C became an important part of the cadence of daily community life.[34]

The Greenville & Columbia benefited from an early interchange with the Laurens Rail Road. Chartered in 1847 and opened seven years later, this cheaply constructed tap road operated the 32 miles between the Laurens District seat of Laurens and Newberry. Although it was hardly built through a mountainous terrain, construction difficulties arose. John Garlington, a Laurens merchant, learned firsthand the challenges associated with building a pioneer road. "About 1853 or 4 he was induced to take a contract on the Laurens R.R. near the river known as the Rock Cut," remembered his daughter Maria Louise Garlington Simpson. "No one else would take it. The rock was very hard and it was almost impossible to cut or drill it but he completed it at a large cost. After it was completed the Directors refused to pay him and there followed a big, albeit successful law suit." Fortunately for investors, which included the state, the company did a respectable freight and passenger business and strengthened traffic revenues for its connecting partner, performing precisely the function of a feeder.[35]

The Greenville & Columbia undertaking largely coincided with another Upstate railroad, the 68-mile Spartanburg & Union Rail Road (S&U). While shorter than the G&C, the Spartanburg road took longer to complete, notwithstanding that its construction standards were generally inferior to those that characterized most railroads built north of the Mason-Dixon Line.[36]

Agricultural and business interests in the greater Spartanburg area, located 25 miles northeast of Greenville, were unwilling to wait for the meandering Greenville & Columbia to reach its upper terminus and to hope for its rails to continue to their community. Rather Spartanburg and several places to the south, including the courthouse community of Unionville (later Union), sought a direct link to Columbia. Yet they were willing to connect with the G&C, creating a less expensive way to reach the outside world. There were options, the most practical being an interchange at Newberry or the Fairfield District settlement of Alston, situated approximately 20 miles south of Newberry on the east bank of the Broad River.[37]

The S&U dated its founding to December 1847. Its organizers, energized by the wealthy Spartanburg District merchant and entrepreneur Gabriel Cannon, obtained a state charter, two years after the granting of the G&C document. Although lawmakers had given the S&U authority to proceed, the official organizational meeting did not take place until mid-1851. Company subscription books, however, had been open for some time. While the undertaking was off to a slow start, optimism reigned. Not only had encouraging investments been occurring, coming mostly from merchants and planters, but the general economy remained healthy, based heavily on cotton. Moreover, company officers anticipated additional financial support. Since the G&C had received both private and public backing, they expected the same. And these men would not be disappointed. In 1854 the state took $150,000 in stock, and it later increased its investment. Surely business interests in Charleston and Columbia, wishing to penetrate still another part of the state, would help to make the project succeed. The editor of the *Charleston Courier* hoped that backers might "find among us a spirit of liberality, equal to the importance of their enterprise." They did, but not in a big way. Between 1854 and 1856 Charleston interests acquired only $30,000 worth of S&U stock, perhaps believing the G&C to be the more attractive proposition.[38]

As with the G&C, the S&U built in the general vicinity of the route expected to be traversed by the LC&C. In fact, organizers of the S&U seriously considered a line from Spartanburg into western North Carolina. The immediate destination would be Rutherfordton, a county-seat village southeast of Asheville. Eventually, though, there might be a hook-up with some transmontane rail project, and the gestating Greeneville & French Broad River Railroad would be the likely candidate. This road, proposed from the greater Asheville area to Greeneville, Tennessee, was expected to connect with the East Tennessee & Virginia Rail Road, a line that in October 1858 opened between Knoxville, Greeneville, and Bristol, Virginia.[39]

The problem that immediately confronted the S&U was not funding so much as locating the route. Disputes among investors and local interests over the exact path delayed construction, so much so that the line was not fixed nor grading seriously begun until 1853. By February 1854 the entire route between Alston and Spartanburg was under contract. In a foolish decision contractors completed grading on the isolated upper Spartanburg portion before crews had finished the lower section, so that right-of-way was ready before any rail could be laid. In the meantime weather and vegetation damaged the naked roadbed.[40]

With the line ready for track gangs, financing woes came to the forefront. A sluggish local economy, which slowed stock subscription payments, had a negative impact. In 1855 the company reported that it required approximately $400,000 to finish the road. The savior of the S&U would be the State of South Carolina, endorsing a substantial amount of its bonds for an investment that had reached $250,000 by 1856.[41]

The little railroad soldiered on. Although it struggled financially and encountered other setbacks, including damaging floods, workers by July 1856 had finished 21 miles from the G&C junction at Alston. At last trains were running and generating revenues, which pleased customers, management, and the connecting G&C. Creditors and investors, too, took heart.[42]

But money troubles continued. A shortage of funds slowed construction to the proverbial snail's pace. As of July 1858 only 25 miles had been completed, and a year later the length totaled 40 miles. It would not be until November 25, 1859, that the iron horse made its long-anticipated entry into Spartanburg. "It was nearly one o'clock before the first train arrived from Union," recalled an onlooker. "The people waited wearily, but their flagging spirits were revived when nearly four miles away the piercing notes of the steam whistle were heard reverberating over the hills. Soon, the crowded train and laboring engine approached, shrieking her summons to the living masses lining the road to clear the track." As with the opening of the Columbia branch (and so many other railroads), residents and visitors participated in a "grand jubilee" or "railroad barbeque." On that November day thousands of well-wishers gorged themselves on an abundance of food: "eight thousand pounds of barbecued flesh of beef, and sheep, and hogs, and kids – with a sprinkling of smaller game – with huge mountains of bread piled like Pelion upon Ossa."[43] Other celebratory activities marked that eventful day, including a party and cotillion held at the Palmetto House hotel. At last Spartanburg, Unionville, and intermediate points had a railroad. Residents along the road took pride and comfort that because of their ironway they were linked to the larger world. And Spartanburg interests now believed that they could compete effectively with Greenville, a town that was their chief commercial rival.[44]

Reflecting the progress in railroad construction nationally during the 1850s – soaring from 9,021 to 30,626 miles – South Carolina trackage rose steadily, increasing from 289 miles at midcentury to 937 miles a decade later. This small state did more than embrace ambitious projects that remained wholly or partially on paper. The building boom produced an impressive statewide railroad network; it was less broken and scattered than the rail grid found in most states east of the Mississippi River outside of the Northeast. Unlike in some parts of the South, 5-foot "Southern gauge" typified Palmetto trackage. Nearly every road enjoyed seamless interline equipment movements. Neighboring North Carolina, however, possessed a hodgepodge of widths, although the standard gauge of 4 feet, 8.5 inches dominated.[45]

Several important additional railroads were in operation by April 12, 1861, when Colonel James Chesnut Jr. ordered the mortar battery at Fort Jackson to fire on Fort Sumter in Charleston harbor, delivering the first shots in the bloodbath that was the Civil War. An important (and strategic) carrier was the interstate Wilmington & Manchester Rail Road (W&M). Chartered in 1846, the company built somewhat faster than neighboring roads. In 1854 it opened a 172-mile line between Eagle Island, opposite the coastal port of Wilmington, North Carolina, and a connection with the Columbia branch of the SCRR at Kingsville, South Carolina. Rumors spread that North Carolina interests, joined by Georgians, planned to sponsor a rail line directly from the Kingsville interchange to Savannah, thus bypassing Charleston completely. Worries about traffic diversions promoted Charlestonians to spearhead a railroad that would meet the Wilmington road at Florence, situated in the heart of the rich agricultural Pee Dee region of the Palmetto State. With fears of a possible Kingsville to Savannah line, the rationale was to prevent the W&M from attracting too much regional trade to Wilmington. Charlestonians thought that the North-eastern Rail Road Company of South Carolina would provide some economic protection. In December 1851 state lawmakers granted organizers a charter to span the 102 miles between Charleston and Florence, a task completed in autumn 1857. Delays resulted, in part, from the time needed to cross swamps and to bridge several streams, including the treacherous Santee River. The North-eastern project sparked what would be a 40-mile extension, but an undertaking that flew the flag of the Cheraw & Darlington Rail Road. Also backed by Charlestonians, this feeder pike began building in 1854 and opened a year later. A few years later the Cheraw & Darlington president thought that if his line were to be extended (probably into North Carolina), it would "make Charleston the great mart for all the region into which this road will penetrate," and in the process "you [will] make her the New York of the Southern country."[46]

A road comparable to the W&M, but better built and equipped, was the interstate Charlotte & South Carolina Rail Road (C&SC), chartered in 1846 and finished eight years later. This 109-mile railroad connected the developing "Queen City of the South," Charlotte, with Columbia, although interests in the Camden area had lobbied to make their town the southern terminus, creating a shorter, less expensive route. Even though the Capital City won out, in either case the road would interchange with the South Carolina Rail Road.[47]

The Charlotte & South Carolina provided a valuable link (but with the inconvenience of a different track gauge) with the North Carolina Rail Road at Charlotte. That state-owned carrier extended in a crude arc from Charlotte eastward to Greensboro and made connections to the expanding Virginia rail network. At the time of secession the Old Dominion boasted the most extensive railroad mileage in the South, claiming more than 1,800 miles. Yet its impressive rail grid had limitations. Virginia roads lacked uniform gauges, and more significantly the state did not have an intersectional trunk line that extended into the expanding markets of the Old Northwest. Although advantageously situated, the C&SC accumulated considerable and potentially dangerous long-term debt. Still, stockholders benefited from the road's brisk business, receiving good dividends until the war.[48]

Helping the profitability of the C&SC was the interchange traffic generated at Chesterville (later Chester), South Carolina, by the 22-mile Kings Mountain Rail Road. This shortline, opened in 1852, extended to the courthouse village of Yorkville, situated in the western portion of the York District. Local interests had pressured the C&SC to be placed on its route, but that did not happen, forcing them to launch an independent road. Such happenings became relatively common during the Railway Age.[49]

At the end of the 1850s another railroad was about to serve Charleston, the 103-mile Charleston & Savannah Railroad (C&S). Although it was chartered by South Carolina in December 1853 and obtained similar rights from Georgia a few months later, construction did not begin until February 1856, and through service did not commence until November 1860, on the eve of secession. At the time the C&S trackage, which featured extensive and expensive bridge and trestle work, operated from Savannah to the south bank of the Ashley River at Charleston. But lacking a bridge into the city and having a gauge of 5 feet, 4 inches, the interconnectiveness of this well-positioned interstate carrier was weakened considerably.[50]

As in much of the story of railroad construction within South Carolina, the elite of Charleston and the city itself invested heavily in the Charleston & Savannah and those railroads that had a direct bearing on their economic interests, seeking always to solidify and strengthen their commercial base. Like private investors in the Savannah road and other carriers, they expected (and usually correctly) that access to the iron horse would offer better, cheaper transport and real-estate appreciation. Initial investments in railroad securities might vanish, but gains, it was believed, outweighed losses, being those prized indirect returns. Throughout their developmental stage railroads often failed to turn a profit, whether in the South or elsewhere. In 1841, during the height of the Demonstration Period, Charles Ellet Jr., a civil engineer, commented on the financials of American railroads. "There are completed, or in process of construction, between three and four thousands miles of rail-roads in the United States. Of these works, some few have thus far sustained themselves, and distributed considerable dividends among their stockholders; the receipts of some others are sufficient to keep them in repair, and pay the interest on the loans incurred for their construction." Then he added, "but of the balance – comprising between one and two hundred rail-roads, having an aggregate length of some two thousands miles – the capitals may be regarded as positively sunk, and many of the companies insolvent."[51]

With the exception of the established and well-situated South Carolina Rail Road, none of these newer roads in the Palmetto State could claim to be money machines. By the eve of hostilities, however, some companies showed a healthy spike in their revenues, aided in part by their monopoly status and a more robust economy. The North-eastern, for one, had receipts in 1859 that were 110 percent greater than they had been for the previous year.[52]

Profitable or not, these carriers in South Carolina offered much to individuals who needed to travel or to ship and receive goods. By 1860 South Carolinians could rely more heavily on their rail network for their passenger and freight transportation needs and less so on roads and waterways. When in February 1860 an Aiken District planter wished to visit a family plantation in the Pee Dee region, he could take a series of intrastate trains. "We left our house yesterday about 8 AM, took the cars at 9; at Branchville took the Columbia train at 1 PM, reached Kingsville about 3 PM – then we took the Wilmington and Manchester train and reached Florence at 7 PM." Unfortunately connecting service at Florence left something to be desired. "Remained there until 2:30 AM, and then took the Northeastern Railroad for Bonneau's station, where we arrived at 6 AM, having travelled about 220 miles."[53]

Even though rail service might be inconvenient, it was superior to alternative forms. After all, roads retained their "horrible" status during most of the year and at times became impassible quagmires, and waterways were hardly improved from previous decades. In some instances water transport actually worsened. "The navigation of the rivers in the South [including South Carolina] is yearly becoming more and more difficult and uncertain," opined a newspaper writer in 1856, "so that it is by no means uncommon to find in many of the best [cotton] planting districts, a good portion of the crop of the previous year still on hand. Rivers have dried up which only a few years ago were navigable for a considerable portion of the year." And the scattered canals, including the Santee Canal, provided limited transport values, being in constant need of repairs and suffering frequently from either too much or too little water.[54]

South Carolinians had failed to achieve that longed-for direct rail linkage from their state to Knoxville, Lexington, Louisville, and Cincinnati. There was some truth in the observation made by the *American Railroad Journal* in 1851 that "the old project of the Charleston & Cincinnati Railroad was founded upon general ideas of the want of our internal commerce, but with the little knowledge which then existed as to the proper route, the limited means at command, and the slight experience which then existed in railroading, a scheme of such magnitude, most of it through a country but thinly settled, could hardly help falling through." Still residents of the Palmetto State had forged an intrastate web of iron rails that traversed much of the most productive countryside, making travel and transport superior to every alternative. Charleston itself had developed into a fledgling rail center. The physical configuration of the South Carolina trackage, as historian Alfred Glaze Smith Jr. has observed, formed a "fan-like appearance with Charleston as a hub." The Railway Age had arrived, but the desire remained strong for ever more railroads, including that long-sought direct connection to the Ohio River.[55]

6 What Happened

BLUE RIDGE RAILROAD

Building schemes during the Railway Age did not always work out as planned. The goals of bold, long-distance lines made by some promoters, including those who backed the Louisville, Cincinnati & Charleston Rail Road (LC&C), were not achieved, but other energetic proposals succeeded. The much publicized New York, Pittsburgh & Chicago Railway was one notable flop. This grandiose project, organized at the turn of the twentieth century, was intended to be a high-density, low-grade freight line that would compete directly with the busy main line of the Pennsylvania Railroad between Gotham and the Windy City. But construction never began. On the other hand, backers of the transcontinental Northern Pacific Railroad embarked on building that difficult route through tamarack swamps, desolate badlands, rugged mountains and mostly unpopulated country between Lake Superior and Puget Sound. "You can't build a railroad from nowhere to nowhere," quipped Cornelius Vanderbilt about the Northern Pacific. But that monumental struggle, begun in 1864 with aid from a federal land grant, ended successfully in 1883, and claimed to be the nation's single greatest corporate undertaking of the era. Then there were those projects that started, sputtered along after completing some mileage, but never achieved their objectives. A good example involved the tireless efforts made by Gilded Age entrepreneur and visionary Arthur Stilwell, who sought to push his Kansas City, Mexico & Orient Railway from Kansas City, Missouri, to Topolobampo, Sinaloa, Mexico. He succeeded in creating a much smaller road, connecting Wichita, Kansas, with Alpine, Texas, and completing modest sections in Mexico under the banner of the Kansas City, Mexico y Oriente Railway.[1]

Similar to the Stilwell road was the more modest Blue Ridge Railroad, a latter-day remnant of the transmontane LC&C scheme. This project, which planned to breach the Appalachian Mountains with iron ribbons, saw some construction, but ultimately it never linked its announced end points.

The Knoxville Railroad Convention wanted to span with rails the nearly 700 miles between the Atlantic Ocean and the Ohio River. This grand interregional undertaking turned out to be more than a paper or "hot-air" proposal. Under the LC&C flag about 10 percent of the projected line was completed, namely between the South-Carolina Canal and Rail-Road Company at Branchville and Columbia. But prior to the outbreak of the Civil War another short piece of this proposed Charleston to Cincinnati road opened, although not along the route fixed by surveyors, approved by directors, and championed by Robert Hayne. This revived project resembled the path that John C. Calhoun had advocated following the Knoxville assembly. Promoters of the Blue Ridge Railroad, led by prominent Charleston merchants Henry Gourdin (first president of the company) and George Trenholm, believed that their choice of how the iron horse should conquer the mountains "offered a more practical route for a railroad to the West than that adopted by the Louisville, Cincinnati and Charleston." Admittedly, the Blue Ridge Railroad was hardly a proud legacy of the Knoxville delegates.[2]

Those dreams so powerfully articulated in Knoxville remained alive. Almost sixteen years to the day later, that persistence sparked another, albeit modest-size, railroad convention. On July 1, 1852, this gathering took place in Anderson Court House (Anderson), South Carolina, seat of Anderson District and not far from the Calhoun family plantation at Fort Hill. Delegates from South Carolina, including a strong and lively contingent from Charleston, joined representatives from neighboring Georgia, North Carolina, and Tennessee to revive the project in a modified form.[3]

Most of the groundwork had already been laid before the convention convened. In hopeful anticipation of the transmontane route, Tennessee lawmakers had incorporated the Knoxville and Charleston Railroad, which would build southeastward from Knoxville to the North Carolina line, or as its charter said, "from the city of Knoxville in the direction of Charleston, South Carolina." The North Carolina legislature had sanctioned a connecting link by creating the Tennessee River Railroad, which would proceed through the valley of the Little Tennessee River "to the point where the line of the State of Georgia crosses said river above the village of Franklin in the County of Macon." Georgia politicians had followed suit, chartering the Blue Ridge Railroad [in Georgia] that would tie the Volunteer and Tar Heel projects to South Carolina by way of Rabun Gap. This natural passageway through the Blue Ridge chain of the Appalachians was near the source of the Little Tennessee River and about a dozen miles north of Clayton, Georgia. Recently cadets from the Military Academy of South Carolina (the Citadel) in Charleston, supervised by an experienced officer, had surveyed through this opening. Their work and subsequent examinations revealed that the South Carolina to Tennessee route was possible, but it would require extensive tunneling: three in South Carolina, two in Georgia, seven in North Carolina, and one in Tennessee, totaling nearly 14,000 feet.[4]

Support for the railroad emanated from several sources. Knoxville interests – individuals and commercial organizations – were determined to bolster the economic position of their hometown. More enthusiastic were Charleston businessmen, who continued to long for direct penetration of interior regions, seeking what the *American Railroad Journal* called "*commercial* greatness as its future" (italics in original). As with virtually every railroad project, those who lived along or close to the projected course expressed their hearty approval.[5]

It would be a South Carolinian who chaired the Anderson Railroad Convention, replicating the role played by another South Carolinian, the late Robert Hayne, who oversaw the Knoxville assembly. Judge John Belton O'Neall, resident of Newberry, veteran of the 1836 Knoxville meeting and president of then building Greenville & Columbia Rail Road (G&C), wielded a friendly gavel. He told a receptive audience of a hundred or so delegates and observers that it was possible to establish this strategic rail link. "It only requires a long pull, a strong pull together, and the neighing of the iron horse will be heard, as he thunders on over the Blue Ridge, and pours his breath of fire on the rich fields of Tennessee. I hope we are here today to write in letters of light, 'prosperity,' on our common country."[6]

Delegates unanimously agreed that they should back this nearly 200-mile railroad between Anderson, western terminus of the G&C, and Knoxville by way of the Rabun Gap, and unite with the three previously chartered carriers. Already a portion in South Carolina had been organized. In December 1851 a localized segment, the Pendleton Rail Road, had obtained its charter, and a year later the state had agreed to subscribe $35,000 to its capital stock. It was expected that the 13 miles between Anderson and Pendleton, the former seat of the Pendleton District (in 1826 the Pendleton District split into the districts of Anderson and Pickens), would be part of this transmontane artery; in fact, there would be a partnership between the Pendleton and the future Blue Ridge companies. If the transmontane project collapsed, the Pendleton would become an operating appendage of the G&C, serving another transportation-starved portion of the Upstate.[7]

Although much of the terrain between Anderson and Pendleton rolled with shallow, intermittent streams, much of the surveyed line beyond Pendleton traversed rough country – "tortuous" was how one commentator described the territory. Several sizable bridges, including a 600-foot span with a 60-foot elevation over the sometimes navigable yet always unpredictable Seneca River, would be needed. And in places extensive embankment work and rock cuts would be required. Multiple tunnels, including several of considerable length, would also be necessary to conquer the mountains. It was believed, however, that the technology of tunnel making had progressed markedly. "Tunnels in our day are no longer obstacles to the construction of railroads, more especially where the grade of the road may be reached by an indefinite number of shafts." True, although boring through rock remained dangerous, time-consuming, and expensive.[8]

The delegates at Anderson named a committee to memorialize South Carolina lawmakers to request a charter and financial aid to build the approximately 50-mile Blue Ridge Railroad [in South Carolina] and to have another committee prepare "an address to the states interested," explaining the agreed-upon plan of action. In reviewing these happenings, the *Palmetto State Banner* in Columbia characterized the convention as being "enthusiastic and harmonious from beginning to end." The newspaper added that "there can no longer be any doubt that the Rabun Gap road *will be built*" (italics in original).[9]

Commercial leaders in Charleston showed a keen interest in establishing a direct rail passage to the northwest through the developing Knoxville gateway, with rail connections provided by the Georgia & East Tennessee and East Tennessee & Virginia railroads. Possibilities looked good for additional lines to radiate out from that city, including the proposed Knoxville & Danville Railroad. If the Anderson to Knoxville project, frequently called the Rabun Gap Route, could be realized, traffic would flow between Charleston and Knoxville through Columbia and Anderson, and connections could be made to points on the Ohio River. Charleston boosters also wanted a "friendlier" road to tap this trade. Although the South Carolina Railroad provided a connection at Augusta with the expanding Georgia rail network, cars could not be physically interchanged with the Georgia Rail Road and Banking Company and had to be unloaded and reloaded. A nightmare scenario became a standard occurrence. "The tax in the form of tolls and drag at the Augusta bridge; the damage done to the merchandise and produce in loading and unloading from the cars, and exposure while passing from depot to depot, the detention and scattering of stocks, etc., are impediments on the line to Charleston," voiced the *Charleston Daily Courier,* "operating perpetually to the annoyance of all those who adopt it as a commercial highway, wholly incompatible with that rapidity and freedom of intercourse with the Atlantic, on which we are embarking, and to our prosperity as an agricultural and commercial people." Also troubling were continuing traffic diversions to Savannah, whether with transshipments to steamboats on the Savannah River at Augusta or directly through the maturing railroad system of Georgia. Furthermore, North Carolina was contemplating extending its state-owned railroad from Salisbury into the valley of the French Broad River. And there were rumors that the proposed Rutherfordton, Charlotte & Wilmington Rail Road might divert traffic. If these Tar Heel State carriers materialized, the volume of freight bound for Charleston would diminish.[10]

Backers of the Rabun Gap Route took heart with the unfolding of events. In November 1852 South Carolina governor John Means told lawmakers that they should back chartering and contribute to the financing the railroad. "It would be a suicidal policy in our State, not to secure this gigantic commerce, now that it is within its reach. I therefore recommend that you subscribe a million of dollars to this road, or even more, if it be necessary to complete it." Continued the governor, "I trust that no sectional feeling will be brought to bear on this question. It is a great State matter. It is true that the interest of Charleston will be more promoted than any other section of our State, but the wealth will be poured into her lap, will be radiated through its entire extent."[11]

The legislature complied, and shortly the Blue Ridge Railroad Company (in South Carolina) won the right to proceed and with adequate capitalization ($4 million). The body further approved the endorsement of $1.25 million in company bonds. Soon the three separate companies, which had been permitted to build in Georgia, North Carolina, and Tennessee, assigned their franchises and financial commitments to the South Carolina enterprise. To reduce confusion and to simplify the corporate structure, the Blue Ridge Railroad of South Carolina absorbed its Georgia counterpart.[12]

But the Anderson to Knoxville railroad project hardly experienced smooth sailing. Negative responses to the Blue Ridge emerged. William Gregg, a wealthy Charleston manufacturer, reminded politicians and fellow citizens, especially those who backed the proposal, about the fate of the LC&C. "I consider the Blue Ridge Rail Road a visionary scheme, and under its present arrangements not an object which ought to induce Charleston to subscribe. I believe that it is destined to almost certain failure." He added: "We have certainly had a sufficient lesson in the signal failure of that splendid project, the Cincinnati enterprise, to guard us against a similar mistake." What Gregg wanted were improvements, including railroads, that focused on developing the resources *within* South Carolina. "Cheap modes of transportation from all quarters of the State could not fail to re-act on the general prosperity of the city [Charleston], the dormant wealth of Charleston might be so directed as to be felt in the remotest parts of the State in stimulating agriculture; draining our swamps and putting into renewed culture our worn-out and waste lands; diversified industry, stimulating the mechanic arts and increasing the population and wealth of the State."[13]

Then there was that old carping about the route. Should it follow the French Broad River or go through the Rabun Gap? Said a Palmetto State lawmaker, "By an examination of the surveys of the old Louisville, Cincinnati and Charleston Railroad Company, we will find that a railroad route has already been surveyed. [That] survey is equal in point of accuracy to any, I have no doubt, that has been made by any company in this State." He went on to point out that the river route would not require costly and time-consuming tunneling, an astute observation since failure to complete the Stump House Tunnel did much to wreck the transmontane endeavor.[14]

Notwithstanding criticisms about the route, backers focused on how to finance the Blue Ridge Railroad. A complicated series of events ensued. Although the State of Tennessee promised to aid in the purchase of rails once roadbed work had been completed, South Carolina ultimately provided most of the funding. Initially Palmetto State politicians guaranteed a portion of Blue Ridge bonds, but railroad sponsors wanted stronger support. In 1854 they got their way. South Carolina agreed to subscribe $500,000 when the company had stock subscriptions that totaled $1 million. The state would commit another $500,000 if the company could raise a like amount and "at least one-fifth of the subscribed capital of the company should be held by responsible individuals or private corporations." There was also a bond guarantee agreement; Columbia would cover $1 million of the $2.5 million worth of debt that the company was authorized to issue. Since the City of Charleston had already subscribed $1,049,000 to the stock for construction in South Carolina and Georgia, the first requirement of the legislative act had been met. Even though there had been scant purchases of stock by private investors, Blue Ridge leaders expected to increase the shareholder pool by using the ploy of paying contractors partly with certificates. In its contract with Anson Bangs and Company of New York, signed in fall 1853, the railroad would follow this payment policy for construction completed: one-half in cash, one-quarter in stock, and one-quarter in unguaranteed bonds. The other key provision: the contractor would have four and one-half years to complete its work.[15]

The inking of the construction document stirred optimism among the railroad hopeful. There still was another reason to believe that the project would flourish: the Georgia legislature in 1854 granted promoters of the North-Eastern Rail Road Company (of Georgia) the right to build from Athens northeastward "to strike the Blue Ridge Rail Road at such a point as the directors may determine." Such a line would make a valuable connection with the Anderson–Knoxville road near Rabun Gap. Even though the North-Eastern would interchange with the Georgia Railroad at Athens, it would more likely be a feeder than a bleeder of traffic.[16]

In another fit of optimism leaders of the Blue Ridge contemplated a major appendage. Their proposed "Southwestern Branch" involved building from the projected main stem at Citico Creek, Georgia, to Athens, Tennessee, creating a rail link with Chattanooga. Such trackage would permit the Blue Ridge to "compete with the Georgia Roads for the trade of Chattanooga."[17]

For a while it appeared that building the Blue Ridge was a viable possibility. Unfortunately, though, company directors selected the wrong contractor; in fact, the Bangs company may have been a colossal fraud. In 1855 for unknown reasons Anson Bangs and his brother Eli sold their interests to other principals, and a replacement firm, A. Birdsall and Company, took charge. But the individuals who were associated with the new operation lacked railroad-building experience. Then in spring 1856 officials of the Blue Ridge, suspecting the Birdsall group to be untrustworthy, voided the contract. This action came about for good reason; the heavy work in South Carolina and Georgia, including deep cuts, tunnels, and bridges, had been largely neglected. "Although, before they forfeited their contract, they had done much earth grading in South Carolina, and Georgia, all that they had done, did not in point of time, expedite the completion of the Road by one day," wrote an exasperated Blue Ridge official. Admitted the contractor: "The work was not prosecuted with vigor." The focus instead had been on the relatively easy and lucrative right-of-way grading, including short sections in both states. Earlier it was discovered that Anson Bangs had made a secret agreement to purchase 25,000 tons of rails from the British firm of Guest and Company, iron that may or may not have been destined for South Carolina. In all likelihood it was a rail scam. Seemingly the $700,000 spent on construction had largely been wasted; already water runoff had damaged the graded sections. The railroad also felt the pain of interest payments that diminished resources as did a lengthy lawsuit with the Bangs group. Moreover, the project was badly delayed. Further hampering construction was that the latest contractor, George Collyer and Company, demanded cash payments, derailing plans for a second state stock subscription. Later the Collyer firm withdrew, although not under a cloud of misconduct.[18]

If actions of the contractors demoralized backers of the Blue Ridge Railroad, so did the financial picture. The paucity of private subscribers, especially from outside South Carolina, forced directors to turn repeatedly to Palmetto State lawmakers for assistance. During their 1856 legislative session opposition for granting additional aid grew stronger. Resolutions were introduced to halt construction, but these measures fizzled. Later a conflict erupted between the company and the controller general over payment of portions of the initial state subscription. Until a court decision brought victory for the Blue Ridge, his action caused concern. Nevertheless, financing remained at best tenuous.[19]

With the money available, Blue Ridge directors decided to concentrate on driving the tunnels in South Carolina and Georgia and opening that short section between Anderson and Pendleton. The greatest obstacle on the entire route involved Stump House Mountain, requiring a bore that would extend nearly 6,000 feet. Hundreds of workers, mostly native-born whites and Irish and German immigrants, toiled on the project with its three shafts and eight working faces. Unfortunately, the dense granite, the not-so-effective black powder, and mandatory hand chiseling hindered progress (nitroglycerin and steam-powered drills were not yet available). "Blasting is tedious and hard work, and the number of workmen must be limited by the contracted space of their operations." By 1858 only about one-third of the job was finished, and it was expected to take at least two more years before ties and rails could be laid. Railroad backers agreed with the *Anderson Gazette* editor, who visited the site in autumn 1857, that completing the tunnel would "remove the want of public confidence." In both South Carolina and Georgia laborers also undertook other tasks, including bridge masonry and stone culverts.[20]

That decision to open the line to Pendleton triggered a positive local response. Directors were delighted when residents of Anderson and the surrounding countryside agreed to take a stock subscription for $24,000, earmarked for this segment. This commitment energized backers and spearheaded a successful drive to generate additional private subscriptions for the entire project. During 1857 the campaign resulted in commitments of more than $225,000, the bulk coming from Charleston patrons. These investments permitted the state to subscribe an additional $500,000, and later in the year more public funds became available. By 1860 the government of South Carolina had committed a hefty $1.31 million ($33 million in 2012 dollars) to the railroad.[21]

Notwithstanding some positive happenings, including more private and state support and completion of the line between Anderson and Pendleton in spring 1858, the Blue Ridge Railroad was running out of money. Even though hundreds of workers had been moving earth, erecting bridge abutments, installing culverts, and chiseling and blasting tons of tunnel rock, much more funding was required if they were to continue. At the annual stockholders meeting, held on November 10, 1858, the body agreed to seek an additional $1 million in stock subscriptions from the legislature. Edward Frost, company president, explained this request: "The Blue Ridge Rail Road must be completed as a State enterprise or it cannot be completed at all. The cost is too great for individual capital to undertake it." Added Frost: "If South Carolina is not prepared to incur the cost of

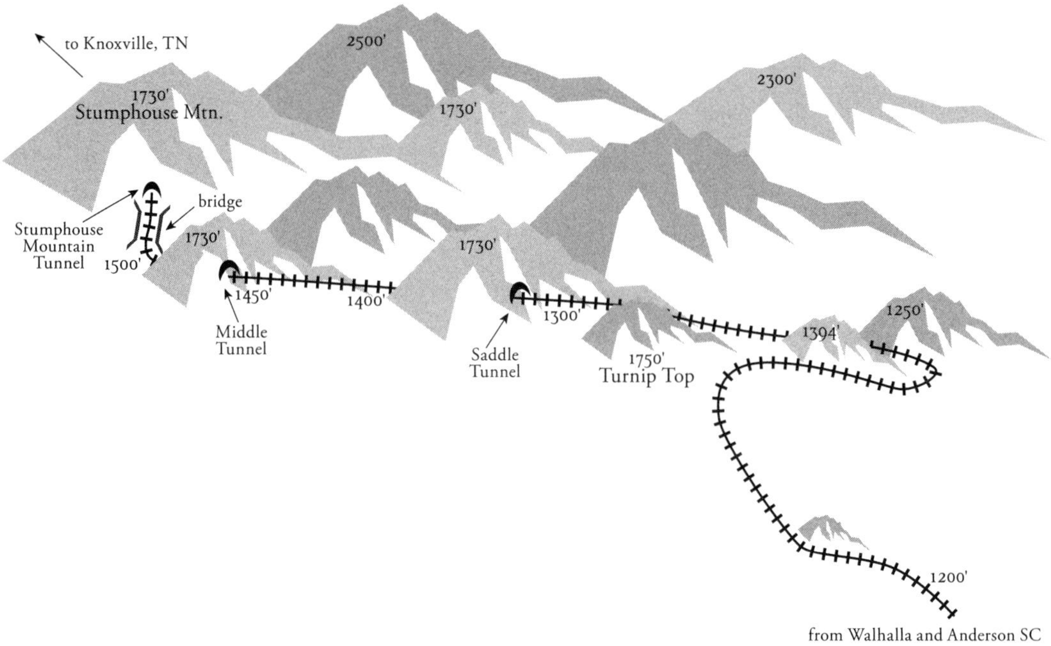

The principal roadblock to completing the Blue Ridge Railroad involved constructing the line across northwestern South Carolina. A particularly challenging (and ultimately disastrous) aspect involved tunneling Stump House Mountain near the German-American settlement of Walhalla in present-day Oconee County.

Created by the Office of Creative Services, Indiana University.

competition for the trade of the West, she should be prepared to recede from the position of moral eminence she has theretofore occupied, and be reconciled to a diminution of her political power and consequence proportioned to her territorial area."[22]

These were strong words. Although friends of the railroad argued for more public support, lawmakers were in no mood to make major commitments, many being tired of the seemingly endless demands for state funds. Opposition built, coming mostly from the northeastern section of the state (Pee Dee region) and other areas removed from the Blue Ridge. The Panic of 1857, which frightened the public, gave politicians pause in making additional expenditures and accumulating more debt. Yet the state could sustain further support, enjoying reasonably good financial health. "Never before has the planting been more profitable than in the last few years," observed a South Carolinian on the eve of the Civil War; "the planters have been everywhere rich, prosperous and happy."[23]

Somewhat grudgingly the state opened its pocketbook. Politicians agreed to a subscription of $310,000, payable in 6 percent bonds. But it came with this iron-clad stipulation: "to complete the road to Walhalla, and for no other purpose; and that the work, beyond the village of Walhalla be immediately suspended, unless further subscriptions be obtained." The destination made good sense. This vibrant town, situated several miles southeast of the tunnel construction, was growing rapidly, having been a planned community started in 1850 by the German Colonization Society of Charleston.[24]

Blue Ridge stockholders agreed that further construction was doubtful. This was understandable, but it may have been a ploy to spark support for state aid to finish building over the mountains into Georgia and beyond. In fact, there was an outpouring of public concern about the stalled railroad. On August 19, 1859, a mass rally took place at an iconic location, the unfinished Stump House Mountain Tunnel. "It was thought that a personal inspection of the operations of the Blue Ridge Railroad Company at Tunnel Hill," wrote the *Charleston Mercury,* "would more satisfactorily inform the public mind of the true merits of this great work than cartloads of speeches and documents." The event may have attracted as many as five thousand people, coming from the Carolinas, Georgia, and Tennessee, including the governor of South Carolina, legislators, and some Blue Ridge opponents.[25]

It was a grand affair at Tunnel Hill. And it was especially memorable for the volume of people who came to this isolated and mostly empty part of the Upstate. "Never before had such a gathering been seen here," observed a participant. "All the horses and mules of the district had been engaged for the three previous days and nights in conveying the crowd from Pendleton, the terminus of the railroad, to the mountain. Every floor and piazza of the houses and cabins on the mountain had been spread with beds." Then the big day arrived, bright and cool. There was more than the customary band music, parade, food, and speeches; visitors had an opportunity either to walk into the largely completed tunnel or to ride a steam-powered elevator that allowed them to descend into "shaft No. 4." All wanted to see the herculean efforts that had been made. The multitudes were told repeatedly about the economic benefits of a completed Blue Ridge Railroad. As one speaker said, "The prosperity of a State sinks precisely with the lethargy with which she treats great enterprise."[26]

About the time of that mass convergence on Stump House Mountain, Walter Gwynn, chief engineer for the railroad, emphasized another advantage that may have been on the minds of visitors to the tunnel site, namely the potential military value of a completed road. As tensions mounted between North and South, civil unrest seemed possible.

> In a military point of view, the Blue Ridge Railroad may be regarded as the "Appian Way," which, by means of its quick transportation, as the "main trunk,' in combination with connecting railroads, within and without the State, would neutralize one of the great advantages of an assailing force, (in almost every part of the State, as well as, over a great extent of a common territory,) that of choosing its point of attack, and possessing the necessary means of reaching it.

Gwynn concluded: "Railroads economize war in money, men and time."[27]

Although trains never ran through the massive Stump House tunnel near Walhalla, South Carolina, the abandoned project eventually had an unusual adaptive use, becoming an aging and warehouse facility for Clemson blue cheese. This image, taken in 1963 by a Clemson University News Bureau photographer, shows the site after the university ended its tunnel storage.

Photograph by William D. Cromer, courtesy of Clemson University Archives.

The chief engineer was hardly alone with such thoughts. An ardent supporter of the Blue Ridge, Christopher Memminger, used the growing fear of war to bolster support for the railroad. Another powerful voice in the political life of the state, Robert Barnwell Rhett Jr., editor of the *Charleston Mercury* and a spokesman for Southern nationalism, echoed Memminger when he underscored the critical need to establish stronger rail links with the "great hives of the white population in Tennessee and Kentucky." A sense of security alone would justify continued construction.[28]

Then came war. Although not long after guns boomed at Charleston, the Blue Ridge had reached Walhalla and adjacent West Union, 21 miles beyond Pendleton, no further work occurred. The $2.9 million expended had resulted in about one-sixth of the line being opened, along with several tunnels either facing an exposed grade or having been only partially bored, and a set of massive stone bridge abutments along Warwoman Creek in Georgia. No work at been done in North Carolina, and only a portion of the grading was completed between Knoxville and Maryville, Tennessee. Outside Knoxville the bridge piers in the Holston River remained largely unfinished. Still, the Blue Ridge ran trains. Between the

Greenville and Columbia Rail Road connection and Walhalla the company dispatched a triweekly mixed freight and passenger accommodation "with occasional extra trips." Three general purpose Norris-built 4-4-0-type locomotives, appropriately named the *Blue Ridge, Fort Hill,* and *Chatuga,* handled the meager amount of freight and passenger traffic.[29]

Following the Civil War there was a revival of the Blue Ridge Railroad dream; the project refused to die. The well-established arguments for this transmontane railroad resurfaced. "Do you want the *quickest* and *cheapest* route to the Atlantic cities? This road will give us about *ninety miles* the advantage over any route we now have" (italics in original), wrote George A. Trenholm, chairman of the board of directors, in the September 1866 issue of *De Bow's Review.*

> As the laws of travel and commerce seek straight lines, so certainly will they pass over our road to Nashville, Memphis, and the points south and west of those cities. Do we wish to open to our markets the inexhaustible stores of mineral and other wealth which have been locked up in eight or ten counties of our State, since the creation of the world to the present time? Would we see flourishing towns and villages, with large mining and manufacturing establishments, spring up?

Trenholm made another cogent point. "To leave it in its present unfinished condition will be to bridge the stream, and stop short of the shore; to win the race, and neglect to take the prize." And memories of the "recent unpleasantness" remained vivid. The railroad would "guard against future sectional jealousies and partisan animosities," opined a Knoxville resident, "which might thereafter arise between sections so remote and so little homogenous, when not united by common interests."[30]

Such thinking rekindled interest. Blue Ridge president J. W. Harrison argued for completion. He thought that it would cost approximately $3.4 million to finish the road to Knoxville, being considerably less than the estimate in 1860 of $4.58 million, and he believed that even in the prostrate South funding could be obtained from domestic and foreign sources. George A. Trenholm had these thoughts: "By way of Rabun Gap there are only one hundred and sixty-four miles of new road to be constructed, and of this, a great deal of the heaviest work had been done in detached sections, so that the cost of completing it, will not exceed $4,500,000, and by this route the whole interior and seaboard of Georgia are rendered as accessible, and brought as near as those of South Carolina."[31]

Others expressed less optimism. They maintained that war-weary Southerners, especially South Carolinians, could not be expected to invest, and the conflict had largely depleted state coffers. Construction money from either the North or Europe, they contended, would be difficult to attract. Amazingly in 1869 South Carolina lawmakers authorized $4 million in bonds. But the widespread corruption associated with federal Reconstruction – that sorry episode between 1866 and 1877 – stymied the building process. It threw what appeared to be adequate financing into a tangle of dishonesty, ineptness, and political wrangling.[32]

Yet before the ravages of the Panic of 1873 took hold and other economic conditions came into play, backers of the Blue Ridge thought that they had a way to reduce their construction and future operating costs. Their railroad would become a narrow-gauge line. In July 1871 James Low, the chief engineer, argued in an exhaustive report for a 3-foot rather than the Southern 5-foot width. "It would be wise to make ourselves as acquainted with the real merits of the 'narrow-gauge' system." As such he was in the vanguard of a narrow-gauge craze that engulfed Great Britain, Europe, North America, and even Latin America, leading to approximately 12,000 miles of slim-width trackage in the United States by the mid-1880s. Low expected substantial savings during the building process. "Areas of the cross sections of cuts and fills are 20 per cent less on the 3 feet gauge" was but one example. He concluded that "the savings in first cost will be immense, enough, in fact, to place the completion of the road within our reach." Yet as economist George W. Hilton has demonstrated, the financial attractiveness of narrow-gauge roads was mostly an illusion. Having a 3-foot width could never have been a panacea for the Blue Ridge; it faced too many challenges.[33]

Naysayers were correct about their expectations for a revitalized Blue Ridge. In 1873 the company went bankrupt. Train service, under court supervision, continued, but it remained minimal, with a single round-trip daily-except-Sunday passenger train between Belton, Anderson, and Walhalla and an "accommodation" or mixed train that operated daily except Sunday between Anderson and Belton. Freight operations became irregular. Still customers appreciated the opportunity to ship cotton, livestock, and miscellaneous commodities and to receive an array of merchandise and to have the U.S. mails. The 32-mile shortline was a failed and broken-down property.[34]

At last it appeared time to write the obituary for a transmontane Blue Ridge Railroad. But some individuals thought not. In January 1876 still another railroad convention took place. The venue was historically significant, Knoxville. Scores of delegates, who represented Georgia, South Carolina, and Tennessee, gathered "in the interest of the Blue Ridge railroad, the most direct route from Knoxville to the sea-board via Rabun Gap and Walhalla, South Carolina." Their intentions, however, did not bring about any additional construction.[35]

Eventually rails would span much of the distance between Anderson and Knoxville; it took several carriers – not one – to make this a reality.

Yet no trains ever steamed through those multiple tunnels in the South Carolina Upstate or Georgia. Even though the Blue Ridge halted its advance at Walhalla, a portion of the Tennessee section opened in 1867 along the prewar survey, stretching 16 miles between Knoxville and Maryville, a county-seat and college town. With funding from the pro-business Reconstruction government of Tennessee, the Knoxville & Charleston Railroad seemed destined to expand, although that would not be a near-term event. In 1869 the property, which was in sorry shape, fell into the hands of a court-appointed receiver. Six years later the newly formed Knoxville & Augusta Railroad took control, but its owners were unable to add mileage. In 1881 the shortline entered the orbit of the Richmond Terminal Company, a recently launched holding company associated with the Richmond & Danville Railroad, and once again talk circulated about reviving the transmontane Blue Ridge scheme.[36]

Part of the Richmond Terminal strategy was to resurrect the North-Eastern Rail Road Company of Georgia. In a series of events, the North-Eastern, a heretofore paper antebellum railroad, was rechartered as the Northeastern Railroad of Georgia with authority to build "to some point on the Blue Ridge Railroad near Clayton." In 1876 the company opened the 36 miles between Athens and Lula, located on the Atlanta & Charlotte Air Line Railroad. Trains then operated over that Richmond Terminal–controlled property between Lula and Cornelia before reaching Clarkesville from Cornelia on its own rails by 1882. Financial difficulties subsequently led to a reorganization of the property beyond Cornelia as the independent Blue Ridge & Atlantic Railroad, a firm with its own plan for forging an intermountain route. Later that carrier faltered, leading to a reorganization that created the Tallulah Falls Railway. Additional building took place in a northerly direction, and by 1907 trackage extended through Tallulah Falls, Clayton, and the Rabun Gap to Franklin, North Carolina. But this 58-mile Georgia pike, controlled by the Southern Railway, was not affiliated with the Richmond Terminal. Earlier, in 1887, the Terminal had become a victim of its own speculative actions. Then seven years later its profitable holdings morphed into the Southern Railway, the creative handiwork of J. P. Morgan Sr., and a triumph of railroad "Morganization."[37]

Adding to the complexity of late-nineteenth-century railroad construction in the projected service territory of the Blue Ridge Railroad was the appearance of the Western North Carolina Railroad. In 1869, after a fourteen-year delay, the road opened between the North Carolina towns of Salisbury, located on the main line of the Richmond & Danville, and Old Fort, east of Asheville. Then in 1882 the Western North Carolina pushed through Asheville and along the French Broad River to a connection with the East Tennessee, Virginia & Georgia Railway (ETV&G) at

Paint Rock, North Carolina, near the state border. The previous year the latter company had reached Paint Rock by installing a 4-mile extension from Wolf Creek, Tennessee. By then the ETV&G operated directly into Knoxville through Morristown, which had been reached from Knoxville in the late 1850s, and Wolf Creek, the eastern terminus of the Cincinnati, Cumberland Gap & Charleston Railroad, a shortline that had begun operations in 1869 between Morristown and Wolf Creek. Not only did the Western North Carolina own a 190-mile main stem, which was famous for its twists and turns in the vicinity of Old Fort, the "Old Fort Loops," but in the mid-1880s the road laid 124 miles of track from Asheville to Murphy, a community in extreme southwestern North Carolina. The company designed this lengthy extension to reach potentially lucrative resources: stands of virgin hardwoods and deposits of coal, copper, and iron. About the time trains rolled over the Murphy branch, the Western North Carolina announced its intention to build to Maryville, Tennessee, and also to Clayton, Georgia. Part of the latter route would follow the Little Tennessee River southward from Almond, North Carolina, and would utilize a portion of the old Blue Ridge survey.[38]

Before any serious work on uniting the Murphy branch with either Maryville or Clayton occurred, a piece of the unbuilt LC&C took shape. The Asheville & Spartanburg Railroad (A&S), one time affiliate of the Richmond Terminal, connected the two places in its corporate name. Begun in 1873, the Asheville & Spartanburg six years later completed the section between Spartanburg (Spartanburg Junction), South Carolina, and Hendersonville, North Carolina. The firm then failed, but after a reorganization the track reached Biltmore (Asheville) in 1886, making for a 70-mile road. The line gained fame for its Saluda Mountain Grade, allegedly the steepest standard-gauge trackage east of the Mississippi River with its 4.8 to 5.1 percent maximum ascents. Yet, more significantly, the A&S linked the old Spartanburg & Union Rail Road and its connection through Columbia with the Western North Carolina, creating a through route via the ETV&G and Cincinnati Southern railroads between Charleston, Knoxville, and Cincinnati.[39]

There continued to be proposals, realized or not, to expand rails in the general area of the Rabun Gap. In 1902 the Southern Railway, which dominated the region's railroad network, decided to revive the Blue Ridge scheme by building down the Little Tennessee River. This plan would connect its Bristol to Memphis line at Knoxville with its Washington, D.C., to Atlanta stem at Cornelia. To achieve this goal the Southern received a North Carolina charter for the Carolina & Tennessee Southern Railway to build between Franklin and the Tennessee state line. The Southern also won a Tennessee charter for the companion Tennessee

& Carolina Southern Railway to extend trackage from Maryville to the North Carolina state line. Southern officials seemed excited about this proposed course of action. "You will recall the old line [Tallulah Falls Railway] stopped at Tallulah Falls, 21 miles from Cornelia," wrote vice president John M. Culp to president William W. Finley in May 1907. "Rabun Gap is 20 miles further on, or 41 miles from Cornelia. The new line is open to Prentiss, 53 miles from Cornelia, and by the end of this month they expect to be open for business to Franklin, the terminus of the line, 60 miles from Cornelia." Remarked Culp, "The country is sparsely settled and comparatively undeveloped, resembling very much our Murphy Branch, but undoubtedly the possibilities of the line are great. From Rabun Gap north the timber is practically untouched, and while forest products will be much the heaviest tonnage for some years to come, the mountain valleys are rich and valuable for the cultivation of corn and wheat." There was more: "I was told that the Southern Railway had filed a mortgage providing sufficient funds to build a line from Bushnell to Franklin, which taken in connection with our extension from Maryville to Bushnell, will, in my opinion, not only give us a good through line from East Tennessee to points in North Georgia and South Carolina, but will provide an immense amount of local traffic." This theme of opportunities continued. In 1914 a promotional public timetable issued by the Tallulah Falls Railway subsidiary extolled the region. "The rich valleys of the Little Tennessee and Rabun Gap are especially fruitful, large yields of corn, wheat, and other crops rewarding the efforts of the thrifty farmers of this section. The mountain side and slopes are ideal for apple growing and many large orchards are now being developed. *Land values are extremely low,* considering the character of the soil" (italics in original).[40]

Not unexpectedly, Colonel Alexander Boyd Andrews, veteran Blue Ridge executive, shared this same sentiment about expansion and linkage. Shortly after his death in 1915, the company minute book recorded these observations: "It having always been his aim to promote its interests and welfare looking to its ultimate completion as, originally projected, to Knoxville, Tennessee, it having ever been his wish to live long enough to accomplish this."[41]

Progress occurred, surely pleasing vice president Culp and president Andrews. By June 1908 the Carolina & Tennessee Southern completed 14 miles northwestward between Bushnell, situated on the Murphy branch and the Little Tennessee River, and Fontana, also on that same stream. Several months later 25 miles of the Tennessee company opened between Maryville and Chilhowee, but not until 1916 did construction crews extend this trackage the nearly 6 miles to Calderwood. Workers then began grading beyond Calderwood eastward toward Fontana, North Carolina.

This left two gaps, the shorter section between Calderwood and Fontana and a longer segment southeast from Almond to Franklin. But no additional building took place, explained largely by the decision of the Aluminum Company of America (Alcoa) to build a power dam on the Little Tennessee that would flood the valley. Later, in the early 1940s the New Deal–created Tennessee Valley Authority became involved in hydroelectric power production in the area, forcing a major line relocation along the Murphy branch.[42]

Even with the Alcoa lake, there remained hope among South Carolinians that a direct connection between the Upstate and Knoxville could somehow be forged. "If you will analyze the proposed Blue Ridge extension, the first in a comparatively advantageous way, the second in a very striking manner," editorialized the *Anderson Tribune* in December 1923, "for we are told this line will not only give additional outlet for the Tennessee and Kentucky coal to the coast, but will also tap a region between Walhalla and Knoxville which is exceedingly rich in mineral deposits, including big quantities of some of the finest marble to be found in the world – mountains of it." But neither the editorial nor the visit by a delegation of Anderson-area businessmen to Southern Railway headquarters in Washington, D.C., could bring about completion of the Blue Ridge Railroad as initially conceived. By the 1920s, after nearly a century, railroad building in the Southeast had virtually ceased.[43]

CINCINNATI SOUTHERN RAILWAY

Despite a string of disappointments, the grand dream of delegates to the Knoxville Railroad Convention would be partially realized. And it did not produce the frustrations that came from that torturous quest experienced by the proponents of the Blue Ridge Railroad to unite South Carolina with Tennessee through the Rabun Gap. During the turbulent Gilded Age a *direct* rail line between Cincinnati and Charleston materialized. This time the catalyst came not from Charleston or some other Southern locality but from Cincinnati, this "Queen City of the West." The result was the Cincinnati Southern Railway (CSRy), the sole long-distance rail line built and owned by an American municipality.[44]

Since the conception of the LC&C much had changed in Cincinnati. Even though the city had expanded once the long depression that followed the Panic of 1837 had lifted, much of the economic luster of this "largest interior town of America" had vanished by the end of the 1850s. Although its population had increased, expectations of robust growth had diminished. "Cincinnati could no longer continue in possession of the trade that was her only reliance for the future," opined a contemporary observer. The opening in 1859 of the north-south Louisville & Nashville Railroad (L&N)

between these two river cities looked threatening. "Louisville, the most active competitor of Cincinnati for Southern trade, was placed in direct communication with Nashville, thence by connecting [railroads] with Knoxville, Chattanooga, Memphis, Augusta, Charleston, and almost every important point in the South," observed Edward Ferguson, a driving force behind the emerging Cincinnati railroad endeavor. Nevertheless, an economic revival of sorts took place in Cincinnati during the Civil War. The Union army created a strong demand for an array of locally produced goods, ranging from meat products to woolen uniforms; however, this stimulus was largely artificial, declining sharply after 1865. The conflict itself severely damaged trade along the Ohio and Mississippi river system and altered, disrupted, or destroyed markets in the Confederacy, and this commerce did not fully return once the war ended.[45]

Following the return of peace, a deep-seated fear of a permanent decline engulfed Cincinnatians. Community leaders realized that much of the regional freight traffic bypassed their metropolis, moving increasingly through the rapidly growing cities situated on the Mississippi River and the Great Lakes – St. Louis, Chicago, and Cleveland. The east-west trunk lines of the Baltimore & Ohio, New York Central (Vanderbilt Lines), and Pennsylvania systems tapped this trade and allowed Baltimore, Boston, New York, and Philadelphia – but not Cincinnati – to benefit from this flow of commerce. When census enumerators made their decennial count in 1870, both St. Louis and Chicago had outpaced Cincinnati. The former claimed populations of 310,864 and 298,977 respectively, while the tally for the later stood at 216,239. And trade south of the Ohio River, at best stagnant, looked as if it might go into a devastating tailspin. The rising position of Louisville prompted the *Cincinnati Commercial* in 1869 to comment: "Its southern railroad [L&N] makes it [Louisville] metropolitan – a funnel through which all our longitudinal railway travel must pass." By then the L&N benefited from a connection with the Nashville & Chattanooga Railroad to Chattanooga, a rail hub with direct links to other points in the former Confederacy. And in 1870 the Louisville Bridge Company opened its iron deck and truss bridge across the Ohio River, creating "the first and only connecting link between the great railway systems of the North and South." To make matters worse for Cincinnati, railroad freight rates favored wholesale jobbers in Louisville. Moreover, shipments from Cincinnati to destinations in the South, traveling through Louisville, were often delayed, even intentionally. A counterresponse followed: "For several years the Board of Trade of Cincinnati maintained a special agent at Louisville to trace out and hurry through Southern consignments."[46]

That "get-up-and-go" spirit still gripped Cincinnatians; they were not about to allow their city's economic position to deteriorate further. Like

an imperial state, Cincinnati sought to carve out (and protect) its own extensive dependencies. If rails were extended into the interior South, exciting opportunities would exist: business and commercial interests could tap consumer and industrial markets, exploit the agricultural (especially cotton and tobacco) and livestock trade, and take advantage of immense stands of timber and extensive deposits of minerals, most of all coal.[47]

Setting sights on the Southlands had been ongoing. Even prior to the Knoxville Railroad Convention, Cincinnatians had contemplated a railroad connection below the Ohio. This thinking continued after the LC&C forever stalled at Columbia. Just as work crews spiked down the last rails on the 185-mile line of the L&N between Louisville and Nashville, there seemed a good chance that Cincinnati might at last achieve its own penetration into Dixie. By 1860 the 99-mile Kentucky Central Railroad had opened between Cincinnati and Lexington, and a connecting 13-mile shortline, the Cincinnati, Lexington & East Tennessee Railroad, anticipated building from its end-of-track at Nicholasville, Kentucky, south of Lexington, to Knoxville. A road that resembled the unbuilt LC&C might yet be possible; after all, the railroad map of the trans-Appalachian West and South was decades away from jelling. War ended that hope, at least for the foreseeable future. Yet Union army General Ambrose Burnside and other federal officials recognized the military value of a rail line from Cincinnati into Kentucky and Tennessee. In fact, these men responded to President Abraham Lincoln's message to Congress in December 1861 that called for the opening of direct rail communication to the South "at government expense and as a war measure." Alas, only surveys were conducted before 1865.[48]

In 1868 prominent Cincinnatians again took up the cause of a railroad into the Southlands. Samuel H. Goodin led the charge, producing a thirty-six-page pamphlet, *Plan for the Construction of the Direct Railroad South, Connecting Cincinnati with the Southern System of Railroads,* which was widely distributed throughout the city and adjoining states. Goodin made clear that it was time to achieve the dreams of the previous decades.

> Through many years of the past the ablest men in all the sections likely to be affected by this work have labored for it; they have spoken and they have written in its advocacy, and plan after plan has been devised and submitted for its accomplishment, by States, counties, cities, conventions, committees, and individuals citizens, until the entire population of the regions interested have become restive, and chafe under the repeated failures of a project so important and so manifestly necessary.

He hoped that in the not-so-distant future, a railroad, financed by investors, would be "delivering freights and passengers at Charleston, Savannah, Pensacola, Mobile, and New Orleans, without break of bulk or change of cars."[49]

If Cincinnati were to become involved in building a southbound railroad, financing needed to come from local capitalists, outside investors, or some combination of these sources. Neither the city nor the county could provide assistance. Delegates to the drawn-out Ohio constitutional convention of 1850–1851 made substantial revisions to a document that had been in effect since statehood. In essence these dominant Jacksonian Democrats strengthened the bulwarks of agrarianism against the onset of the new economic order. When the soon-to-be ratified constitution dealt with public support for business ventures, including internal improvements, it took this position: "The General Assembly shall never authorize any county, city or township, by vote of its members or otherwise, to become a stockholder in any joint stock company, corporation or association whatever, or to raise money for, or loan its credit to or in aid of such company, corporation or association [Article 8, Section 6]." No longer could cities, towns, counties, or townships assist private corporations by becoming stock and bond holders. Ohio government itself would surely embrace this anti-investment stance. Such a provision would protect state credit and forever end investments in projects that were expensive, unneeded, or failed. Financial commitments to internal improvements, especially canals, had nearly bankrupted several states, and Ohioans had been frightened by their close brush with financial disaster. No one wanted to become an Illinois or an Indiana, places that had

A goal of the backers of the Louisville, Cincinnati & Charleston Rail Road involved bridging the Ohio River, forging that all-important connection between the South and the Old Northwest. That dream became reality on March 1, 1870, when the Louisville Bridge Company, closely tied to the Louisville & Nashville Railroad, opened the first rail link between northern and southern railways. Quickly the span bolstered the prosperity of both the city and the railroad. The importance of the Louisville bridge prompted D. Appleton and Company of New York to produce a steel engraving, *City of Louisville,* that showed two trains, one freight and one passenger, steaming over this most impressive structure.

Author's collection.

succumbed to the siren songs for better transportation. Vivid, unpleasant memories remained about the Ohio law, enacted in 1837, that allowed state government to loan money and subscribe to stock in canals, railroads, and turnpikes.[50]

Notwithstanding the legal roadblock created by the revised Ohio constitution, Cincinnati still wanted a direct railroad to the South. Private investors, however, hesitated to commit to such a project, fearing the cost of building through a difficult terrain and the likelihood in the near term of limited local or short-haul traffic. Furthermore, government sources in Kentucky and Tennessee could not be expected to make major contributions, being hard-pressed to meet their own financial obligations. Toward the end of the 1860s a solution was forthcoming, and it came from the fertile mind of a Cincinnati lawyer, Edward Ferguson, "Father of the Cincinnati Southern Railway."[51]

What Ferguson proposed was brilliant. Even though Cincinnati could not become a stockholder in a corporation, including a railroad, the Ohio constitution did not prevent the city from *owning* such an enterprise. "I thought of the project [railroad], and sat down one day [in 1868] to see how I could draft a bill to meet the case. I roughly sketched the first section. When I had done that, I became satisfied that it could be done." This led to a measure entitled: "A bill relating to cities of the first-class, having a population exceeding one hundred and fifty thousand inhabitants." (Cincinnati was the only Ohio metropolis that met this qualification.) Support was strong, winning backing from the Cincinnati City Council, Board of Trade, and Chamber of Commerce. "The bill, as drawn, meets the approval of our people, irrespective of party lines or political complexion," observed the *Cincinnati Daily Enquirer.* "It is approved as the true and only solution of a great problem, and the achievement of a great purpose. Cincinnati needs this Southern railroad." In April 1869 the proposal went before state lawmakers, and good news followed. Both the house and senate overwhelmingly approved this enabling measure, and on May 4, 1869, with the governor's signature, it became law.[52]

The specifics of the Ferguson handiwork were straightforward. To launch a railroad the Cincinnati City Council needed to pass a resolution declaring it a necessity and designating terminals (one of which had to be Cincinnati). Then local voters would make their decision. If they gave the proposal the green light, the Superior Court of Cincinnati would appoint five trustees to supervise surveys, approve purchases of rights-of-way and support sites, and arrange financing.[53]

Although there was some sentiment among council members to select Knoxville or Nashville as the southern end point, the body chose Chattanooga instead. This Tennessee River town of 6,093 had already become an important node on the railroad map. Lines, including the pioneer Nashville & Chattanooga, radiated out of Chattanooga in a spoke-like fashion. The community also benefited from a direct connection to an even faster growing railroad center, Atlanta. Furthermore, the population of Chattanooga continued to spike: 12,892 in 1880 and 29,100 a decade later.[54]

For the next decade Cincinnatians strove to make their railroad a reality, and they encountered the predictable ups and downs. Since the trustees agreed that the directness of the route would be a prime consideration, problems developed with right-of-way acquisitions. As with the LC&C, Tennesseans favored the Cincinnati project, and land matters never became troublesome. In autumn 1869 Tennessee lawmakers granted permission to build in the state, namely "to enter, survey, and acquire by gift, purchase or condemnation, land or portions of constructed railways, in such amount as might be necessary for the construction and maintenance of the Railway." In fact, residents of the railroad-starved eastern section, desirous of a northern outlet, earlier had taken action. Following the war, area interests had organized the Cincinnati & Chattanooga Railway. Although this paper company conducted a preliminary survey from Chattanooga northward toward Emory Gap on Tennessee's Emory River, work stopped in joyful anticipation of the CSRy.[55]

The legal right for the Cincinnati railroad to build through Kentucky, however, became a monumental struggle. The notion that "what is past is prologue" held true. Bluegrass State lawmakers expressed feelings similar to those of their predecessors when they refused to nurture the LC&C. The old bugaboo of urban jealousy reappeared. Businessmen, politicians, and others from greater Louisville, most of all, objected to granting economic advantages to Cincinnati. "The railroad is a bad thing for Louisville," editorialized the *Louisville Courier-Journal*. "It gives Cincinnati, our natural rival, a direct line of connection with two or three points worth connecting with, and imposes upon us the necessity of looking after our communications rather more actively than we have done recently." The writer continued, "Grass will certainly not grow in the streets of Cincinnati in our day. The merchants of Cincinnati, the railroad men of Cincinnati, are a thoroughly live and ingenious set of Yankee plotters, who propose to swarm upon the Southern country like ducks upon June-bugs." In March 1870 the Kentucky legislature denied the charter.[56]

An aggressive response followed. Cincinnatians turned to the long-established practice of organizing a railroad convention. In October 1870 this meeting took place in Lexington, a city destined to be on the path of the CSRy, and that well-attended gathering went off as expected. Representatives, who came from numerous counties in Kentucky and also from Alabama, Georgia, and Tennessee, agreed that the railroad would offer both direct and indirect benefits to a large region. By the end of their sessions, delegates appointed a committee to arrange a series of public meetings to be held throughout the Bluegrass State. The object was to explain the advantages of the CSRy, particularly to Kentuckians who lived outside the projected service area. Stock raisers became a principal target group. The existing network of rail lines allowed these shippers to reach lucrative southern markets only indirectly via Nashville, and they "suffered heavy losses from the longer confinement of cattle which this made necessary." The lobbying crusade became extensive. "During the winter months of 1870[–1871], the State had been canvassed from end to end in the interest of the project."[57]

Despite a well-orchestrated drive to convince Commonwealth lawmakers to charter the CSRy with the needed powers to establish a corridor, a second setback came in early 1871. This time the margin of defeat was less than with the earlier attempt. There was reason for guarded optimism.[58]

Not wanting to wait for Kentucky politicians to bestow their blessings, the always imaginative Edward Ferguson launched an effort to win federal approval for the stalled project. Specifically the CSRy sought permission in February 1871 to bridge the Ohio River and to gain the right to build in Kentucky and Tennessee. The title explained the rationale: "A bill to promote commerce and to cheapen the transportation of the mails and military and naval stores between Cincinnati and Chattanooga." Although the measure sailed through the U.S. House of Representatives by a two-thirds vote, it failed in the Senate for want of time.[59]

By mid-1871 conventional wisdom considered the Cincinnati to Chattanooga line stillborn. Not only had access been denied twice in Frankfort and postponed in Washington, but opposition mounted among fiscally conservative Cincinnatians. These individuals argued that if construction ever began, the project would become a costly burden on taxpayers. Some contended that citizens should not be taxed for enterprises that could not benefit everyone equally, a legacy of the Jeffersonian-Jacksonian political culture. This outlook led to legal action that challenged the constitutionality of the Ferguson Act. But the attack failed. In the case of *Walker v. City of Cincinnati* the Ohio Supreme Court ruled in December 1871 that the municipality unequivocally had the right to build a railroad.[60]

The battleground next shifted back to Kentucky. In not employing Cincinnati lobbyists and relying instead on "Kentucky friends of the Railway," CSRy backers hoped that this tactic would make the importance of this railroad to a rival commercial center less obvious. In February 1872 victory came, but unfortunately a measure "laden with burdensome conditions." Most troubling were the financial requirements. The state demanded that the company pay more than regular property taxes and franchise fees. Instead a charge of fifty cents would be levied for every passenger who crossed the Commonwealth and twenty-five cents for each person who traveled 100 miles within it. A penny levy was also placed on every 100 pounds of freight.[61]

After the pyrrhic victory in Kentucky, trustees and friends of the CSRy discussed their options. And they had much to consider, including the reappearance of the ugly head of local taxpayer opposition. Still, the project remained alive. Then good news came: the federal government approved the "Ohio River Bridge Act," allowing the railroad to span that active waterway, and Kentucky lawmakers, pressured by representatives from eastern and southern counties, repealed the odious features of earlier law. By spring 1873 the company had secured the necessary enabling legislation.[62]

While proponents and opponents of the Cincinnati to Chattanooga railroad wrangled, surveyors explored possible paths between Lexington and Chattanooga (at the time it was expected that the road would acquire trackage rights over the Kentucky Central). In March 1873 their exhaustive field report became available. The essence of the document was that no matter the route chosen – three major possibilities with some twenty-six variations were suggested – the geography in Kentucky and Tennessee presented expensive obstacles. There were mountains, hills and valleys, and three major rivers to cross. After considerable discussion, the board of trustees selected the "Military Route" that had been partially located by Union Army surveyors in 1863. This line ran from Cincinnati to Chattanooga through Lexington, Danville, and Somerset, Kentucky, and Emory Gap and Dayton, Tennessee.[63]

Financing now became the paramount issue. The timing for finding funding was awful; the Panic of 1873 had thrown the national economy into a long and painful depression. For several years the board of directors struggled to raise construction money, being frustrated by the general economic malaise, the weak national and international bond markets, and hometown opposition. But proceeds of a $10 million bond sale through a New York City bank, which took months to arrange, permitted the building process to commence. During the early months of 1874 contracts for about 150 parcels were let for grading, masonry, and bridge and tunnel work, and by that fall preparation of the roadbed in the rugged terrain of southern Kentucky and northern Tennessee was underway. The following year trustees awarded additional contracts, including one for an iron-truss bridge over the Ohio River and another for a cantilever-truss bridge (the first in North America) over a deep gorge carved by the Kentucky River.[64]

Building the CSRy required more money than originally anticipated. Happily for supporters another successful bond sale occurred.

The placement in 1876 of an additional $6 million dollars of securities, again endorsed by the City of Cincinnati, produced tangible results. This cash infusion permitted the railroad to open the 158 miles between the Kentucky communities of Ludlow, opposite Cincinnati (the 5,100-foot Ohio River bridge to Cincinnati would not be ready until December 1877), and Somerset, about 40 miles north of the Tennessee border. A privately operating firm, the Cincinnati Southern Rail*road* Company, functioning under a temporary arrangement with the trustees, instituted passenger service on July 23, 1877. About the same time freight began to move the length of the completed line. This lease meant that revenues were finally flowing into the municipal treasury. And the financial picture looked promising; as of June 30, 1878, gross earnings for the operator exceeded $365,000, and the economy was on the mend.[65]

Although heavy investments had been made, Chattanooga still had not been reached. By the end of 1877 expenditures on the physical plant neared $16 million; nevertheless, that southern goal seemed likely in the near future. Already work crews had finished grading from Somerset to within 5 miles of Chattanooga, a point where a connection was planned with the Western & Atlantic Railroad. (Trustees later decided to build their own line into Chattanooga, paralleling the Western & Atlantic.) The superstructure for the bridges and viaducts had also been completed.[66]

Then another crisis brewed. Trustees estimated that it would cost $3.25 million to finish construction, and the rub again became funding. With legislative approval in April 1878 trustees won authority to issue $2 million in bonds, *if* voters approved. Although far less than what was wanted, this money would place the railroad within striking distance of completion. But on May 3, 1878, there was no victory celebration; the measure failed in a tight municipal election – 11,237 for and 11,456 against. According to one chronicler, this was the "result mainly attributable to an unfriendly feeling toward the Trustees and the great doubt as to whether the two millions would finish the work." Again company representatives returned to Columbus, and a second authorization for $2 million was granted, but it came with the provision that the lowest construction bid *must* be accepted. This requirement was followed, and fortunately the lowest bid, $1,671.998.11, was well within the set financial limits. On August 14 another city bond election occurred, and this time there were 16,224 ballots cast in favor and 10,425 in opposition. Shortly thereafter the trustees approved the construction contract. Yet trouble lurked; opponents challenged the constitutionality of the financial arrangements. Then in December 1878 the railroad overcame that obstacle. This litigation, though, had wasted time and resources. The contractor suffered from uncertainty and the rising costs of labor and materials that came with a

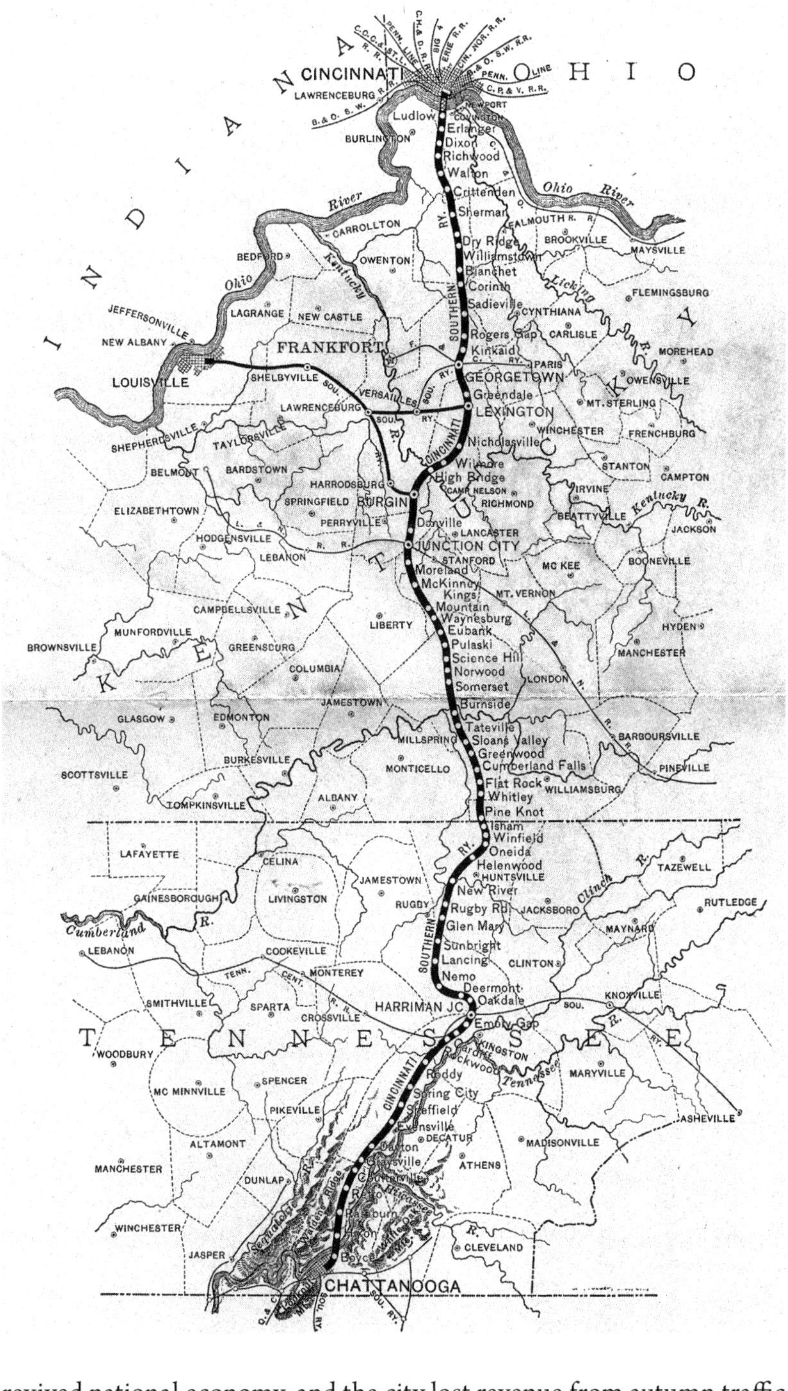

This map, made not long after the Cincinnati Southern Railway opened, depicts a railroad that operated in a mostly "air-line" fashion between its sponsoring city, Cincinnati, and Chattanooga, Tennessee.

Author's collection.

revived national economy, and the city lost revenue from autumn traffic as better times took hold.[67]

At last completion was within sight. Soon the 336-mile line with its 27 tunnels, which featured the 3,984-foot long Kings Mountain bore, and 105 bridges, including its signature structures over the Ohio and Kentucky Rivers, began operations. As built, this route through Kentucky and Tennessee was a far cry from what Major William McNeill and his surveyors had envisioned more than four decades earlier. By June 1879 the short section into Chattanooga was being finished, and workers prepared depots, yards, and other support facilities. In early February 1880 the entire railroad was done, adding to that explosion of railroad mileage that marked the Gilded Age. Although the depression of the 1870s had diminished construction, the 1880s saw an annual average of 7,000 miles of new track.[68]

Soon this strategic north-south route allowed through movements. On the evening of February 21, the first two southbound freight trains departed the Cincinnati terminal, with boxcars containing clothing, drugs, furniture, meats, starch, and whiskey, destined for Chattanooga and other southern locations. Five days later a train load of cotton from Birmingham arrived in Cincinnati. But more track work, especially ballasting and tie-tamping, was required to enhance train speeds. On March 8 the first passenger train left Cincinnati on a trial run to Chattanooga, and not long afterward regular service began.[69]

It was time for a gala celebration; the dream of the 1830s for Cincinnatians had come true. Residents would outdo themselves in officially commemorating the opening of their railroad to the South. On the evening of March 17, 1880, the extravaganza commenced. "The whole city had given itself up to the festivities of the hour," reported a guest from Macon, Georgia, "and everything beautiful in the way of fireworks, bunting and Chinese lanterns." The following afternoon there was "a grand police and firemen's parade" and that evening the formal ceremonies. "The largest banquet ever spread in the United States, up to that date, was given by the citizens of Cincinnati at the Music Hall. When prominent residents gathered at the food-laden tables, not less than seventeen hundred and seventy-six Southern men, leading merchants, manufacturers, politicians, governors and other invited guests sat down to this magnificent feast." Speeches and toasts followed. In a lengthy presentation Edward Ferguson proudly told the audience, many of whom had arrived on special trains from Chattanooga and intermediate points: "You have seen its graceful trestles, easy curves, nowhere a single reverse one, its low grades and substantial permanent way – this marvel of the engineer's skill in linking nature to civilization. The road has been made, and it will stand."[70]

No one disputed Ferguson's glowing assessment; the CSRy had embraced good, contemporary trunk-line construction standards. In fact, the former commissioner of public works in France, E. Lavoinne, made this comment: "The road approaches nearer to the European roads in its construction than of the railways as generally built in America; its great importance led its engineers to introduce at considerable cost, improvements which were only realized on older lines after the development of

One of the great civic events in the history of Cincinnati, Ohio, took place on the evening of March 17, 1880, when hundreds of local dignitaries and invited guests dined in splendor at the city's spacious and opulent Music Hall. It was a "Grand Banquet," indeed.

Courtesy of the Library of Congress.

the traffic, when competition forced their adoption as a means to arrive at a more economical operation."[71]

While the CSRy was an impressive achievement, no one at the celebration mentioned the great risk that the city had taken. Maybe that fact was fully understood among attendees, but the dangers prompted H. P. Boyden, who in 1901 chronicled the road, to remark: "As one looks back over the history of the tremendous undertaking, the gay and almost reckless confidence of the [backers] seems well nigh incredible. The few notes of warning that were thrown out were all but unheeded in the presence of a great popular impulse." The explanation for that enthusiasm was simple. "For thirty years Cincinnati had been talking about a Southern railroad," and that powerful sentiment led to widespread public approbation. Boyden admitted that the story of the CSRy had a happy ending.[72]

In one of the earliest public timetables issued by the Cincinnati Southern, the company made much of its "superior" passenger service and "delightful" scenic sights. The schedule boasted: "A perfect system of Parlor, Drawing Room and Sleeping Cars is operated on Express Trains." Even the non-limiteds offered much to the traveler, "being first-class passenger trains running on express time." For vacationers it was practical to "stop off at places of interest on the line, or in certain cases securing day trains and obtaining a view of the scenery, for which the Line is noted."[73]

Representing the fancy artwork commonly found on railroad public timetables during the Gilded Age, this schedule for April 15, 1881, was issued by the Cincinnati Southern Railway. The road's claim as the "Direct Route South" was no exaggeration.

Author's collection.

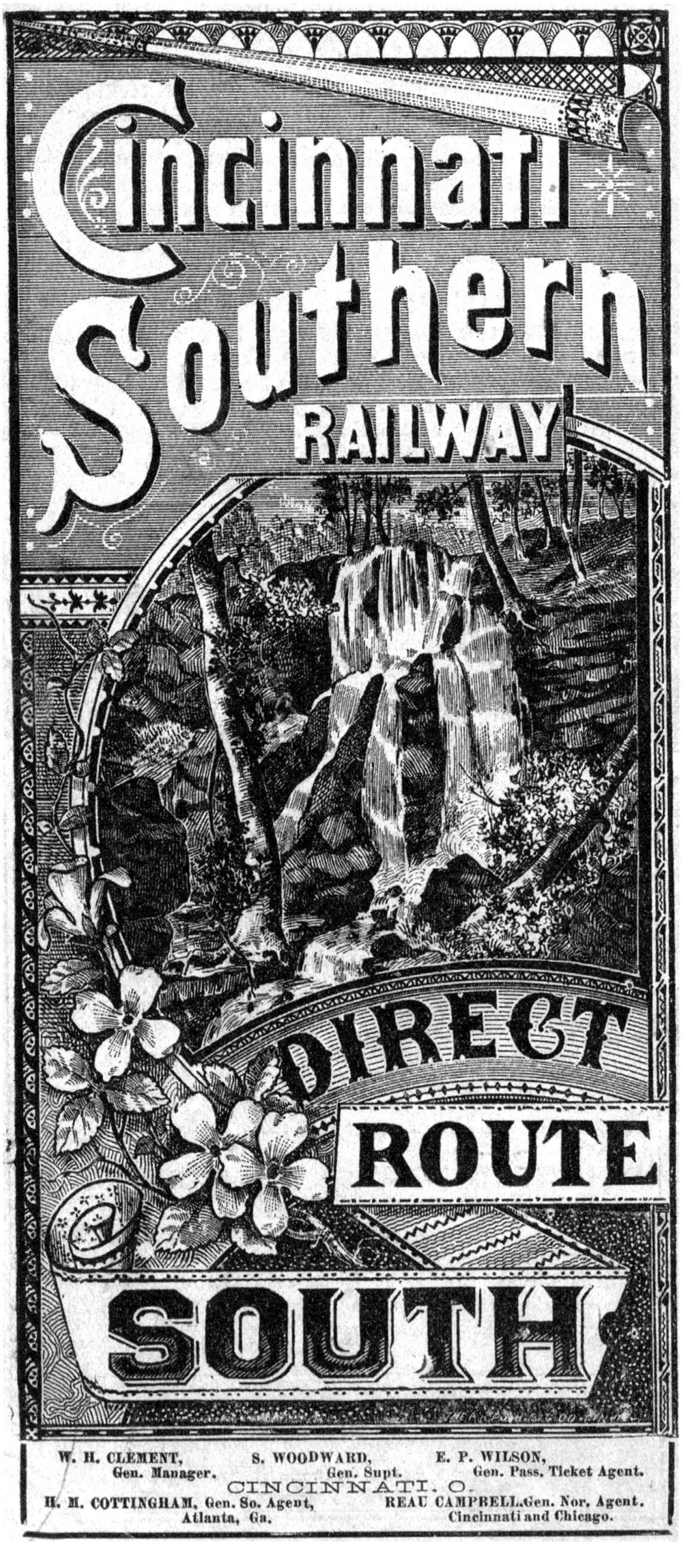

Once service began, the trustees needed to determine the future of their railroad. City fathers never planned to be both owner *and* operator. One option involved granting a long-term rental to either a syndicate of private interests or an established carrier. A year or so before the line opened, a group of Cincinnati investors had assumed operations from the Cincinnati Southern Railroad, taking the name of the Cincinnati Railroad Company. Its lease, though, could be extended. And legally the trustees could sell the property. Eventually the decision was made for the rental-lease choice. Ten proposals were received, including one from the current operator. "If any of the bids which the city will this year realize from the [Cincinnati] Southern," observed the *Cincinnati Enquirer,* "they will be much larger than is anticipated." A robust economy resulted in terms that exceeded expectations. On October 12, 1881, the CSRy was leased to the Erlanger Syndicate, a group headed by German-born banker Frederic Emile d'Erlanger and his multi-national banking house of Emile Erlanger and Company, but with a range of investors from Great Britain, France, the Netherlands, and the United States, including Cincinnati. Already the Erlanger organization had become involved in American railroads, notably the Alabama Great Southern and East Tennessee, Virginia & Georgia.[74]

The contract contained several key provisions. At its core was the twenty-five-year progressive rental structure: $800,000 for the each of the first five years, $900,000 annually for the second five years, $1 million annually for the next five years, $1.09 million annually for the fourth and $1.25 million annually for the final five-year period. The lessee also agreed to make yearly payments of $12,000 to defray expenses of the trustees and, more importantly, to maintain the line and to pay property taxes and assessments. This appeared to be an equitable arrangement for both parties.[75]

The leased property became the Cincinnati, New Orleans & Texas Pacific Railway Company (CNO&TP), commonly (and appropriately) known as the "Queen and Crescent Route." This agreement allowed its management to control an unbroken line from Cincinnati through Chattanooga to New Orleans. The future looked promising; it did not take long for the Erlanger franchise to generate respectable returns. In 1884, for example, earnings totaled $7,907 per mile and expenses stood at $5,470 per mile. And after May 30, 1886, traffic and revenues increased when the track gauge was realigned from Southern (5-foot) to standard, being no longer at odds with the rest of the country. This change, which cost approximately $54,000, was completed in only thirteen hours. Now the railroad could take on more the nature of a "bridge line" between northern and southern destinations, as other Dixie carriers at the same time also abandoned the wider Southern gauge.[76]

Yet hard times came; the CNO&TP fell into receivership in March 1893. Several factors precipitated this financial crisis. Most pronounced was the deepening agricultural depression in the South that had drastically reduced freight and passenger traffic and hence slashed revenues. Management also faced the increasing costs of that 1881 progressive rental agreement. And in the minds of investors the ever-shorting term of the lease caused a nagging uncertainty about the future relationship between the Syndicate and Cincinnati fathers.[77]

Although the Erlanger operating firm failed, all was not lost for this well-positioned, municipally owned trunk line. Not long after the downfall of the Cincinnati, New Orleans & Texas Pacific Railway, the Cincinnati Southern entered the orbit of the Southern Railway Company. Part of the ongoing system-building phenomenon, this giant regional carrier made its debut on July 1, 1894, following the consolidation of several southeastern railroads. What emerged was a dynamic enterprise financed by J. P. Morgan and Company and led by Samuel Spencer, an able railroad executive and Morgan associate.[78]

Under Morgan-Spencer control the Southern Railway became aggressive in expanding and protecting its system. In 1895 the company leased for ninety-nine years another publicly built road, the 223-mile, state-owned North Carolina Railroad, which replaced a previous agreement between North Carolina and the Richmond & Danville Railroad, the core of the Southern. That same year the Southern acquired stock control of the Alabama Great Southern Railway, which in turn controlled the CNO&TP (lessor of the CSRy from the City of Cincinnati). Four years later the Southern took over the South Carolina & Georgia Railroad (successor to the South Carolina Railroad) and placed the entire route between Cincinnati and Charleston under a single management. This Washington, D.C.-based company best typified the classic J. P. Morgan and Company quest for a self-sustaining and integrated railroad system.[79]

The Southern Railway relationship endured. When that robust road became part of Norfolk Southern Corporation in 1982, the lease with the City of Cincinnati remained. By then the trackage between Cincinnati and Chattanooga had been repeatedly improved, including line relocations and tunnel abandonments. These betterments made less accurate the term employees had long used: the "Rat Hole Division." The Cincinnati Southern had become a modern freight artery.[80]

Cincinnati itself continued to benefit from its direct access to the South. In the 1920s a contributor to *Forbes* magazine argued that excellent railroad connections, including those provided by the Cincinnati Southern, shaped this modern metropolis. "She is a city of great industries, but her genius has been not so much the genius of production as of distribution." That legacy remained. The Queen City of the Ohio, its rival

Louisville, and Baltimore, which by the late nineteenth century considered itself the "Southern Gateway," each profited from its rail penetration of the South.[81]

If delegates to the Knoxville Railroad Convention could have boarded a time machine to the twenty-first century, they surely would have been awed by the flourishing rail route between Charleston and Cincinnati. In all likelihood they would have found the CSRy the most inspiring, even breathtaking, especially with its monster bridges, deep cuts, magnificent tunnels, and heavy continuously welded steel rails. For these backers of the LC&C, their dream had come true.

7 What Might Have Happened

A GREATER CHARLESTON

Suggesting what might have happened if something did not occur or occurred only partially – that is counterfactual or virtual history – is a risky business. Yet the question "What if?" can lead to insights. The case might be made that Charleston, which once enjoyed an envied status as a dominant Atlantic port, might have retained its position for decades, even permanently, had the Louisville, Cincinnati & Charleston Rail Road (LC&C) been completed. "There is every reason to believe, that CHARLESTON possesses some peculiar advantages, which will entitle her to command a larger share of this [Western] trade, than *rightfully belongs,* to any other city in the union" (italics in original), stated the 1835 pamphlet on *The Proposed Rail-Road from Cincinnati to Charleston.* "SHE STANDS IN THE FRONT RANK, and [with the transmontane railroad] she will enter the list when she finds the course clear for Southern competition. AND SHE WILL WIN" (capitalization in original). Even in distant Boston, observers perceived that the LC&C was destined to make Charleston *the* American seaboard port. "To this end was Charleston to be forthwith converted into the great commercial rival of New York, and that the importing and exporting for the South and West was to be done no longer by the Northern cities." Yet a consensus existed that Charleston would never again regain its once enormous wealth. In the late eighteenth century it was said that nine of America's ten wealthiest men lived in the greater Charleston area. Still, Charlestonians expected to benefit from the LC&C, perhaps regaining for their hometown the status of the "Commercial Emporium of the South." The feeling went that "the more prosperous my beloved city, the more prosperous the beloved I."[1]

No one denied that nature had blessed Charleston. For generations this historic center of Palmetto State commerce had prospered because of its protected, deep-water harbor that permitted easy access to coastal and transoceanic sea lanes. Coastal sloops and schooners and much larger oceangoing sailing vessels made Charleston a port of call. "The city of Charleston is situated within two hours sail of the Ocean," noted Charlestonian Christopher G. Memminger in 1839, "accessible at all times and seasons of the year, and by merchant vessels of every class." The city, though, did have a geographical shortcoming. Unlike Savannah, its chief rival, located on the Savannah River approximately twenty miles inland from the ocean, Charleston lacked a navigable river that penetrated the heart of South Carolina or beyond. The Santee Canal and interior river improvements had helped, but only a railroad could effectively alter that disadvantage. After all, the opening in 1833 of the trans-state South-Carolina Canal & Rail-Road produced a positive impact, siphoning off trade from Savannah for Charleston that had earlier moved by flatboats, steamboats, and other watercraft along the long-flowing and meandering Savannah River. "Sixteen or eighteen steamboats once plied the Savannah River, greatly to the convenience and advantage of those whose property was situated there," recalled a prominent lower Savannah River planter. "[Since then] lands and houses have been depreciated, industries checked, and many honest citizens deprived in a measure of their livelihood."[2]

Although Charleston eventually obtained that rail route to the Ohio River, which dramatically collapsed distances, it would take decades, but initially it would not be that coveted *direct* path to the "West." On the other hand, Cincinnati interests, through imaginative, determined municipal efforts, created their own "air-line" to Chattanooga and that city's advantageous access to Southland destinations. Not until formation of the Southern Railway did a single management operate what became a through line, via the leased Cincinnati Southern, between Charleston and Cincinnati.[3]

Just as Cincinnatians knew the value of reaching markets in the South, at the dawn of the Railway Age Charlestonians understood the importance of a direct rail artery to the Ohio River, even though such an undertaking would be expensive, risky, and fraught with engineering and financial problems. Building the first long-distance interregional carrier in America might have had a monumental impact, improving the economic position of the city and in the process damaging arch-rival Savannah and other lesser Atlantic seaports, whether Wilmington, North Carolina, or Brunswick, Georgia. Charlestonians battled unsuccessfully to achieve that goal, first with the LC&C and later with the less ambitious Blue Ridge Railroad.

There is that haunting question: what *if* the LC&C had been completed by the 1840s? Although the impact that this first transmontane railroad would have had on Charleston and its environs is speculation, vast possibilities existed for economic growth in Charleston and nearby areas.

With the LC&C in operation there would be a stream of inbound goods from Cincinnati and other places along its extensive mileage. One dimension of the railroad would have been developmental, taking time – perhaps decades – to exploit fully the traffic potential. Still, carloads of agricultural products – barreled pork, cotton, grain, flour, livestock, especially mules – lumber (cedar, chestnut, locust, oak, and pine) and naval stores, cotton bagging and rope, minerals, salt, tobacco, and whiskey would travel over LC&C rails. Such commodities might have contributed to a diverse manufacturing sector. Take those heavy bales of cotton, undoubtedly a staple of the company's traffic mix. Instead of some of the first textile mills in the South appearing along or near the Savannah River, they might have popped up on the outskirts of Charleston, and perhaps a large cloth-producing firm, which began locally in the 1840s, might not have failed so quickly. Cotton, too, would likely have continued to flow along the established export routes, principally to destinations in Great Britain and New England. Conceivably piles of raw or processed mineral products, including coal, marble slabs, and iron and zinc ingots, might have crowded public wharves. Likely logs and milled lumber would have been stacked nearby. Certainly brick-making operations, utilizing an abundance of commercial clay, would have expanded at numerous locations, meaning that this popular, albeit bulky, building material would have moved through the Charleston port.[4]

Then there would be that increased flow of goods consigned for interior destinations. Undeniably it would have been wide and diverse, ranging from English-made crockery to Connecticut-manufactured hardware. The volume and variety would be more than items such as the window glass or coffee, tea, and spices that historically were destined for plantations and farms. Traditionally these agricultural units were known for their high degree of self-sufficiency, producing most of the things that were consumed, used or worn. If the subsistence level at which slaves and poor whites lived could be altered, demand would grow for more consumer goods. The market existed, but it would take time to evolve. In places the LC&C would act as a classic developmental railroad, operating in advance of actual transportation requirements. Yet early on it would be able to exploit an existing clientele. Increased inbound traffic would have enlarged the size of the Charleston merchant-jobber class and expanded the city's warehouse district. "The foreign trade of Charleston has been limited by the want of communications with the interior," said a company spokesman. "It is impossible that she can carry on an advantageous importing trade, unless that trade can find outlets by internal communications. But if this great avenue were opened, a change would at once be effected."[5]

The LC&C would have been an unusual operation. What would make the LC&C stand out from most other railroads in the South (and elsewhere) was that it was designed to generate *long-distance* traffic and not to rely solely or heavily on short hauls. Most carriers in the region experienced a seasonal surge in transporting agricultural products – cotton most of all – and not a balanced in- and outbound flow of commodities and goods. As development occurred along LC&C rails, the traffic mix could be expected to undergo important shifts. Also the Charleston to Cincinnati road, unlike typical antebellum carriers, would not have emphasized passenger movements over freight, but would have sought both types.

Just as the Erie Canal molded commerce and manufacturing and stimulated urban growth and development in the Empire State, this first railroad penetration from a South Atlantic seaport to the Ohio River country and its various intermediate points could have created a lively corridor. Local economies, including those of Charleston, Columbia, Asheville, Knoxville, Lexington, and other places, would benefit from their location on an *established,* premier rail route just as several Upstate New York communities blossomed into cities because of the Erie Canal and later the largely parallel New York Central Railroad. An enormous difference existed between a tap line or intrastate road and a long-distance, interregional carrier. Admittedly, some villages and towns that would be missed by LC&C rails would surely wither and die.

Even after plans to extend the LC&C beyond Columbia had fizzled, some supporters expected that the South Carolina metropolis could still achieve a degree of economic dominance as the railroad network matured, becoming even the hub of southern commerce. "Then if Charleston, as is at present indicated, should assert her proper position as a commercial city," editorialized the *American Railroad Journal* in 1851, "and established lines of ocean steamers to and from the principal ports of Europe, the merchant or planter of the Mississippi valley need go no farther than the 'emporium of the south' to ship his produce or receive his imported cargo."[6]

What actually happened *without* the LC&C or similar direct rail connections was less than impressive. Although Charleston continued to refer to itself as that "Commercial Emporium of the South" or the "Queen City of the South" (but more appropriately called the "Holy City" because of the proliferation of church steeples), the place struggled. For much of the period that followed the Knoxville Railroad Convention population figures remained relatively stable, never really spiking. Census statistics tell much: 30,289 in 1830; 29,261 in 1840; 42,985 in 1850; 40,522 in 1860 (these included whites, free blacks, and slaves); 48,956 in 1870; 49,984 in 1880, 54,955 in 1890; and 55,807 in 1900. While events outside its control hurt the community – the yellow fever outbreak of 1854, the disastrous fire of 1861, a 7.3 magnitude earthquake in 1886, and the Great Hurricane of 1893 – the damages suffered from the ravages of the Civil War and the city's negative image among non-Southerners as the "Spiritual Capital of the Confederacy" collectively took their toll. Consequently Charleston fell into a long slumber. The city did not fully awake until the era of World War II and the Sunbelt renaissance that followed, making locations in the region popular for investors and newcomers from the North and elsewhere. For generations Charleston had languished, staying a sleepy, albeit charming, Old South backwater. No wonder it became known – at least to outsiders – as the "City of the Past."[7]

The topography of the Charleston core suggests that it might have been a challenge for the city to emerge as a premier rail hub. It lay between the ocean and the coastal plain on an isolated three-mile-long peninsula surrounded by two relatively broad, shallow, and short rivers, Ashley and Cooper. There were also miles of swamplands between the coastline and the extensive interior pine barrens. Yet the LC&C could have found space (perhaps requiring earthen and rock fill) for the required railroad facilities. After all, rail yards in the antebellum period appeared in the vicinity of other compact coastal ports such as Baltimore, Boston, and New York City.

The honor of railroad Mecca, which eluded Charleston, went elsewhere, notably to Atlanta, a town site that had ample room for expansion and claimed an advantageous regional location. A writer for *Harper's New Monthly Magazine* succinctly explained how the city came into being: "The answer is one word – railways." Ultimately, thanks to the iron horse, Atlanta became one of the few great American cities not to be situated on a navigable waterway, whether ocean, lake, river, or canal. Long-distance goods, if destined for export or internal consumption, commonly moved by train through Atlanta. And so did that constant stream of travelers. This Georgia community emerged as the crossroads for goods and people passing through the Southeast. Not only did Atlanta become a beehive of railroad-related activities – with an army of workers who labored in train service and yards, shops, and other facilities – but businesses benefited from freight rates that favored manufacturers, jobbers, and other customers. This advantageous pricing was more pronounced here than in any other place in the Southeast, including Charleston. By the 1880s the Georgia capital immodestly claimed to be the "Gate City of the South," and it would never be seriously challenged for that distinction, not by Birmingham, Charlotte, Jacksonville, Mobile, Nashville, New Orleans, Richmond, or Tampa. The statistics, which reveal steady growth, are impressive: 9,554 residents on the eve of the Civil War, soaring to 65,533 by 1890 and reaching 154,839 in 1910. A combination of strategic location and civic boosterism – the work of those all-important "livewires" – made Atlanta a grand metropolis. Ironically, as historian Ulrich B. Phillips notes, "the town itself originated as an incidental result of the building of [rail]roads intended exclusively for the benefit of other cities."[8]

Even without the LC&C, as conceived, Charlestonians expected that the developing network of iron rails in the Southlands would create lasting prosperity. In 1846, several years after the plug had been pulled on the transmontane project, officials of the South Carolina Railroad thought that their well-positioned trans-state line would funnel to and from Charleston and its port freight from locations in Georgia, Alabama, and adjoining states. "Each railroad west of Charleston in turn may become the parent of others, indefinitely reproducing others and spreading their arms in every direction gathering and bearing on their tracks the products of countless farms and manufactories to be exchanged at our Seaport for the merchandise of other lands, which in turn are to be re-conveyed by the same channels to the places of their consumption." This was positive thinking at its best.[9]

It was never ordained that Atlanta would become that giant railroad center of the South. Unquestionably, Knoxville would have been a key node on the LC&C between Charleston, Lexington, Cincinnati, and Louisville. Georgia promoters planned to connect their developing railroads with the LC&C at Knoxville, and perhaps the state-owned Western & Atlantic, which did much to energize Atlanta, would have been postponed or not built at all. There would be additional roads that radiated out of Knoxville, penetrating agricultural lands, including the fertile upper Shenandoah Valley of Virginia, and tapping extensive stands of timber and rich mineral deposits. A connection also would be made with Chattanooga, another potential rival to Atlanta, and local and through traffic could have catapulted that Tennessee River town into the ranks of a dominant metropolis. Writing in 1913, John Bomar Cleveland, an amateur historian who studied the conflict between John C. Calhoun and Robert Hayne, believed that if the LC&C had succeeded, Greenville or Spartanburg, not Atlanta, would have become the vital railroad center. "It has been one of the greatest misfortunes to South Carolina that the differences between Calhoun and Hayne were so great as to the respective routes that it postponed for many years the completion of the line down the French Broad," he contended, "and the result has been that Georgia has been built up at the expense of South Carolina, and Atlanta made possible, whereas the great distributing point should have been in upper South Carolina."[10]

Historically railroads have either created or stimulated urban centers. But without that pioneer LC&C, Charleston (or any other place in South Carolina) did not get a leg up on other communities of the Southeast. Its businessmen, led by powerful, forward-thinking merchant-capitalists, tried mightily to achieve the goal of the Knoxville Railroad Convention.

But, alas, for years they depended heavily on their intrastate ribbons of iron, which most of all handled shipments of upland cotton to their port facilities.

PREVENTING CIVIL WAR

"Mobility of population is death to localism." This perception, argued by America's foremost historian, Frederick Jackson Turner, suggests a possibility unrealized by the ill-fated Louisville, Cincinnati & Charleston Rail Road. Localism, which can be extended to regionalism or sectionalism, played a critical role in the coming of the nation's greatest bloodbath, the Civil War, or officially the War of the Rebellion. As Turner's collective writings suggest, two great conflicting forces shaped the course of American history – the frontier that helped to bind the nation and the sectionalism that tore it apart. These two elements, he believed, explained the distinctiveness of the American civilization.[11]

Before canal mania, fueled by the opening of the Erie Canal, internal trade largely traveled on a north-south axis rather than following the east-west continental land mass. These traditional movements involved more than the intercostal waters, which had been active since colonial times, but centered on the flourishing river commerce that developed along the Ohio-Mississippi river system. Merchants in Cincinnati and Louisville developed strong business relationships with their counterparts in Memphis and New Orleans, helping to forge commercial alliances between the Old Northwest and the South. There was also migration along these riverways, whether between Cincinnati and New Orleans or Pittsburgh and Natchez, creating and strengthening social, cultural, and political ties. Direct and indirect communications added to this cohesion, especially after the advent of steamboats, and ranged from travelers to letters and newspapers. As for the latter, daily and weekly publications printed extensive "exchanges" from news sources in places along these busy rivers and their principal tributary streams. Readers of an Indiana newspaper may have had a better sense of what was happening in Louisiana and Mississippi business and politics than they did of comparable affairs in Connecticut or New Jersey. "Trade along the Mississippi and its tributaries," observed historian Marc Egnal, "gave the Northwest and Southwest a shared outlook and common set of interests."[12]

But in the 1830s new transportation routes started to alter that north-south connectedness. A combination of trunk canals and railroads began to link the older states of the Old Northwest and adjoining places with the East, including New England, New York, and the Mid-Atlantic states. For residents of the West, events in Boston, New York, and Philadelphia took on greater importance than happenings in Charleston, Mobile, and New

Orleans. By midcentury not only did several long canals exist in Ohio, Indiana, and Illinois, but additional "ditches," including some lengthy lateral or feeder ones, had opened. More importantly, the iron horse was poised to penetrate the Appalachian barrier from Baltimore, New York, and Philadelphia. Every mile of railroad built across the mountains and in the Old Northwest shifted a portion of the commerce from the West to the East and reduced the flow of products along the interior drainage system. A revolution of internal trade routes was at hand. Some shippers learned that even though steamboat companies might charge less than railroads for freight, the risks associated with river travel meant that insurance coverage absorbed much of the rate differential between these two transport modes. But as the network of canals and railroads matured, haulage charges declined substantially. "The transportation revolution reduced shipping costs between the East and West," concluded financial scholar John J. Binder, who carefully examined contemporary rate structures. And this trend had a real impact: "[It] changed the direction of East-West trade from the U-shaped southern routes to direct northern routes." Moreover, railroads were faster, safer, and operable in most weather conditions, and they conveniently served popular markets in both the East and the Old Northwest. These iron rails spurred the remarkable growth of Chicago, Cincinnati, Cleveland, Detroit, and Indianapolis, and their industries – consumer durables, farm machinery, food processing, machine tools, and railroad equipment – strengthened bonds with the East. "Boston and New York have spread over the northwestern States a net work of improvements which has entirely diverted their trade from its natural channel," lamented the editor of a New Orleans newspaper in 1850. "The tobacco, flour, and trade of the State of Ohio, are already gone, or at least we receive but little from her beyond what is necessary for our own consumption. Indiana has forgotten, and Illinois holds but slight intercourse with us." His sad reflections continued. "The fine rivers which are tributary to the Mississippi, and stretch their arms through these States, should naturally have given us their trade; but the eastern cities look upon the rich field of commerce which they have presented by their internal improvements, [and have] overcome our natural advantages and deprived us of their trade." This journalist may have recalled that following the War of 1812 80 percent of the receipts by river at New Orleans involved produce from the Old Northwest. The Crescent City was that meeting place of flatboats and tall-masted ships.[13]

Yet a completed LC&C could have enhanced that earlier closeness that water commerce had forged between the Old Northwest and the South. Before, during, and after the Knoxville meeting the advantages of expanding markets between the two regions were repeatedly emphasized. These arguments involved more than Charleston and its environs benefiting from a larger sphere of lucrative in- and outbound trade; they included commercial expansion in Asheville, Columbia, Knoxville, Lexington, and other places as well. Once the LC&C had opened, it would not have been long before telegraph wires were strung along its length, further enhancing business and personal connectedness. During the 1850s this communication technology took hold at a phenomenal rate, making possible virtually instant messaging.

That burning desire for the Charleston to Cincinnati rail line drew from multiple rationales. One motivation involved slavery, the primary cause of the Civil War. As early as 1833 Elias Horry, president of the South-Carolina Canal and Rail-Road Company, publically commented on a "Rail Road up the French Broad River." This respected railroad executive considered such an undertaking "so indissolubly connecting the Southern and Western interests, strengthening the bonds of union and thereby perpetuating all the blessings of our valuable institutions [including slavery]." On the eve of the Knoxville Railroad Convention Abram Blanding told an assembly in Charleston, "The South would then be able [with the railroad] to compete with Eastern cities for the trade of Ohio, and, with a branch to Louisville, for the trade of Indiana. The connection with Cincinnati, from a political point of view, meant detaching a powerful confederate from the east, as far as commerce and social relations could do it, and might keep Ohio a friend of the South on the slavery question, as she would receive all the benefits of slave labor, indirectly, without any of its evils." Added Blanding, "If the road ended at Louisville in a slave state, it would not be attended with so many advantages." Responding to attacks on the "peculiar institution" by abolitionists somewhat later, Robert Hayne remarked: "Slavery, as it now exists in the Southern States, which we all feel and know to be essential to the prosperity and welfare – nay to the very existence of the States – is so little understood in other portions of the Union that it has been lately assailed in a spirit which threatens, unless speedily arrested, to lead eventually to the destruction of the Union and all the evils which must attend so lamentable an occurrence." If "free social intercourse" could be achieved between the "South and the West," then the negative impact of antislavery advocates could be thwarted. As Hayne elaborated, "Reciprocal dependence from Michigan to Florida, by establishing connection in business, promoting friendships, abolishing prejudices, creating greater uniformity in political opinions and blending the feeling of distant portions of the country into a union of heart" would accomplish much. At the time of the Knoxville Railroad Convention Judge John B. O'Neall, Newbury, South Carolina, resident, railroad activist, and ardent unionist, chimed in with these comments: "If it [LC&C] succeeds, South Carolina will be prosperous beyond all former calculations, and the Union of States will be as lasting as the rocks and mountains which will be passed and overcome by the contemplated road." O'Neall merely reiterated what railroad promoters had been arguing for some time, namely that iron rails would forever unite the country.[14]

Other supporters of the LC&C echoed the Hayne perception, contending that a combination of personal contacts and commercial commitments to be brought about by the intersectional railroad would prevent outsiders from altering the status quo, and therefore the federal union would be preserved. Support for slavery existed in the Old Northwest, with Illinois being an example. The Prairie State went so far as to vote in 1824 on whether to legalize bondage, but this ballot measure failed. More than a decade later the Illinois river town of Alton made national headlines when local slavery supporters murdered Elijah Lovejoy, an abolitionist newspaper publisher. A sizable number of residents who lived north of the Ohio River, many of whom hailed from the South or had personal ties to the region, had no moral objections to slavery. As late as 1840 the federal census revealed that in Illinois, for example, the population included more than three hundred slaves. And throughout the Old Northwest there existed much antiblack feeling. Take the statement made by a Virginia-born person of color about his experiences in antebellum Cincinnati. He "found every door closed against the colored man in a free state, excepting the jails and penitentiaries, the doors of which were thrown wide open to receive him." He added, "From the treatment I received by the people generally, I found it little better than in Virginia."[15]

Southern advocates of the LC&C who thought that direct transport connections with citizens of the Old Northwest could diminish, although not likely silence, the shrill cries made by a vocal minority for slave emancipation found others in the South who shared that conviction. Declared a state senator from Virginia in 1838: "The opening of one lone line of communication between the James River and the Ohio, will do more to check the progress of abolition in the free states of the west than all the appeals which eloquence can make, and all the arguments that ingenuity can urge." His timing was appropriate. In the 1830s the antislavery movement was heightening its demands for immediate and total abolition. When it came to the political positions taken by Illinois, Indiana, and Ohio, most of all, in the wake of the South's threatened secession, the Virginia lawmaker's line of thinking might have made a difference.[16]

A functioning Charleston to Cincinnati railroad would have done more than produce an important commercial relationship between the Old Northwest and South: it would have affected patterns of internal migration. One would suspect that thousands of free whites from the Old Northwest, foreign lands, and other locales would have taken temporary railroad construction jobs and then accepted permanent maintenance and operating positions. With a developmental road, potentially many more individuals would been attracted to business and professional opportunities in new or expanding settlements. Considering the mileage involved and the fact that railroads typically established stations every 8 to 10 miles, scores of trackside locations would have morphed into thriving communities. "The railroads made small-town America," as historian Albro Martin has aptly stated. "Not even the haughtiest river city during the steamboat era had quite the easy intercourse with the world around the bend or beyond the vanishing point on the straightaway that the railroad brought to the 'small' town." Even more jobs would exist in commercial agriculture and extractive industries; thousands upon thousands of able-bodied men could have made their livelihood from these endeavors.[17]

The presence of more financially independent whites likely would not have thrilled slaveholders, because these individuals might have shaped political and social sentiments. In western North Carolina, eastern Tennessee, and eastern Kentucky there already existed a majority population who had little or no sympathy for the slaveholding class, or what they called "the Slave Power." It is not an overstatement to suggest that railroads fostered a burgeoning middle class and in the process created a more diverse population. J. Fred Rippy, the biographer of Joel Poinsett, the prominent South Carolina politician, diplomat, and delegate to the Knoxville Railroad Convention, concluded that "such a means of communication [LC&C] between the two sections might have made possible the gradual emancipation of the slaves by causing a large influx of free whites into the South and removing the menace of free Negroes by creating a numerical preponderance of Anglo-Saxons." Surmised Rippy, "In a word, it might have prevented the Civil War and its terrible aftermath!"[18]

There were Northerners who saw the advantages of railroads that would tie their home region not just with the Old Northwest but directly with the South. In 1854 a contributor to a Washington, D.C., newspaper advocated such rail connections, especially a direct iron way between Boston and New Orleans. Such a linkage, he contended, would enhance "bonds of union," preventing any possible breakup of the Republic. That core rail line never became an antebellum reality. Nor did one that was intended to link Sandusky, Ohio, on the shores of Lake Erie, with Charleston and Savannah, but at midcentury a Buffalo, New York, newspaperman saw the value in such a railroad. "To create a *oneness* of feeling and interest between the North and the South, nothing will contribute more than the construction of an iron way from Lake Erie to Savannah and Charleston" (italics in original). The New York–based *American Railroad Journal* took a similar position. "The various roads now under construction [1852], and in contemplation, extending through various states of our Union from north to south, will, when completed, serve as an additional bond of union to the confederacy."[19]

Interestingly after the failure of the LC&C to push beyond South Carolina, efforts by such Southerners as John C. Calhoun and James Gadsden focused on uniting the slaveholding South not with the Old Northwest but with Texas, adjoining territories, and California. The goal became a Southern transcontinental railroad. In 1853 surveys made under the direction of Secretary of War Jefferson Davis indicated that the best route for a Southern railroad ran south of the Gila River in Mexican territory, and later that year the Gadsden Purchase secured this desired land. Ideally an east-west trunk line would bind the Old South with the slaveholding lower Mississippi River Valley and westward to the Pacific Ocean. Several options received consideration, including the more northerly, but still southern, 35th-parallel route. This obsession with protection of sectionalism was hardly what delegates in Knoxville had in mind or, probably, wanted.[20]

Every transcontinental railroad proposal became contentious; after all, several cities along the Mississippi River sought to become the eastern terminus, including New Orleans, Memphis, St. Louis, and Rock Island. In fact, Memphis and St. Louis would each hold their own railroad conventions to consider routing strategies. But the ensuing controversy involved more than what place would become the departure point for a Pacific railroad; it pitted free states against slave states. Later, as the war began, merchants and their associates in Charleston felt confident that direct linkage with a Southern transcontinental line would produce a "golden era" for their home city in the newly constituted Confederate States of America. The South Carolina port would become the New York City equivalent in a sprawling Southern slave republic.[21]

The failure of the LC&C, the delay in building other north-south rail arteries, controversy over the route for a Pacific railway, and the growing rail network between states of the Old Northwest and the East intensified sectional rivalries. Already extremists and agitators, whether abolitionists in the North or "fire-eaters" in the South, fueled these debates over free versus slave labor, whipping up anger in the process. In the minds of some Northerners *all* Southerners embraced slavery, and similarly there were those Southerners who believed that *everyone* who did not support the peculiar institution was as an abolitionist. In 1858 the *Charleston Mercury* said it best: "On the subject of slavery the North and South are not only two Peoples, but they are rival, hostile Peoples." [22]

By the 1850s the railroad map revealed a growing commercial linkage between Ohio and New York and not Ohio and South Carolina. In the Old Northwest an expansion of railroad construction took place, soaring during the decade from 1,235 to 10,333 miles. At midcentury trackage averaged 442 miles per free state but only 112 miles per slave state. "This expanding transportation system was binding the Northwest closer to the Eastern states while divorcing it from the earlier alliance with the South," wrote Charles S. Sydnor in his History of the South series volume. "Transportation developments in the first half of the nineteenth century increased the differences between slave and free states and contributed to the isolation of the South." Fellow historian Ray Allen Billington reached a similar conclusion. "The two sections were bound by such firm economic ties that they merged into one section, the North. The new alignment, which arrayed two giant sections against each other, made civil war inevitable; only the emotional excitement bred of the efforts of each to control new frontiers beyond the Mississippi was needed to touch off the irrepressible conflict."[23]

Whether the Civil War was an irrepressible or repressible conflict remains debatable, as Civil War historians ranging from Charles A. and Mary R. Beard and Kenneth M. Stampp to Avery O. Craven, David Herbert Donald, and J. G. Randall have contended. But the union between the Old Northwest and the East, which created that economic interdependence, may well have been offset by a more powerful economic and social relationship between the Old Northwest and the South. Developments in the transportation infrastructure did much to produce two dramatically different societies that featured their own peculiar social structures and cultural values. In part because of growing isolation between the regions, meaningful firsthand experiences of each other's institutions and outlooks diminished. A completed Louisville, Cincinnati & Charleston Rail Road might have mitigated that separation, altering the course of American history and achieving a legacy of inestimable significance. There is truth in the observation made by one railroad commentator that "parochialism, the source of so much ignorance, superstition, fear, bigotry, and strife, is always diminished by travel." But Abraham Lincoln said it best. In 1876 Henry Charles Carey, who served as the chief economic adviser to Lincoln during his presidency, recounted a conversation he had had in May 1861 with the newly inaugurated chief executive:

> "What it was that even then held the Union together? Was it not the Mississippi?" "Yes," said he [Lincoln], "that is the cross-tie." "Well, then," as I continued, "if you had an iron cross-tie [railroad] down the Valley and through the mountain region to Alabama and the Gulf, and another from the Ohio through East Tenneessee [*sic*] to Charleston and Savannah, do you think it would be possible to dissolve the Union?" "No," said he, "it would then be entirely impossible."

Carey added his own belief that such "hooks of steel" would have produced "a feeling of brotherhood throughout the Union."[24]

Could it be that a failed LC&C helped to cause the Civil War?

Notes

1. SLOW, DIFFICULT, AND DANGEROUS TRAVEL

1. Henry Adams, *The Education of Henry Adams* (New York: Heritage Press, 1942), 441–54.

2. In the antebellum decades the Old Northwest, which by 1848 consisted of the states of Illinois, Indiana, Michigan, Ohio, and Wisconsin, was commonly called "the West." Contemporaries might also consider all or parts of Arkansas, Kentucky, Louisiana, Mississippi, and Tennessee to be included in "the West."

3. Robert Mills, *Inland Navigation Plan for a Great Canal between Charleston and Columbia, and for Connecting Our Waters with Those of the Western Country* (Charleston, S.C.: Telescope Company, 1821); George Rogers Taylor, *The Transportation Revolution, 1815–1860* (New York: Holt, Rinehart and Winston, 1951), 20–22; Ronald E. Shaw, *Canals for a Nation: The Canal Era in the United States, 1790–1860* (Lexington: University Press of Kentucky, 1990), 18.

4. Seymour Dunbar, *A History of Travel in America* (New York: Tudor Publishing, 1937), 19–20; Randle Bond Truett, *Trade and Travel around the Southern Appalachians before 1830* (Chapel Hill: University of North Carolina Press, 1935), 4–6.

5. George W. Knepper, ed., *Travels in the Southland 1822–1823* (Columbus: Ohio State University Press, 1966), 6, 49, 82; Parmenas Taylor Turnley, *Reminiscences of Parmenas Taylor Turnley: From the Cradle to Three-Score and Ten* (Chicago: Henneberry, 1892), 32–36.

6. George R. Wilson, *Early Indiana Trails and Surveys* (Indianapolis: Indiana Historical Society, 1919), 1, 22, 24, 29; William C. Davis, *A Way through the Wilderness: The Natchez Trace and the Civilization of the Southern Frontier* (New York: HarperCollins, 1995), 11–17, 25, 51–53; J. L. Ringwalt, *Development of Transportation Systems in the United States* (Philadelphia: By the author, 1888), 25; Mills Lane, ed., *The Rambler in Georgia* (Savannah, Ga.: Beehive Press, 1973), 36, 69–70.

7. Rebecca Solnit, *Wanderlust: A History of Walking* (New York: Viking Penguin, 2000), 5–6; John A. Jakle, *Images of the Ohio Valley: A Historical Geography of Travel, 1740 to 1860* (New York: Oxford University Press, 1977), 22.

8. Lewis Condict, ed., "Journal of a Trip to Kentucky in 1795," *Proceedings of the New Jersey Historical Society* (1919): 122.

9. See W. M. Gillespie, *A Manual of the Principles and Practice of Road-Making* (New York: A. S. Barnes, 1852).

10. *American Railroad Journal,* January 12, 1833.

11. R. Carlyle Buley, *The Old Northwest: Pioneer Period, 1815–1840,* 2 vols. (Indianapolis: Indiana Historical Society Press, 1950), 1:474–75; Howard D. Dozier, *A History of the Atlantic Coast Line Railroad* (Boston: Houghton Mifflin, 1920), 4; Dunbar, *A History of Travel in America,* 717–40; Ezra M. Stratton, *The World on Wheels, or, Carriages, with Their Historical Association from the Earliest to the Present Time* (New York, 1878; reprint, New York: B. Blom, 1972).

12. Stratton, *The World on Wheels,* 424; Lawrence Fay Brewster, "Ante-bellum Planters and Their Means of Transportation," *Proceedings of the South Carolina Historical Association* (1948): 21; Norman G. Raiford, "South Carolina and the Issue of Internal Improvement, 1776–1860" (PhD diss., University of Virginia, 1974), 229–30.

13. William F. Gephart, *Transportation and Industrial Development in the Middle West* (New York: Columbia University Press, 1909), 44, 46; John H. White Jr., *Wet Britches and Muddy Boots: A History of Travel in Victorian America* (Bloomington: Indiana University Press, 2013), 32.

14. *Charleston (S.C.) Southern Patriot,* March 1, 1822; John C. Trautwine, *Some Remarks on the Internal Improvement System of the South* (Philadelphia,

1839); William Elejius Martin, *Internal Improvements in Alabama* (Baltimore: Johns Hopkins University Press, 1902), 23–24.

15. Ethel Conrad, ed., "Touring Ohio in 1811: The Journal of Charity Rotch," *Ohio History* 99 (Autumn 1990): 144; Emily Foster, ed., *The Ohio Frontier: An Anthology of Early Writings* (Lexington: University of Kentucky Press, 1996), 182; Louis A. Garavaglia, *To the Wide Missouri: Traveling in America during the First Decades of Westward Expansion* (Yardley, Pa.: Westholme Publishing, 2011), 51.

16. Philip D. Jordan, *The National Road* (Indianapolis: Bobbs-Merrill, 1948); William Jackson, *Lecture on Railroads Delivered January 12, 1829 before the Massachusetts Charitable Mechanic Association* (Boston: Henry Bowen, 1829), 4.

17. John Alexander Williams, *Appalachia: History* (Chapel Hill: University of North Carolina Press, 2002), 146–47; Ellen Eslinger, ed., *Running Mad for Kentucky: Frontier Travel Accounts* (Lexington: University Press of Kentucky, 2004), 6–12; Trautwine, *Some Remarks on the Internal Improvement System of the South.*

18. Taylor, *The Transportation Revolution,* 16; William T. Utter, *The Frontier State, 1803–1825,* vol. 2: *The History of Ohio* (Columbus: Ohio State Archaeological and Historical Society, 1942), 206–207; David E. Paterson, *Frontier Link with the World: Upson County's Railroad* (Mercer, Ga.: Mercer University Press, 1998), 6; Craig Thompson Friend, *Along the Maysville Road: The Early American Republic in the Trans-Appalachian West* (Knoxville: University of Tennessee Press, 2005), 25–26.

19. Karl Raitz, ed., *The National Road* (Baltimore: Johns Hopkins University Press, 1996), 140–42; Charles Singer, et al., *A History of Technology,* vol. 4: *The Industrial Revolution* (New York: Oxford University Press, 1958), 534; Taylor, *The Transportation Revolution,* 28–31; H. Roger Grant, *Ohio on the Move: Transportation in the Buckeye State* (Athens: Ohio University Press, 2000), 10–11.

20. Moina W. Large, *History of Ashtabula County, Ohio* (Topeka, Kans.: Historical Publishing Company, 1924), 99.

21. Richard S. Simons, *The Rivers of Indiana* (Bloomington: Indiana University Press, 1985), 4; Donald Davidson, *The Tennessee: The Old River,* vol. 1 (New York: Rinehart, 1946); Stanley John Folmsbee, *Sectionalism and Internal Improvements in Tennessee, 1796–1845* (Knoxville: East Tennessee Historical Society, 1939), 80–81; Mary U. Rothrock, ed., *The French Broad-Holston Country: A History of Knox County, Tennessee* (Knoxville: East Tennessee Historical Society, 1946), 95–97.

22. Alice Wright, *The Ohio River* (Marietta, Ohio: Prettit-Seevers Printing, 1964), 4–5; Charles Henry Ambler, *A History of Transportation in the Ohio Valley* (Glendale, Calif.: Arthur H. Clark, 1932), 25–26; H. E. Chambers, *Mississippi Valley Beginnings* (New York: G. P. Putnam's Sons, 1922), 22.

23. Brian P. Birch, "Taking the Breaks and Working the Boats: An English Family's Impressions of Ohio in the 1830's," *Ohio History* 95 (Winter–Spring 1986): 107; J. C. Ainsworth, "Steamboating on the Columbia River: The Pioneer Journal of Captain J. C. Ainsworth," ed. Henry H. Clifford and Lucetta A. Clifford, in *Brand Book* 9 (Los Angeles: Los Angeles Corral of Westerners, 1961), 3; Guillaume Tell Poussin, *The United States: Its Power and Progress* (Philadelphia: Lippincott, Grambo, 1851), 348.

24. Ringwalt, *Development of Transportation Systems in the United States,* 10; Turnley, *Reminiscences of Parmenas Taylor Turnley,* 26, 28.

25. James Flint, *Letters from America Containing Observations on the Climate and Agriculture of the Western States* (Endinburgh: Tait, 1822), 13; Leland D. Baldwin, *The Keelboat Age on Western Waters* (Pittsburgh: University of Pittsburgh Press, 1941), 47–50, 52; Charles B. Duncan, *The Beautiful Ohio* (Privately printed, 1971), 8.

26. Ringwalt, *Development of Transportation Systems in the United States,* 14; Christian Schultz, *Travels on an Inland Voyage through the States of New-York, Pennsylvania, Virginia, Ohio, Kentucky and Tennessee and through the Territories of Indiana, Louisiana, Mississippi and New-Orleans* (reprint, Ridgewood, N.J.: Gregg Press, 1968), 130–31; Erik F. Haites, James Mak, and Gary M. Walton, *Western River Transportation: The Era of Early Internal Development, 1810–1860* (Baltimore: Johns Hopkins University Press, 1975), 17–18.

27. F. Daniel Larkin, *John B. Jervis: An American Engineering Pioneer* (Ames: Iowa State University Press, 1990), 6.

28. Balthasar Henry Meyer, *History of Transportation in the United States before 1860* (reprint, Boston: Peter Smith, 1948), 96–98; Haites et al., *Western River Transportation,* 14, 16.

29. T. J. Stiles, *The First Tycoon: The Epic Life of Cornelius Vanderbilt* (New York: Alfred A. Knopf, 2009), 41–43; *Liberty Hall* (Cincinnati, Ohio), October 30, 1811; Patricia Mooney Melvin, "Steamboat West: The Legacy of a Transportation Revolution," *Old Northwest* 7 (Winter 1981): 342; Ambler, *A History of Transportation in the Ohio Valley,* 107–31.

30. *American Railroad Journal,* July 7, 1849; William Rule, *Standard History of Knoxville, Tennessee* (Chicago: Lewis Publishing, 1900), 276–77; *Knoxville (Tenn.) Register,* March 5, March 12, 1828; Rothrock,

The French Broad-Holston County, 96–97; Tod J. Butler, "The Cincinnati Southern Railway: A City's Response to Relative Commercial Decline" (PhD diss., Ohio State University, 1971), 12; Haites et al., *Western River Transportation,* 1.

31. Ambler, *A History of Transportation in the Ohio Valley,* 127; Frederick C. Gamst, ed., *Early American Railroads: Frannz Anton Ritter von Gerstner's Die innern Communication (1842–1843)* (Stanford, Calif.: Stanford University Press, 1997), 416.

32. Leslie S. Henshaw, "Early Steamboat Travel on the Ohio River," *Ohio Archaeological and Historical Publications* 20 (1911): 380; Jakle, *Images of the Ohio Valley,* 32–33; Haites et al., *Western River Travel,* 18–19.

33. Jakle, *Images of the Ohio Valley,* 32–33; Margaret L. Coit, *John C. Calhoun: American Portrait* (New York: Houghton Mifflin, 1950), 415; Louis C. Hunter, *Steamboats on the Western Rivers: An Economic and Technological History* (Cambridge, Mass.: Harvard University Press, 1949), 412–15.

34. Jakle, *Images of the Ohio Valley,* 32–33.

35. Wolfgang Schivelbusch, *The Railway Journey: The Industrialization of Time and Space in the 19th Century* (Berkeley: University of California Press, 1977), 95; Thomas J. Kirkland and Robert M. Kennedy, *Historic Camden,* part 2: *Nineteenth Century* (Columbia, S.C.: State Company, 1926), 39; Guillaume Tell Poussin, *Travaux d'améliorations intérieures, projetés ou exécutés par le gouvernment général des États-Unis d'Amérique, de 1824 à 1831* (Paris: Anselin, 1834); *Speech of Mr. Memminger, The Commissioner from South Carolina, before the Legislature of Kentucky, upon the Proposition to Co-operate in Making a Railroad from Charleston to the Ohio River* (Frankfort, Ky.: A. G. Hodges, 1839), 4.

36. Shaw, *Canals for a Nation,* 1–29; Carol Sheriff, *The Artificial River: The Erie Canal and the Paradox of Progress, 1817–1862* (New York: Hill & Wang, 1996), 52; Elting Morison, *From Know-How to Nowhere: The Development of American Technology* (New York: Basic Books, 1974), 35–39; Robert J. Kapsch, *Historic Canals and Waterways of South Carolina* (Columbia: University of South Carolina Press, 2010), 6–9.

37. Grant, *Ohio on the Move,* 52–67; Frank E. Hargrave, *A Pioneer Indiana Railroad: The Origin and Development of the Monon* (Indianapolis: Privately printed, 1932), 13, 16.

38. Shaw, *Canals for a Nation,* 143; Paul Fatout, *Indiana Canals* (West Layfayette, Ind.: Purdue University Press, 1972), 149–55.

39. Shaw, *Canals for a Nation,* 112–15; *American Railroad Journal,* April 14, 1832; T. Gibson Hobbs Jr., *The Canal on the James: An Illustrated Guide to the James River and Kanawha Canal* (Lynchburg, Va.: Blackwell Press, 2009); Wayland Fuller Dunaway, *History of the James River and Kanawha Company* (reprint, New York: AMS Press, 1969), 132–33, 163, 170–74; Gamst, *Early American Railroads,* 672–74; Kenneth W. Noe, *Southwest Virginia's Railroad: Modernization and the Sectional Crisis* (Urbana: University of Illinois Press, 1994), 14; John Majewski, *A House Dividing: Economic Development in Pennsylvania and Virginia before the Civil War* (New York: Cambridge University Press, 2000), 126; Daniel W. Crofts, *Reluctant Confederates: Upper South Unionists in the Secession Crisis* (Chapel Hill: University of North Carolina Press, 1989), 108.

40. Kapsch, *Historic Canals and Waterways of South Carolina,* 18, 21–53.

41. Ibid., 76–77, 93, 134.

42. S. Augustus Mitchell, *Mitchell's Compendium of the Internal Improvements of the United States* (Philadelphia: Mitchell & Hinman, 1838), 51, 55; Shaw, *Canals for a Nation,* 117.

43. Shaw, *Canals for a Nation,* 22–24

44. Ibid., 153–54; Jack Gieck, *A Photo Album of Ohio's Canal Era* (Kent, Ohio: Kent State University Press, 1988), 37; Taylor, *The Transportation Revolution,* 132–33.

45. *Athens (Ohio) Mirror and Literary Register,* July 16, 1825.

46. Shaw, *Canals for a Nation,* 171, 173; *American Railroad Journal,* January 2, 1831.

47. Fatout, *Indiana Canals,* 118.

48. George W. Bagby, *Canal Reminiscences: Recollections of Travel in the Old Days on the James River and Kanawha Canal* (Richmond: West, Johnson, 1879).

49. Friend, *Along the Maysville Road,* 260–62.

2. A RAIL ROAD?

1. At the dawn of the Railway Age "railroad" was commonly spelled as two words or perhaps as a hyphenated word. Not until the mid-nineteenth century did usage turn "railroad" into a single word.

2. Charles E. Lee, *The Evolution of Railways* (London: Railway Gazette, 1937), 7–10; Jackson, *Lecture on Railroads Delivered January 12, 1829,* 10. See also Richard D. Heffner, ed., *Democracy in America* (New York: New American Library, 1956).

3. Charles E. Lee, "Some Railway Facts and Fallacies," in *The Civil Engineering of Canals and Railways before 1850,* ed. Mike Chrimes (Aldershot, England: Ashgate, 1997), 219, 222–23, 225–38; H. Roger Grant, *The Railroad: The Life Story of a Technology* (Westport, Conn.: Greenwood Press, 2005), 1–2.

4. Frederick C. Gamst, "The Context and Significance of America's First Railroad, on Boston's Beacon Hill," *Technology and Culture* 33 (1992): 66–100; *The*

First Railroad in America: A History of the Origins and Development of the Granite Railway at Quincy, Massachusetts (Privately printed, 1927).

5. *The First Railroad in America*; "Granite Railway," in William D. Middleton, George M. Smerk, and Roberta L. Diehl, eds., *Encyclopedia of North American Railroads* (Bloomington: Indiana University Press, 2007), 501–502; Gamst, *Early American Railroads*, 295; Stephen Salsbury, *The State, the Investor, and the Railroad: The Boston & Albany, 1825–1867* (Cambridge, Mass.: Harvard University Press, 1967), 45.

6. William Jackson, *Lecture on Rail Roads* (Boston: Henry Bowen, 1829).

7. George L. Vose, "Notes Relating to the Early History of Transportation in Massachusetts," *Journal of the Association of Engineering Societies* 4 (1884):67–68.

8. Frederick C. Gamst and Marilou Gamst, "Virginia's First Railroad, on Falling Creek, about 1810," *Railroad History* 168 (Spring 1993): 13–14.

9. Gamst and Gamst, "Virginia's First Railroad, 7–12.

10. Alfred Glaze Smith Jr., *Economic Readjustment of an Old Cotton State: South Carolina, 1820–1860* (Columbia: University of South Carolina Press, 1958), 156.

11. Adrian Vaughan, *Railwaymen, Politics and Money: The Great Age of Railways in Britain* (London: John Murray, 1997), 6–7, 10; J. T. Shackleton, *History of Railways* (London: New English Library, 1976), 14; Robert H. Thurston, *A History of the Growth of the Steam Engine* (New York: Appleton, 1897), 159–60; H. W. Dickinson, *A Short History of the Steam Engine* (New York: Cambridge University Press, 1939), 93–97.

12. Anthony Burton, *Richard Trevithick: Giant of Steam* (London: Aurum Press, 2000).

13. L. T. C. Rolt, *The Railway Revolution: George and Robert Stephenson* (New York: St. Martin's Press, 1962).

14. Shackleton, *History of Railways*, 17–23; Vaughan, *Railwaymen, Politics and Money*, 68–72.

15. Christian Barman, *Early British Railways* (Middlesex, England: Penguin Books, 1950), 5.

16. "Col. John Stevens (1749–1838)," in Middleton et al., *Encyclopedia of North American Railroads*, 1033–34; Alfred W. Bruce, *The Steam Locomotive in America: Its Development in the Twentieth Century* (New York: Bonanza Books, 1952), 21.

17. Gamst, *Early American Railroads*, 122–27; Jim Shaughnessy, *Delaware & Hudson* (Syracuse, N.Y.: Syracuse University Press, 1997), 31–57; Larkin, *John B. Jervis*, 35–38.

18. Ray Slate, "The Truth behind the *Pride of Newcastle*," *Railroad History* 201 (Fall–Winter, 2009): 71–85; Horatio Allen, *The Railroad Era: First Five Years of Its Development* (New York, 1884), 20–22; William H. Brown, *History of the First Locomotive in America: From Original Documents and the Testimony of Living Witnesses* (New York: D. Appleton, 1874), 88–92; William Conrad Kessler, ed., "Horatio Allen's Impressions of English Railway," *Bulletin of the Railway and Locomotive Historical Society* 61 (May 1943): 47.

19. Slate, "The Truth behind the *Pride of Newcastle*," 80; "Delaware & Hudson," in Middleton, *Encyclopedia of North American Railroads*, 353; *New York Times*, August 9, 1877.

20. *First Semi-Annual Report to the President and Directors of the South-Carolina Canal and Rail-Road Company by Their Committee of Inquiry* (Charleston, S.C.: A. E. Miller, 1828), 7.

21. *Report of the Commissioners Appointed by the Legislature of South Carolina to Cause Examinations, Surveys and Estimates to Be Made for a Rail Road between Charleston and Cincinnati* (Columbia, S.C.: Telescope Office, 1836), 25.

22. James D. Dilts, *The Great Road: The Building of the Baltimore & Ohio, the Nation's First Railroad, 1828–1853* (Stanford, Calif.: Stanford University Press, 1993), 36–99; John F. Stover, *History of the Baltimore and Ohio Railroad* (West Lafayette, Ind.: Purdue University Press, 1987), 29–39.

It is always dangerous to state when a particular "first" occurred in American railroading. In December 1825 a pioneer rail project was announced, calling for "the construction of a Rail Road betwixt the Mohawk and Hudson rivers." Then in April 1826 New York lawmakers granted a charter for the Mohawk & Hudson Rail Road, but construction did not begin until July 1830; finally on August 10, 1831, operations commenced on this 16-mile pike. See Frank Walter Stevens, *The Beginnings of the New York Central Railroad: A History* (New York: G. P. Putnam's Sons, 1926), 1–26.

23. *Charleston (S.C.) Courier*, December 5, 1827; Gregory Allen Greb, "Charleston, South Carolina, Merchants, 1815–1860: Urban Leadership in the Antebellum South" (PhD diss., University of California, San Diego, 1978), 90, 92, 94; Ulrich B. Phillips, *A History of Transportation in the Eastern Cotton Belt* (New York: Columbia University Press, 1908), 137.

24. Fairfax Harrison, *A History of the Legal Development of the Railroad System of the Southern Railway Company* (Washington, D.C.: Southern Railway Co., 1901), 4–5; *First Semi-Annual Report to the President*

and Directors of the South-Carolina Canal and Rail-Road Company, 5.

25. *Proceedings of the Citizens of Charleston, Embracing the Report of the Committee and the Address and Resolutions Adopted at a General Meeting in Reference to the Proposed Railroad from Charleston to Cincinnati* (Charleston, S.C.: A. E. Miller, 1835), 15–16; George Rogers Taylor and Irene D. Neu, *The American Railroad Network, 1861–1890* (Cambridge, Mass.: Harvard University Press, 1956), 41–42.

26. Robert Mills, *Statistics of South Carolina, Including a View of Its Natural Civil, and Military History, General and Particular* (Charleston, S.C.: Hurlbut and Lloyd, 1826), 168–68; Samuel Melanchthon Derrick, *Centennial History of South Carolina Railroad* (Columbia, S.C.: State Company, 1930), 1–10; *Charleston (S.C.) Courier,* October 27, 1827; March 13, 1828.

27. Kapsch, *Historic Canals and Waterways of South Carolina,* 21–53, 121–41; "Internal Improvement in South Carolina," *North American Review* 4 (July 1821): 146; Mitchell, *Mitchell's Compendium of the Internal Improvements of the United States,* 52–53.

28. Kapsch, *Historic Canals and Waterways of South Carolina,* 71.

29. John F. Stover, *American Railroads,* 2nd ed. (Chicago: University of Chicago Press, 1997), 12–15.

30. J. Parker Lamb, *Perfecting the American Steam Locomotive* (Bloomington: Indiana University Press, 2003), 9; Derrick, *Centennial History of South Carolina Railroad,* 46.

31. Stover, *American Railroads,* 13; Taylor and Neu, *The American Railroad Network, 1861–1890,* 43–45; Brown, *History of the First Locomotive in America,* 135–42, 156.

32. Derrick, *Centennial History of South Carolina Railroad,* 29, 31–32; David Kohn, comp. and ed., *Internal Improvement in South Carolina, 1817–1828* (Washington, D.C.: Privately printed, 1938), 587–89.

33. *First Semi-Annual Report to the President and Directors of the South-Carolina Canal and Rail-Road Company,* 7–9.

34. *Columbia (S.C.) State,* March 1, 1914.

35. Derrick, *Centennial History of South Carolina Railroad,* 82–97; Stover, *History of the Baltimore and Ohio Railroad,* 35–36.

36. John H. White Jr., *American Locomotives: An Engineering History, 1830–1880* (Baltimore: Johns Hopkins University Press, 1997), 13–14.

37. Steam locomotives are commonly referred to by their classification in the Whyte System, developed by F. H. Whyte, an official from the New York Central Lines. Whyte used the number of pilot-truck wheels, drivers, and trailing-truck wheels to identify most kinds of steam locomotives. Thus the "American" or "8-wheeler" locomotive is a 4-4-0, which means it has a four-wheel pilot truck, two pairs of coupled drivers, and no trailing truck.

38. White, *American Locomotives,* 512–13.

39. *Charleston (S.C.) Courier,* December 29, 1830.

40. Brown, *History of the First Locomotive in America,* 153–54; *Charleston (S.C.) Mercury,* June 18, 1831; Derrick, *Centennial History of South Carolina Railroad,* 84.

41. *Charleston (S.C.) Courier,* August 1, 1831.

42. *The American Railway: Its Construction, Development, Management and Appliances* (Secaucus, N.J.: Castle, 1988), 104–05; White, *American Locomotives,* 167, 509–11.

43. White, *American Locomotives,* 33–46.

44. Derrick, *Centennial History of South Carolina Railroad,* 101–102; *American Railroad Journal,* June 2, 1832.

45. *Annual Report of the Board of Directors of the South-Carolina Canal and Rail-Road Company* (Charleston, S.C.: A. E. Miller, 1836), 4–5; Aaron W. Marrs, *Railroads in the Old South: Pursuing Progress in a Slave Society* (Baltimore, Md.: Johns Hopkins University Press, 2009), 36; *Semi-Annual Report to the Stockholders of the South-Carolina Canal and Rail-Road Company* (Charleston, S.C.: A. E. Miller, 1843); Edward Hungerford, *Men of Erie: A Story of Human Effort* (New York: Random House, 1946), 53–54; Grant, *Ohio on the Move,* 80.

The SCC&RRCo gained attention for development of an usual piece of rolling stock, the "Barrel Car." "These cars [for both freight and passenger], we believe, will be invaluable to the Company, and to others who use them, being much lighter, cheaper, and more durable than the square form," commented President T. Tupper. Novel yes, but popular no. *Semi-Annual Report to the Stockholders of the South-Carolina Canal and Rail-Road Company* (Charleston, S.C.: A. E. Miller, 1840), 6–7.

46. Derrick, *Centennial History of South Carolina Railroad,* 104–105, 202–204.

47. *Charleston (S.C.) Courier,* August 24, 1834; Derrick, *Centennial History of South Carolina Railroad,* 101.

48. Nicholas Wood, *A Practical Treatise on Railroads and Interior Communications in General* (Philadelphia: Carey & Lea, 1832); Derrick, *Centennial History of South Carolina,* 22–23, 119–22; Majewski, *A House Dividing,* 73; Gustav Metzman, *Cincinnati and Ohio: Their Early Railroads* (New York: The Newcomen Society of England, American Branch, 1948), 9; John G. Van Deusen, *Economic Bases of Disunion in South Carolina* (New York: Columbia University Press, 1928), 222; Donald A. Grinde Jr., "Building the

South Carolina Railroad," *South Carolina Historical Magazine* 77 (April 1976): 86–87, 92.

49. Craig Miner, *A Most Magnificent Machine: American Adopts the Railroad, 1825–1862* (Lawrence: University Press of Kansas, 2010), 156–60.

50. Albert J. Churella, *The Pennsylvania Railroad: Building an Empire, 1846–1917* (Philadelphia: University of Pennsylvania Press, 2013), 73; John F. Stover, *Iron Road to the West: American Railroads in the 1850's* (New York: Columbia University Press, 1977), 5–16; Poussin, *The United States*, 345; Glenn Hoffman, *Building a Great Railroad: A History of the Atlantic Coast Line Railroad Company* (Jacksonville, Fla.: CSX Corporate Communications and Public Affairs, 1998), 2.

3. KNOXVILLE, 1836

1. H. Roger Grant, *Twilight Rails: The Final Era of Railroad Building in the Midwest* (Minneapolis: University of Minnesota Press, 2010); Robert S. Cotterill, "Memphis Railroad Convention, 1849," *Tennessee Historical Magazine* 4 (June 1918): 89; *New York Herald*, August 6, 1859.

Antebellum commentators believed that railroad conventions had a strong appeal to Southerners, although the reasons why are not clear. Before the Civil War numerous organized gatherings occurred throughout the Southlands, including one held in Charleston, South Carolina, in 1854 that "promoters expected might be the greatest in all convention history." See Jere W. Roberson, "To Build a Pacific Railroad: Congress, Texas, and the Charleston Convention of 1854," *Southwestern Historical Quarterly* 78 (October 1974): 117–39.

2. Allen W. Trelease, *The North Carolina Railroad, 1849–1871 and the Modernization of North Carolina* (Chapel Hill: University of North Carolina Press, 1991), 12.

3. "Railroad Conventions before 1860," *Bulletin of the Business Historical Society* 7 (December 1933): 6–9; *Seventeenth Annual Report of the President and Directors of the Board of Public Works to the General Assembly of Virginia* (Richmond, Va.: Samuel Shepherd, 1833), 278–85; Robert F. Hunter and Edwin L. Dooley Jr., *Claudius Crozet: French Engineer in America, 1790–1864* (Charlottesville: University Press of Virginia, 1989), 68; *Knoxville (Tenn.) Register*, September 7, 1831; *Washington (D.C.) Daily National Intelligencer*, September 21, 1831.

The first recorded railroad meetings that occurred in Virginia were held in 1829 and 1830 in Frederick, Jefferson, and Shenandoah Counties, where proponents discussed a line from the Potomac River to Staunton and then to the Ohio River, making for a 350-mile railroad. See Charles W. Turner, "The Early Railroad Movement in Virginia," *Virginia Magazine of History and Biography* 35 (October 1947): 354.

4. Milton Sydney Heath, *Constructive Liberalism: The Role of the State in Economic Development in Georgia to 1860* (Cambridge, Mass.: Harvard University Press, 1954), 255–57.

5. Meyer, *History of Transportation in the United States before 1860*, 427; Phillips, *A History of Transportation in the Eastern Cotton Belt*, 169–70.

6. Robert Y. Hayne, *Address in Behalf of the Knoxville Convention, to the Citizens of the Several States Interested in the Proposed Louisville, Cincinnati and Charleston Rail Road* (Charleston, 1836), 34.

Although there has not been a systematic examination of the early railroad meetings and conventions that took place in the South, it is likely that they numbered several score, possibly more. In another early example, Memphis-area citizens met in 1831 to discuss a rail line that would extend east from their Mississippi River docks. On December 17, 1831, these rail advocates received a state charter for their Atlantic and Mississippi Rail Road. "Apparently the vision and enthusiasm of the group exceeded their resources, as no construction was ever accomplished." See Gordon W. Lindsay, "Southern Railway System–Memphis Division," *Bulletin of the Railway and Locomotive Historical Society* 90 (May 1954): 70.

7. Clipping in the Bureau of Railway Economics Coll., John W. Barriger III National Railroad Library of the St. Louis Mercantile Library, St. Louis, Mo.

8. *American Rail-Road Journal*, March 17, 1832.

9. J. Fred Rippy, *Joel R. Poinsett, Versatile American* (Durham, N.C.: Duke University Press, 1935), 163, 166; Joel Poinsett, *Statement of the Comparative Advantages of Charleston over the Cities South of New York* (Charleston, S.C.: J. S. Burges, 1833).

10. Marrs, *Railroads in the Old South*, 11; *Rail-Road Journal*, March 10, 1832, March 17, 1832; Stover, *American Railroads*, 13; Ebenezer Smith Thomas, *Reminiscences of the Last Sixty-Five Years* (Hartford, Conn.: Privately printed, 1840), 2:104–11.

11. William C. Redfield, *Sketch of the Geographical Rout of a Great Railway by Which It Is Proposed to Connect the Canals and Navigable Waters of New-York, Pennsylvania, Ohio, Indiana, Illinois, Michigan, Missouri, and the Adjacent States and Territories*, 2nd rev. ed. (New York: Carvill, 1830); Hungerford, *Men of Erie*, 5–7; George Leslie Albright, *Official Explorations for Pacific Railroads, 1853–1855* (Berkeley: University of California Press, 1921), 10–20; David Haward Bain, *Empire Express: Building the First Transcontinental*

Railroad (New York: Penguin Putnam, 1999), 3–10, 16.

12. *Proceedings of the Citizens of Charleston Embracing the Report of the Committee and the Address and Resolutions Adopted at a General Meeting in Reference to the Proposed Rail-Road from Cincinnati to Charleston* (Charleston, S.C.: A. E. Miller, 1835), 6–7; *Southern Quarterly Review* 1 (January 1842): 39.

13. Richard C. Wade, *The Urban Frontier: Pioneer Life in Early Pittsburgh, Cincinnati, Lexington, Louisville, and St. Louis* (Cambridge, Mass.: Harvard University Press, 1959), 155; Emmet Field Horine, *Daniel Drake (1785–1852): Pioneer Physician of the Midwest* (Philadelphia: University of Pennsylvania Press, 1961); Edward D. Mansfield, ed., *Memories of the Life and Services of Daniel Drake, M.D.* (Cincinnati, Ohio: Applegate, 1855).

14. "Robert Y. Hayne," in Allen Johnson and Dumas Malone, eds., *Dictionary of American Biography* (New York, 1931), 4:456–59; Theodore D. Jervey, *Robert Y. Hayne and His Times* (1909; reprint, New York: Da Capio Press, 1970); William W. Freehling, *Prelude to Civil War: The Nullification Controversy in South Carolina, 1816–1836* (New York: Harper & Row, 1966), 104.

15. J. G. M. Ramsey, *Dr. J. G. M. Ramsey: Autobiography and Letters,* ed. William B. Hesseltine (Knoxville: University of Tennessee Press, 2002); David Lawson Eubanks, "Dr. J. G. M. Ramsey of East Tennessee: A Career of Public Service" (PhD diss., University of Tennessee, 1965).

16. *Goodspeed's History of Tennessee* (1887), 878; *American Railroad Journal,* September 1, 1832.

17. W. T. Porter, "History of the Cincinnati Southern Railway, 1837–1937," ms., Cincinnati Historical Society Library, Cincinnati, Ohio; Thornton M. Hinkle, *The Movement of 1835–36 to Construct a Cincinnati Southern Railway* (Cincinnati: W. H. Anderson, 1901), 3; J. H. Hollander, *The Cincinnati Southern Railway: A Study in Municipal Activity,* Johns Hopkins University Studies in Historical and Political Science 12 (Baltimore: Johns Hopkins University Press, 1894; reprint, New York: Johnson Reprint Corp., 1973), 10; *Rail-Road from the Banks of the Ohio River to the Tide Waters of the Carolinas and Georgia* (Cincinnati, 1835), 3–12.

18. Charles M. Wiltse, *John C. Calhoun: Nullifier, 1829–1839* (Indianapolis, Ind.: Bobbs-Merrill, 1949), 324; *Rail-Road from the Banks of the Ohio River to the Tide Waters of the Carolinas and Georgia,* 3–12; Charles Theodore Greve, *Centennial History of Cincinnati and Representative Citizens* (Chicago: Biographical Publishing Company, 1904), 1:590.

19. *Rail-Road from the Banks of the Ohio River to the Tide Waters of the Carolinas and Georgia.*

20. Charles Roy Schultz, "Hayne's Magnificent Dream: Factors Which Influenced Efforts to Join Cincinnati and Charleston by Railroad, 1835–1860" (PhD diss., Ohio State University, 1966), 18–21; Daniel W. Hollis, "Costly Delusion: Inland Navigation in the South Carolina Piedmont," *Proceedings of the South Carolina Historical Association* (1968): 42; *Proceedings of the Citizens of Charleston Embracing the Report of the Committee and the Address & Resolutions; American Railroad Journal,* December 6, 1835; *Charleston (S.C.) Courier,* November 26, 1835.

21. Butler, "The Cincinnati Southern Railway," 19.

22. *American Railroad Journal,* November 14, 1841.

23. *Charter of the Louisville, Cincinnati and Charleston Rail-Road Company as Passed by the Legislatures of Kentucky, Tennessee, No. & So. Carolina with the Amendments; also the Charter of the South-Western Rail-Road Bank and the Bye-Laws* (Charleston, S.C.: A. E. Miller, 1838), 3–16.

24. *American Railroad Journal,* March 19, 1836.

25. Folmsbee, *Sectionalism and Internal Improvements in Tennessee,* 117; *Rogersville (Tenn.) Railroad Advocate,* June 7, 1832.

26. Charles G. Hall, ed., *The Cincinnati Southern Railway: A History* (Cincinnati, Ohio, 1902), 26.

27. William J. MacArthur Jr., *Knoxville's History: An Interpretation* (Knoxville: East Tennessee Historical Society, 1978), 19–20; Issac Patton Martin, *Church Street Methodists, Children of Francis Asbery: A History of Church Street Methodist Church, Knoxville, Tennessee, 1816–1947* (Knoxville, 1947), 21–22; *Proceedings of the Knoxville Convention, Relation to the Proposed Louisville, Cincinnati & Charleston Rail-Road, Assembled at Knoxville, Tennessee, July 4th, 1836* (Knoxville, 1836), 42.

28. *Knoxville Register,* June 15, 1836; *Boston Courier,* July 28, 1836.

29. Senator John C. Calhoun had been named a delegate from South Carolina, but he did not attend. Yet "he did the cause perhaps greater service by remaining at his post in Washington to see the distribution bill [Surplus Revenue Act] through Congress." Wiltse, *John C. Calhoun,* 330.

30. Hayne, *Address in Behalf of the Knoxville Convention,* 32; "Cincinnati and Charleston Rail-Road," *Western Monthly Magazine* 5 (September 1836): 538–40.

31. *Knoxville Register,* July 6, 1836; Martin, *Church Street Methodists,* 23.

The Church Street Methodist Episcopal Church would also be the site of the much smaller "General Internal Improvement Meeting" that took place in

September 1847, composed of delegates from Tennessee and South Carolina. Their discussions again centered on "the advantages and importance of a Railroad connection between Tennessee and the Southern Atlantic coast." *Proceedings of the General Internal Improvement Meeting, Held at Knoxville, Tennessee, On Friday and Saturday, September 24th and 25th, 1847* (Knoxville, Tenn.: Printed at the Register Office, 1847), 1–15.

32. *Proceedings of the Knoxville Convention,* 3; *Denver Rocky Mountain News,* March 28, 1886; *American Railroad Journal,* September 3, 1836; John Belton O'Neall, *Biographical Sketches of the Bench and Bar of South Carolina* (n.p., 1859), 2:241; "Ramsey Scraps," Special Collections, University of Tennessee, Knoxville; *Washington (D.C.) Daily National Intelligencer,* July 22, 1836.

33. *Proceedings of the Knoxville Convention,* 4–7; *Report of the Commissioners Appointed by the Legislature of South Carolina to Cause Examinations, Surveys and Estimates to Be Made for a Rail Road between Charleston and Cincinnati* (Columbia, S.C.: Telescope Office, 1836), 3; *American Railroad Journal,* April 9, 1836; May 21, 1836; Meyer, *History of Transportation in the United States before 1860,* 427.

34. *American Railroad Journal,* August 20, 1836.

35. *Proceedings of the Knoxville Convention,* 20–26.

A year prior to the Knoxville Railroad Convention, Georgia governor Wilson Lumpkin, a staunch advocate of railroads, in his valedictory message to lawmakers indicated that the best route for the Charleston to Cincinnati project would be to build through the northeastern part of his state, utilizing Rabun Gap, and to forge a connection with the Georgia Rail Road & Banking Company by an extension of that road from Athens. See Heath, *Constructive Liberalism,* 260–61.

36. Heath, *Constructive Liberalism,* 30–33; *American Railroad Journal,* August 20, 1836; September 3, 1836.

37. Phillips, *A History of Transportation in the Eastern Cotton Belt,* 307–10; *Macon Georgia Messenger,* November 10, 1836; *American Railroad Journal,* September 3, 1836; March 10, 1838.

38. Ralph D. Gray, "Philadelphia and the Chesapeake and Delaware Canal, 1769–1823," *Pennsylvania Magazine of History and Biography* 84 (October 1960): 401–23; Ralph D. Gray, *The National Waterway: A History of the Chesapeake and Delaware Canal, 1769–1985* (Urbana: University of Illinois Press, 1969), 53–55; Carter Goodrich, *Government Promotion of American Canals and Railroads, 1800–1860* (New York: Columbia University Press, 1960); Carter Goodrich, "American Development Policy: The Case of Internal Improvements," *Journal of Economic History* 16 (December 1956): 449–60; Carter Goodrich, "Internal Improvement Reconsidered," *Journal of Economic History* 30 (June 1970): 289–311.

39. *American Railroad Journal,* September 3, 1836; Peter Temin, "The Jacksonian Economy," in *The Many-Faceted Jacksonian Era: New Interpretations,* ed. Edward Pessen (Westport, Conn.: Greenwood Press, 1977), 102–13; James W. Holland, "The East Tennessee and Georgia Railroad, 1836–1860," *East Tennessee Historical Society's Publications* (January 1931): 91; Douglas C. North, *The Economic Growth of the United States, 1790–1860* (Englewood, N.J.: Prentice-Hall, 1966), 198–201.

40. Robert G. Angevine, "Individuals, Organizations, and Engineering: U.S. Army Officers and the American Railroads, 1827–1838," *Technology and Culture* 42 (April 2001): 296.

41. *Proceedings of the Knoxville Convention,* 45–48.

42. *Knoxville Register,* July 13, 1836.

43. *Proceedings of the Knoxville Convention,* 47–48; *American Railroad Journal,* September 3, 1836.

44. *First Annual Report of the President and Directors to the Stockholders of the East Tennessee and Virginia Rail Road Company* (Jonesborough, Tenn.: Rail Road Journal Office, 1850), 4; Michael J. Connolly, *Capitalism, Politics, and Railroads in Jacksonian New England* (Columbia: University of Missouri Press, 2003), 10.

45. *American Railroad Journal,* August 20, 1836; *Knoxville Register,* October 5, 1836.

46. Cotterill, "Memphis Railroad Convention, 1849," 88–89.

47. Hayne, *Address in Behalf of the Knoxville Convention,* 4–5.

48. Herbert H. Harwood Jr., *The Railroad That Never Was: Vanderbilt, Morgan, and the South Pennsylvania Railroad* (Bloomington: Indiana University Press, 2010), 14–15.

49. Phillips, *A History of Transportation in the Eastern Cotton Bell to 1860,* 186.

50. *Columbia (S.C.) Telescope,* March 17, 1838.

The actions of the Knoxville Convention firmly support the argument made by Aaron W. Marrs in *Railroads in the Old South* that "before the Civil War southerners were on a trajectory that embraced railroads," 8.

4. SURVEYS, FINANCES, AND CONSTRUCTION

1. John Bomar Cleveland, *Controversy between John C. Calhoun and Robt. Y. Hayne as to the Proper Route of a Railroad from South Carolina to the West* (Spartanburg, S.C.: n.p., 1913), 4, 6; *Report of the*

Commissioners Appointed by the Legislature of South Carolina to Cause Examinations, Surveys and Estimates to Be Made for a Rail Road between Charleston and Cincinnati, 6–7.

2. See *Knoxville (Tenn.) Register*, March 8, 1837.

3. James A. Ward, "J. Edgar Thomson and the Georgia Railroad, 1834–1847," *Railroad History* 134 (Spring 1976): 14.

4. See *Report of the South Carolina Commissioners to the Knoxville Convention, on the Subject of the Proposed Railroad from Charleston to Cincinnati* (July 1836); *Report of the Commissioners Appointed by the Legislature of South Carolina to Cause Examinations, Surveys and Estimates to be Made for a Rail Road between Charleston and Cincinnati*, 3.

5. Forest G. Hill, *Roads, Rails and Waterways: The Army Engineers and Early Transportation* (Norman: University of Oklahoma Press, 1957), 41–43.

6. Angevine, "Individuals, Organizations, and Engineering," 298.

7. Hill, *Roads, Rails and Waterways*, 41–42; Emory Q. Hawk, *Economic History of the South* (New York: Prentice-Hall, 1934), 320.

8. Daniel Hovey Calhoun, *The American Civil Engineer: Origins and Conflict* (Cambridge, Mass.: Technology Press, Massachusetts Institute of Technology, 1900), 17–22; Angevine, "Individuals, Organizations, and Engineering," 293; Churella, *The Pennsylvania Railroad*, 129.

9. *American Railroad Journal*, October 17, 1835; Wiltse, *John C. Calhoun*, 142–54; Edmund P. Gaines, *To the Young Men of the States of the American Union, Civil and Military* (n.p., n.d.), 38.

10. "William Gibbs McNeill," in George W. Cullum, *Biographical Register of the Officers and Graduates of the United States Military Academy* (n.d., n.p.), 1:161; William D. Middleton, *Landmarks on the Iron Road: Two Centuries of North American Railroad Engineering* (Bloomington: Indiana University Press, 1999), 15–16.

11. "William Gibbs McNeill"; Hill, *Roads, Rails and Waterways*, 114–15, 117, 123, 144, 147; *Raleigh and North-Carolina Gazette*, November 6, 1837; Robert G. Angevine, *The Railroad and the State: War, Politics, and Technology in Nineteenth Century America* (Stanford, Calif.: Stanford University Press, 2004), 94, 97.

12. Angevine, *The Railroad and the State*, xiv; Lewis Henry Haney, *A Congressional History of Railways in the United States to 1850* (New York: A. M. Kelley, 1968), 282; Alasdair Roberts, *America's First Great Depression: Economic Crisis and Political Disorder after the Panic of 1837* (Ithaca, N.Y.: Cornell University Press, 2012), 114.

13. *First Annual Report of the President and Directors of the Louisville, Cincinnati & Charleston Rail-Road Company* (Charleston, S.C.: A. E. Miller, 1837), 4.

14. Ibid.

15. John G. Smedberg to Hugh C. Young, November 23, 1837, South Caroliniana Library, Columbia.

16. Allan Nevins, *Fremont: Pathmaker of the West* (New York: D. Appleton-Century Company, 1939), 24; Smedberg to Young.

17. *American Railroad Journal*, December 15, 1838; October 16, 1852; Capt. William G. Williams, Letter Copy-Book, April 8–August 26, 1837, South Caroliniana Library, Columbia; *First Annual Report of the President and Directors of the Louisville, Cincinnati & Charleston Rail-Road Company*, 5–6; Derrick, *Centennial History of South Carolina Railroad*, 140–43.

18. John Preston Arthur, *Western North Carolina: A History, from 1730–1913* (Raleigh, N.C.: Edwards & Broughton, 1914), 237; Edmund Cody Burnett, "Hog Raising and Hog Driving in the Region of the French Broad River," *Agricultural History* 20 (April 1946): 86–87.

19. *First Annual Report of the President and Directors of the Louisville, Cincinnati & Charleston Rail-Road Company*, 19–20; *Speech of Mr. Memminger, the Commissioner from South Carolina, before the Legislature of Kentucky upon the Proposition to Co-operate in Making a Railroad from Charleston to the Ohio River*, 10.

20. *First Annual Report of the President and Directors of the Louisville, Cincinnati & Charleston Rail-Road Company*, 19–20; *Journal of the Senate of the Commonwealth of Kentucky* (Frankfort, Ky: A. G. Hodges, 1837), 204–208.

21. "Experimental Surveys, Profile of Routes for the LC&C RR, from Knoxville, Tennessee, to Lexington, Kentucky, 1837–1838, Major William Gibbs McNeill, Chief Engineer," Norfolk Southern Corporation Archive, Norfolk, Va.; *American Railroad Journal*, October 1, 1838.

22. Thomas D. Clark, "The Lexington and Ohio Railroad: A Pioneer Venture," *Register of the Kentucky State Historical Society* 31 (1933):9–28; Gamst, *Early American Railroads*, 770–72; H. S. Tanner, *Memoir on the Recent Surveys, Observations and Internal Improvements in the United States* (Philadelphia: Privately printed, 1830), 76–77; *American Railroad Journal*, November 11, 1854.

23. *Speech of Mr. Memminger*, 13.

24. John C. Calhoun to S. D. Ingham, December 28, 1833, in Clyde N. Wilson, ed., *The Papers of John C. Calhoun*, vol. 12: *1833–1835* (Columbia: University of South Carolina Press, 1979), 196; John C. Calhoun to J. S. Williams, September 1835, in Wilson, *The Papers of John C. Calhoun*, 12:557.

25. Irving H. Bartlett, *John C. Calhoun: A Biography* (New York: W. W. Norton, 1993), 231.

26. Ramsey "Scraps," University of Tennessee Special Collections Library, Knoxville, hereafter cited as Ramsey "Scraps"; Wiltse, *John C. Calhoun,* 331.

27. *American Railroad Journal,* August 6, 1836; Wiltse, *John C. Calhoun,* 331–32; John C. Calhoun to Editor of the *Pendleton Messenger* [Frederick W. Symmes], September 22, 1836, in Clyde N. Wilson, ed., *The Papers of John C. Calhoun,* vol. 13: *1835–1837* (Columbia: University of South Carolina Press, 1980), 286, 293.

The Savannah River officially begins where the Tugaloo and the Seneca Rivers meet.

28. Calhoun to Editor of the *Pendleton Messenger,* in Wilson, *The Papers of John C. Calhoun,* 13:296–93.

29. Both South Carolina and national newspapers reprinted the Calhoun letter to the *Pendleton Messenger;* see, for example, *Charleston (S.C.) Mercury,* October 4, 1836, and *Washington, D.C., Daily National Intelligencer,* October 6, 1836. John C. Calhoun to J Ed Colhoun, September 19, 1836, and October 2, 1836, in Wilson, *The Papers of John C. Calhoun,* 13:285–86, 296; Wiltse, *John C. Calhoun: Nullifier,* 333.

30. Clyde N. Wilson, ed., *The Papers of John C. Calhoun,* vol. 17: *1844* (Columbia: University of South Carolina Press, 1988), 201; Ramsey "Scraps"; Charles E. Orser Jr., *The Material Basis of the Post-bellum Tenant Plantation* (Athens: University of Georgia Press, 1988), 21–46; *American Railroad Journal,* February 15, 1839; David Williams, *The Georgia Gold Rush: Twenty-Niners, Cherokees, and Gold Fever* (Columbia: University of South Carolina Press, 1993), 74–75, 90.

31. John C. Calhoun to Jas Ed Colhoun, December 9, 1836, and December 6, 1836, in Wilson, *The Papers of John C. Calhoun,* 13:307, 308; *American Railroad Journal,* December 15, 1838.

32. Rob Y. Hayne to John C. Calhoun, November 1, 1838, in Clyde N. Wilson, ed., *The Papers of John C. Calhoun,* vol. 14: *1837–1838* (Columbia: University of South Carolina Press, 1981), 454–59; John C. Calhoun to Gen'l R. Y. Hayne, November 17, 1838, in Wilson, *The Papers of John C. Calhoun,* 14:465–58.

33. John C. Calhoun to Robert Y. Hayne, November 17, 1838, in John C. Calhoun, *Correspondence of John C. Calhoun,* ed. J. Franklin Jameson (Washington, D.C.: Fourth Annual Report of the Historical Manuscripts Commission of the American Historical Association, 1900), 413–15.

34. Clyde N. Wilson, ed., *The Papers of John C. Calhoun,* vol. 15: *1839–1841* (Columbia: University of South Carolina Press, 1983), 776–77, 807–808, 815.

35. Gamst, *Early American Railroads,* 732–33.

36. Wallace P. Reed, ed., *History of Atlanta, Georgia* (Syracuse, N.Y.: D. Mason, 1889), 429–30, 431; Gamst, *Early American Railroads,* 721–25; James A. Ward, *J. Edgar Thomson: Master of the Pennsylvania* (Westport, Conn.: Greenwood Press, 1980), 28–30, 42.

37. *Charleston* (SC) *Courier,* December 1, 1836; Wiltse, *John C. Calhoun,* 337–38.

38. John C. Calhoun to George Cox, January 10, 1844, in Wilson, *The Papers of John C. Calhoun,* 17:690; Coit, *John C. Calhoun,* 416–18; Cleveland, *Controversy between John C. Calhoun and Robt. Y. Hayne as to the Proper Route of a Railroad from South Carolina to the West,* 381.

39. *Poor's Manual of Railroads of the United States* (New York: H. V. and H. W. Poor, 1885), 448, 484.

40. Ramsey "Scraps"; *American Railroad Journal,* June 3, 1837; November 15, 1839.

41. Carl Schurz, *Life of Henry Clay* (New York, 1887), 2:114, 126; Peter Temin, "The Jacksonian Economy," in *The Many-Faceted Jacksonian Era: New Interpretations,* ed. Edward Pessen (Westport, Conn.: Greenwood Press, 1977), 102–13; Paul B. Trescott, *Financing American Enterprise: The Story of Commercial Banking* (New York: Harper & Row, 1963), 16–40; "Message of the Governor [of Kentucky]," *Journal of the Senate of the Commonwealth of Kentucky* (December 4, 1838): 11.

42. *Athens (Ga.) Southern Banner,* January 21, 1837; Irene D. Neu, *Erastus Corning: Merchant and Financier, 1794–1872* (Ithaca, N.Y.: Cornell University Press, 1960), 62–63.

43. Theodore Kornweibel Jr., *Railroads in the African American Experience* (Baltimore: Johns Hopkins University Press, 2010), 11–28; Ramsey "Scraps."

Not everyone associated with antebellum Southern railroads endorsed the use of company-owned slaves. President T. Tupper of the SCC&RRCo explained his lack of enthusiasm: "The privilege of promptly dismissing an inferior, vicious, or otherwise worthless negro from our service, is a very great one, which would not be had if they belonged to the company. It is also important to have the eye of an owner to look to the treatment as well as the conduct of the slaves." He continued: "If the Company owned them, the overseers might be cruel to them without redress; and it could not be expected they would attend much to their habits. But it is different where there is a master to appeal to, or to inquire after them, who feels nearly the same for them, he does for his children, besides the protection of their value, which is a great stimulant to see they are not abused." *Semi-Annual Report to the Stockholders of the South-Carolina Canal and Rail-Road Company,* 11.

44. Derrick, *Centennial History of South Carolina Railroad,* 145–46.

45. Dolores Greenberg, *Financiers and Railroads, 1869–1889* (Newark: University of Delaware Press, 1980), 22–23; Dorothy R. Adler, *British Investment in American Railways, 1834–1898* (Charlottesville: University of Virginia Press, 1970), 4; Augustus J. Veenendaal Jr., *Slow Train to Paradise: How Dutch Investment Helped Build American Railroads* (Stanford, Calif.: Stanford University Press, 1996), 10–11; Reginald C. McGrane, *Foreign Bondholders and American State Debt* (New York: Macmillan, 1935), 11; *American Railroad Journal,* June 25, 1853; Paul Wallace Gates, *The Illinois Central and Its Colonization Work* (Cambridge, Mass.: Harvard University Press, 1934), 76.

46. *Charleston (S.C.) Courier,* October 21, 1836.

47. *Knoxville Register,* November 16, 1836; *Charleston (S.C.) Courier,* December 1, 1836; Derrick, *Centennial History of South Carolina Railroad,* 154; Phillips, *A History of Transportation in the Eastern Cotton Belt to 1860,* 187.

48. Wade, *The Urban Frontier,* 190–91; Shaw, *Canals for a Nation,* 131, 133–34.

49. *American Railroad Journal,* October 1, 1838; Salsbury, *The State, the Investor, and the Railroad,* 32; Marrs, *Railroads in the Old South,* 21.

50. *Charleston (S.C.) Courier,* October 29, 1836; November 25, 1836; December 17, 1836.

51. Schultz, "Hayne's Magnificent Dream," 47–47a; Bray Hammond, *Banks and Politics in America from the Revolution to the Civil War* (Princeton, N.J.: Princeton University Press, 1957), 168.

52. *Speech of Mr. Memminger,* 9; *Exposition of the Claims of the Louisville, Cincinnati and Charleston Railroad Company to the Support of the Legislature and People of the State of Kentucky* (n.p., n.d.), 2–3.

53. Derrick, *Centennial History of South Carolina Railroad,* 157; *Exposition of the Claims of the Louisville, Cincinnati and Charleston Railroad Company to the Support of the Legislature and People of the State of Kentucky,* 2–5.

54. *Charter of the Louisville, Cincinnati & Charleston Rail-Road Company as Passed by the Legislatures of Kentucky, Tennessee, No. & So. Carolina with the Amendments; also the Charter of the South-Western Rail-Road Bank and the Bylaws* (Charleston, S.C.: A. E. Miller, 1838), 16–26.

55. Derrick, *Centennial History of South Carolina Railroad,* 158; *Charleston (S.C.) Courier,* January 11, 1837.

56. Schultz, "Hayne's Magnificent Dream," 49.

57. Phillips, *A History of Transportation in the Eastern Cotton Belt to 1860,* 191.

58. *Charter of the Louisville, Cincinnati & Charleston Rail Road Company,* 27–28.

59. Phillips, *A History of Transportation in the Eastern Cotton Belt to 1860,* 193; Folmsbee, *Sectionalism and Internal Improvement in Tennessee,* 160–61; *Knoxville Register,* December 13, 1847.

60. *Exposition of the Claims of the Louisville, Cincinnati and Charleston Railroad to the Support of the Legislature and People of the State of Kentucky,* 1–7.

61. Derrick, *Centennial History of South Carolina Railroad,* 163.

62. *American Railroad Journal,* November 1, 1838; *Boston Atlas,* April 23, 1839.

63. Derrick, *Centennial History of South Carolina Railroad,* 164–65; *American Railroad Journal,* October 1, 1838.

64. Derrick, *Centennial History of the South Carolina Railroad,* 156–58.

65. Phillips, *A History of Transportation in the Eastern Cotton Belt to 1860,* 189–94.

66. *American Railroad Journal,* July 15, 1839.

67. Phillips, *A History of Transportation in the Eastern Cotton Belt to 1860,* 172.

68. *American Railroad Journal,* November 1, 1838.

69. Derrick, *Centennial History of South Carolina Railroad,* 179–82.

70. Derrick, *Centennial History of South Carolina Railroad,* 102–103, 182–83; Gamst, *Early American Railroads,* 535, 632, 647, 649.

71. *American Railroad Journal,* November 1, 1839.

72. Dilts, *The Great Road,* 7–12.

73. Derrick, *Centennial History of South Carolina,* 183–84.

74. Ibid., 185–87; Minute Book, South-Carolina Canal and Rail-Road Company, October 22, 1835, 51; "Historical Documentation, St. Matthews Railroad Cut," 31, Calhoun County Museum Archive, St. Mathews, S.C.

75. Derrick, *Centennial History of South Carolina,* 187–89.

76. Kirkland and Kennedy, *Historic Camden,* pt. 2: *Nineteenth Century,* 39–41; *American Railroad Journal,* June 27, 1846; Phillips, *A History of Transportation in the Eastern Cotton Belt to 1860,* 174, 211.

77. *American Railroad Journal,* December 1, 1840.

78. *Proceedings of the Stockholders of the Louisville, Cincinnati and Charleston Rail Road Company* (Charleston, S.C., 1841); *Proceedings of the Stockholders of the South-Carolina Rail-Road Company, and of the South-Western Rail-Road Bank* (Charleston, S.C.: Miller & Browne, 1847), 33.

79. *Proceedings of the Stockholders of the Louisville, Cincinnati and Charleston Rail Road Company.*

80. Derrick, *Centennial History of South Carolina,* 188.

5. CRISIS AND CONTRACTION

1. Jean Strouse, *Morgan: American Financier* (New York: Random House, 1999), 24; H. Roger Grant, *Self-Help in the 1890's Depression* (Ames: Iowa State University Press, 1983), 5–11.

2. Roberts, *America's First Great Depression,* 13; Stiles, *The First Tycoon,* 112–15; Philip Hone, *The Diary of Philip Hone, 1828–1851,* ed. Allan Nevins (New York: Dodd, Mead and Co., 1927), 234–37, 241–42, 248–59.

3. Claude A. Campbell, "Banking and Finance in Tennessee during the Depression of 1837," *East Tennessee Historical Society's Publications* 9 (1937): 19–30; Miles S. Richards, "Pierce Marion Butler: The South Carolina Years, 1830–1841," *South Carolina Historical Magazine* 87 (January 1986): 24; David S. Reynolds, *Waking Giant: America in the Age of Jackson* (New York: HarperCollins, 2008), 109, 310–11; Roberts, *America's First Great Depression,* 23, 36.

4. Charles Schultz, ed., "Glimpses into Cincinnati's Past: The Gest Letters, 1834–1842," *Ohio History* 73 (Summer 1964): 167, 172; *Semi-Annual Report to the Stockholders of the South-Carolina Canal and Rail Road Company* (Charleston, S.C.: A. E. Miller, 1841), 7; *Annual Report of the Petersburg Rail Road Company* (Petersburg, Va.; Intelligencer Job Office, 1849), 6.

5. *Washington, D.C., Daily National Intelligencer,* May 27, 1837; *American Railroad Journal,* March 15, 1839; December 1, 1840; Gamst, *Early American Railroads,* 757–59.

6. *Proceedings of the Louisville, Cincinnati and Charleston Rail Road Company, 1839.*

7. Jim Cohen, "Divergent Paths, United States and France: Capital Markets, the State, and Differentiation in Transportation Systems, 1840–1940," *Enterprise and Society* 10, no. 3 (Sept. 2009): 449–97.

8. Charles Roy Schultz, "Hayne's Magnificent Dream," 58–59; Ramsey "Scraps."

9. *Charleston (S.C.) Courier,* September 30, 1839; *Philadelphia Niles National Register,* October 12, 1839; Jervey, *Robert Y. Hayne and His Times,* 515, 530; Sadie Smathers Patton, *Sketches of Polk County History* (Hendersonville, N.C.: Historical Commission of Polk County, 1950), 20; Yates Snowden, ed., *History of South Carolina* (Chicago: Lewis Publishing, 1920), 2:614.

10. Gregory Allen Grep, "Charleston, South Carolina, Merchants, 1815–1860: Urban Leadership in the Ante-bellum South" (PhD diss., University of California, San Diego, 1978), 95–96.

11. Snowden, *History of South Carolina,* 2:2, 614; Phillips, *A History of Transportation in the Eastern Cotton Belt,* 197; Derrick, *Centennial History of South Carolina Railroad,* 171; *Charleston (S.C.) Courier,* October 24, 1839.

12. Ramsey "Scraps."

13. *The National Cyclopaedia of American Biography* (New York: James T. White, 1904), 68–69.

14. *Philadelphia North American,* July 1, 1839.

Toward the end of 1839 not everyone had given up hope for a completed LC&C. Dr. J. G. M. Ramsey in a letter to James K. Polk, written on October 26, realized that the Panic of 1837 had caused grave financial problems, but believed that "sooner or later [the railroad] will be carried through." J. G. M. Ramsey Papers, University of Tennessee Special Collection Library, Knoxville.

15. Henry D. Crapers, *The Life and Times of C. G. Memminger* (Richmond, Va.: Everett Waddey, 1893); *The National Cyclopaedia of American Biography,* 200.

16. Ramsey "Scraps."

17. *American Railroad Journal,* November 15, 1841; Wiltse, *John C. Calhoun,* 342.

18. Holland, "The East Tennessee and Georgia Railroad," 90–92; *American Railroad Journal,* May 6, 1837; Gamst, *Early American Railroads,* 764–65.

19. Hiwassee Railroad Company, "Proceedings of the President and Board of Directors, August 13, 1836–April 28, 1848," Norfolk Southern Archive, Norfolk, Va.

20. Phillips, *A History of Transportation in the Eastern Cotton Belt,* 194–96; *American Railroad Journal,* November 1, November 15, 1840.

21. Phillips, *A History of Transportation in the Eastern Cotton Belt,* 203.

22. *American Railroad Journal,* February 15, 1842.

23. Derrick, *Centennial History of South Carolina Railroad,* 182, 190; *Proceedings of the Stockholders of the Louisville, Cincinnati and Charleston Rail Road Company* (Charleston, S.C., 1843).

24. Charles Roy Schultz, "Hayne's Magnificent Dream," 75–179; *American Railroad Journal,* July 5, 1851.

25. Harrison, *A History of the Legal Development of the Railroad System of Southern Railway Company,* 268.

26. Alfred Glaze Smith Jr., *Economic Readjustment of an Old Cotton State: South Carolina, 1820–1860* (Columbia: University of South Carolina Press, 1958), 179–87.

27. Harrison, *A History of the Legal Development of the Railroad System of Southern Railway Company,* 311; Smith, *Economic Readjustment of an Old Cotton State,* 179–81.

28. Phillips, *A History of Transportation in the Eastern Cotton Belt,* 340–42; Tommy W. Rogers, "The Great Population Exodus from South Carolina, 1850–1860," *South Carolina Historical Magazine* 68 (January 1967): 14–21; Roy McBee Smith, *Vardry McBee, 1795–1864: Man of Reason in an Age of Extremes* (Spartanburg, S.C.: Laurel Heritage Press, 1997), 195–209.

29. Lillian Kibler, *Benjamin F. Perry: South Carolina Unionist* (Durham, N.C.: Duke University Press, 1946), 209–16; *American Railroad Journal,* June 19, 1852; October 16, 1852.

30. *American Railroad Journal,* August 1, 1849; October 6, 1849; August 19, 1853; Thomas H. Pope, *The History of Newberry County, South Carolina, 1799–1860* (Columbia: University of South Carolina Press, 1973), 40–146; *Charleston (S.C.) Courier,* April 4, 1851; May 17, 1851.

31. *American Railroad Journal,* November 24, 1849; Smith, *Economic Readjustment of an Old Cotton State,* 179–83; Phillips, *A History of Transportation in the Eastern Cotton Belt to 1860,* 345–46.

32. Harrison, *A History of the Legal Development of the Railroad System of Southern Railway Company,* 316–17.

33. *American Railroad Journal,* April 23, 1859; *Annual Report of the President and Directors of the Greenville and Columbia Rail Road Company to the Stockholders* (Columbia, S.C., 1859).

34. Pope, *The History of Newberry County,* 40–146; Ramsey "Scraps"; *American Railroad Journal,* June 29, 1850.

35. Harrison, *A History of the Legal Development of the Railroad System of Southern Railway Company,* 359–60; Lacy K. Ford, *Origins of Southern Radicalism: The South Carolina Upcountry, 1800–1860* (New York: Oxford University Press, 1988), 226–27; Phillips, *A History of Transportation in the Eastern Cotton Belt,* 347; Maria Louise Simpson papers, 1895, William Klugh collection, Clemson, S.C.

36. Harrison, *A History of the Legal Development of the Railroad System of Southern Railway Company,* 370–71.

37. Phillips, *A History of Transportation in the Eastern Cotton Belt,* 347–48; *American Railroad Journal,* August 16, 1851; August 27, 1851.

38. Charles Roy Schultz, "Hayne's Magnificent Dream," 106–107; Smith, *Economic Readjustment of an Old Cotton State,* 183.

39. Harrison, *A History of the Legal Development of the Railroad System of Southern Railway Company,* 369, 375–80.

40. Charles Roy Schultz, "Hayne's Magnificent Dream," 116.

41. Ibid., 120–21; Smith, *Economic Readjustment of an Old Cotton State,* 180.

42. *Report of the President of the Spartanburg & Union Rail Road Company to the Stockholders at Their Annual Meeting, August 13 and 14, 1856* (Spartanburg, S.C.: Spartanburg Express, 1856).

43. "Pelion upon Ossa" comes from Greek mythology, being an allusion to the attempt of the giants to scale heaven by piling Mount Ossa upon Mount Pelion.

44. *American Railroad Journal,* July 31, 1858; September 11, 1858; Charles Roy Schultz, "Hayne's Magnificent Dream," 131; Works Progress Administration, *A History of Spartanburg County* (Spartanburg, S.C.: Band and White, 1940), 114–16; J. B. O. Landrum, *History of Spartanburg County* (Atlanta, Ga.: Franklin Printing and Publishing, 1900), 40–41.

45. Stover, *Iron Road to the West,* 11, 61.

46. Phillips, *A History of Transportation in the Eastern Cotton Belt,* 349–50, 352–55; Dozier, *A History of the Atlantic Coast Line Railroad,* 75–79; *American Railroad Journal,* April 25, 1857.

47. Harrison, *A History of the Legal Development of the Railroad System of Southern Railway Company,* 153–54; Trelease, *The North Carolina Railroad,* 13–15, 35.

48. Phillips, *A History of Transportation in the Eastern Cotton Belt,* 337–40; Charles Turner, "Virginia Railroad Development, 1845–1860," *Historian* 10 (Autumn 1947): 50–52.

49. Phillips, *A History of Transportation in the Eastern Cotton Belt,* 346–47.

50. H. David Stone Jr., *Vital Rails: The Charleston & Savannah Railroad and the Civil War in Coastal South Carolina* (Columbia: University of South Carolina Press, 2008), 24–39; Dozier, *A History of the Atlantic Coast Line Railroad,* 81–82.

51. Smith, *Economic Readjustment of an Old Cotton State,* 181; Charles Ellet Jr., *Exposition of the Causes Which Have Conduced to the Failure of Many Rail-Roads in the United States* (Philadelphia: John C. Clark, 1841), 3.

52. Hoffman, *Building a Great Railroad,* 18.

53. Brewster, "Ante-bellum Planters and Their Means of Transportation," 25.

54. *American Railroad Journal,* October 11, 1856.

55. *American Railroad Journal,* November 1, 1851; Smith, *Economic Readjustment of an Old Cotton State,* 129, 191.

6. WHAT HAPPENED

1. Grant, *Twilight Rails,* 30; Robin W. Winks, *Frederick Billings: A Life* (New York: Oxford University Press, 1991); Keith L. Bryant Jr., *Arthur E. Stilwell:*

Promoter with a Hunch (Nashville, Tenn.: Vanderbilt University Press, 1971), 170–77, 221–22. Also useful is Robert E. Pounds and John B. McCall, *The Orient* (Midwest City, Ok.: Santa Fe Railway Historical & Modeling Society, 2011).

2. *Columbia Daily South Carolinian,* August 28, 1854.

3. *Charleston (S.C.) Daily Courier,* July 17, 1852.

4. Harrison, *A History of the Legal Development of the Railroad System of Southern Railway Company,* 334–36; *Columbia Tri-Weekly South Carolinian,* May 27, 1852; *Annual Report of the President and the Directors to the Stockholders of the Blue Ridge Railroad Company in South Carolina, Held in Charleston, the 22nd of November, 1856* (Charleston, S.C.: Walker, Evans, 1856), 3; *American Railroad Journal,* May 29, 1852; Ethel B. Mitchel, *The Romance of the Blue Ridge Railroad* (Pendleton, S.C.: Southern Printing Company, 1972), 7.

5. American Railroad *Journal,* August 5, 1854.

6. *Charleston (S.C.) Daily Courier,* July 17, 1852.

7. Harrison, *A History of the Legal Development of the Railroad System of the Southern Railway Company,* 337; *Charleston (S.C.) Mercury,* March 18, 1853.

8. *Report of the President and Directors to the Annual Meeting of the Stockholders of the Blue Ridge Rail Road Company in South Carolina* (Charleston, S.C.: Walker, Evans, 1857), 4; Betty L. Plisco, *The Rocky Road to Nowhere: A History of the Blue Ridge Railroad in South Carolina* (Salem, S.C.: Blue Granite Books, 2002), 33; "Rabun Gap Railroad," Ramsey Scraps, University of Tennessee Library, Special Collections, Knoxville, hereafter cited as "Rabun Gap Railroad"; *American Railroad Journal,* October 27, 1855.

9. *American Railroad Journal,* July 17, 1852.

10. *Charleston (S.C.) Daily Courier,* March 1, 1852; Van Deusen, *Economic Bases of Disunion in South Carolina,* 248.

11. *Journal of the House of Representatives of the State of South Carolina, Being the Annual Session of 1852,* 25–26 (Columbia, S.C.: State Printers, 1852).

12. *Charleston (S.C.) Mercury,* February 2, 1853.

13. *Charleston (S.C.) Daily Courier,* April 12, 1853.

14. *America Railroad Journal,* September 16, 1854.

15. *American Railroad Journal,* August 5, 1854; George DeWitt Brown, "A History of the Blue Ridge Railroad, 1852–1874" (MA thesis, University of South Carolina, 1967), 24–49; Henry D. Capers, *The Life and Times of C. G. Memminger* (Richmond, Va.: Everett Waddey, 1893), 515.

16. Harrison, *A History of the Legal Development of the Railroad System of the Southern Railway Company,* 397–98.

17. *Report of the President and Directors to the Annual Meeting of the Stockholders of the Blue Ridge Rail Road Company in South Carolina* (1857), 17.

18. Ibid., 3; *Annual Report of the President and Directors of the Blue Ridge R. R. Company in South Carolina* (Charleston, S.C.: Evans & Cogswell, 1860), 7–9; Plisco, *The Rocky Road to Nowhere,* 19–22.

19. Brown, "A History of the Blue Ridge Railroad, 1852–1874," 36–40.

20. *American Railroad Journal,* October 2, 1857; *Report of the President and Directors to the Annual Meeting of the Stockholders of the Blue Ridge Rail Road Company in South Carolina* (1857), 12; Plisco, *The Rocky Road to Nowhere,* 34.

21. *Charleston (S.C.) Daily Courier,* January 30, February 11, 1857; Smith, *Economic Readjustment of an Old Cotton State,* 181.

22. *Report of the President and Directors and of the Chief Engineer to the Annual Meeting of the Stockholders of the Blue Ridge Rail Road Company, in South Carolina, Held in Charleston, the 10th November, 1858* (Charleston, S.C.: Walker, Evans, 1858), 5, 28–29.

23. Christopher M. Poteat, "A Frontier Not Extended: South Carolina, the Blue Ridge Railroad, and the Failure to Connect with the West, 1852–1860," *Proceedings of the South Carolina Historical Association* (1990): 36; Michael Perman, ed., *The Coming of the American Civil War* (Lexington, Mass.: D. C. Heath, 1993), 165.

24. *Annual Report of the President and Directors of the Blue Ridge R. R. Company in South Carolina* (1860), 5; George Benet Shealy, *Walhalla: A German Settlement in Upstate South Carolina: "The Garden of the Gods,"* (Seneca, S.C.: Blue Ridge Art Association, 1990), 89–101.

25. *Charleston (S.C.) Mercury,* August 22, 1859.

26. Ibid.

27. *Annual Report of the President and Directors of the Blue Ridge R. R. Company in South Carolina* (1860), 26.

28. Steven A. Channing, *Crisis of Fear: Secession in South Carolina* (New York: Simon and Schuster, 1970), 55.

29. Brian A. Boyd, *The Tallulah Falls Railroad: A Photographic Remembrance* (Clayton, Ga.: Fern Creek Press, 1998), 13; *Report of the President and Directors to the Annual Meeting of the Stockholders of the Blue Ridge Rail Road Company in South Carolina* (1857), 10; *Annual Report of the President and Directors of the Blue Ridge R.R. Company in South Carolina* (1860), 16, 21, 25–26.

30. G. A. Trenholm, "Charleston, S.C. and Her Great Railroad Connection with the North-West,"

DeBow's Review (September 1866): 314, 316; "The Rabun Gap Railroad."

31. Brown, "A History of the Blue Ridge Railroad, 1852–1874," 57–81; *Report on the Subject of the Blue Ridge Railroad, and in Reference to the Railroad Connection with Cincinnati and Louisville via Knoxville, Tenn.* (Charleston, S.C.: Joseph Walker, 1866), 9–10.

32. Brown, "A History of the Blue Ridge Railroad, 1852–1874," 57–8; Harrison, *A History of the Legal Development of the Railroad System of Southern Railway Company*, 340–41.

33. James P. Low, *The Narrow Gauge: A Report of the Chief Engineer of the Blue Ridge Railroad* (Columbia, S.C.: Carolina Printing, 1871), 3, 17, 30; George W. Hilton, *American Narrow Gauge Railroads* (Stanford, Calif.: Stanford University Press, 1990), 48–117.

34. *Charleston (S.C.) Daily News*, June 20, 1873; *Charleston (S.C.) News and Courier*, July 1, 1873; *Travelers' Office Guide of the Railway and Steam Navigation Lines in the United States and Canada* (Philadelphia: National Railway Publication Company, July 1874), 542.

According to the June 1868 issue of the *Travelers Official Railway Guide of the United States and Canada*, the railroad dispatched only one train between Anderson and Walhalla, although it met connecting Columbia passenger trains on the Greenville & Columbia. Patrons who wished to leave Walhalla for Columbia had only the option of the 4:00 AM train, but a return from Columbia meant arrival at a more desirable time, 8:00 PM. In the 1870s Blue Ridge service was somewhat better than what was provided in the late 1860s.

35. *Macon Georgia Weekly Telegraph and Georgia Journal and Messenger*, February 1, 1876.

36. Harrison, *A History of the Legal Development of the Railroad System of the Southern Railway Company*, 930–39; Maury Klein, *The Great Richmond Terminal: A Study in Businessmen and Business Strategy* (Charlottesville: University Press of Virginia, 1970), 91.

37. Harrison, *A History of the Legal Development of the Railroad System of the Southern Railway Company*, 397–405; Klein, *The Great Richmond Terminal*, 284.

38. *Poor's Manual of Railroads of the United States for 1885*, 413–14, 479–82; Richard L. Kimball Jr., "The Carolina & Tennessee Southern Railway Company," *Ties* (March–April 2009): 22.

39. Harrison, *A History of the Legal Development of the Railroad System of the Southern Railway Company*, 380–85.

40. Kimball, "The Carolina & Tennessee Southern Railway Company," 22–23; J. M. Culp to W. W. Finley, May 28, 1907, Presidential Files, Southern Railway Company, Southern Railway Historical Association Archive, Kennesaw, Ga.; *Tallulah Falls and the Rabun Gap Country* (Tallulah Falls Railway, July 1914).

41. Blue Ridge Railroad Minute Book, #1, April 20, 1915, 325, Norfolk Southern Corporation Archive, Tucker, Ga..

42. Kimball, "The Carolina & Tennessee Southern Railway Company," 21, 23, 25.

43. *Anderson (S.C.) Tribune*, December 14, 1923.

44. See Scott R. Fletcher, "Public Dreams, Private Means: Cincinnati and Its Southern Railway, 1869–1901," *Journal of Transport History* 24 (March 2003): 38–58.

45. *American Railroad Journal*, November 30, 1850; Sherry O. Hessler, "'The Great Disturbing Cause' and the Decline of the Queen City," *Bulletin of the Historical and Philosophical Society of Ohio* 20 (July 1962): 170–85; Butler, "The Cincinnati Southern Railway," iii, 16–17; E. A. Ferguson, *Founding of the Cincinnati Southern Railway with an Autobiographical Sketch* (Cincinnati: Robert Clarke, 1905), 9.

46. Greve, *Centennial History of Cincinnati and Representative Citizens*, 1:860; Hollander, *The Cincinnati Southern Railway*, 10; Maury Klein, *History of the Louisville & Nashville Railroad* (New York: Macmillan, 1972), 90–91; Robert Selph Henry, *Railroad Business* (Indianapolis: Bobbs-Merrill, 1942),110; *Cincinnati Commercial*, 1869, clipping in Cincinnati and Southern Railway Papers, Cincinnati Historical Society, Cincinnati, Ohio, hereafter cited as CSRy papers; Charles G. Hall, ed., *The Cincinnati Southern Railway: A History* (Cincinnati, 1902), 31.

47. Hall, *The Cincinnati Southern Railway*, 20.

48. Hollander, *The Cincinnati Southern Railway*, 14–15; *Poor's Manual of the Railroads of the United States for 1868–69* (New York: H. V. & H. W. Poor, 1868), 84, 170; Ambler, *A History of Transportation in the Ohio Valley*, 234.

49. S. H. Goodin, *Plan for the Construction of the Direct Railroad South, Connecting Cincinnati with the Southern System of Railroads* (Cincinnati: Wrightson, 1868), 3, 18.

50. George W. Knepper, *Ohio and Its People* (Kent, Ohio: Kent State University Press, 1989), 212–14; Hinkle, *The Movement of 1835–36 to Construct a Cincinnati Southern Railway*, 12; Gates, *The Illinois Central Railroad and Its Colonization Work*, 17; Hollander, *The Cincinnati Southern Railway*, 12.

51. *Cincinnati Commercial*, April 22, 1869.

52. Hollander, *The Cincinnati Southern Railway*, 19–20, 22–23, 89–92; *Cincinnati Daily Enquirer*, November 25, 1868; *Laws of Ohio, Kentucky and Tennessee Authorizing the Construction of the Cincinnati Southern Railway* (Cincinnati: n.p., 1881), 3–9.

53. Hollander, *The Cincinnati Southern Railway*, 23–24.

54. Ellis Merton Coulter, *The Cincinnati Southern Railroad and the Struggle for Southern Commerce, 1865–1872* (Chicago: American Historical Society, 1922), 35–37; *Compendium of the Eleventh Census, 1890* (Washington, D.C.: Government Printing Office, 1892), 377.

55. Hollander, *The Cincinnati Southern Railway*, 25–26.

56. *Louisville Courier-Journal*, n.d., clipping in CSRy papers; Hollander, *The Cincinnati Southern Railway*, 26–27.

57. Coulter, *The Cincinnati Southern Railroad and the Struggle for Southern Commerce*, 49–50; Hollander, *The Cincinnati Southern Railway*, 27, 29.

58. Hollander, *The Cincinnati Southern Railway*, 29–30.

59. Coulter, *The Cincinnati Southern Railroad and the Struggle for Southern Commerce*, 54; *Congressional Globe*, 41st Congress, 2nd Session, 1869–1870, 1948.

60. Hollander, *The Cincinnati Southern Railway*, 30–31.

61. Hall, *The Cincinnati Southern Railway*, 38; Hollander, *The Cincinnati Southern Railway*, 32.

62. Coulter, *The Cincinnati Southern Railroad and the Struggle for Southern Commerce*, 60–61; Hollander, *The Cincinnati Southern Railway*, 33.

63. *Surveys for the Cincinnati Southern Railway: A Preliminary Report of the Chief Engineer* (n.p., March 1873), 3–65; Hollander, *The Cincinnati Southern Railway*, 33–34.

64. Hall, *The Cincinnati Southern Railway*, 38–40; Hollander, *The Cincinnati Southern*, 38–39, 40, 44.

65. Hollander, *The Cincinnati Southern Railway*, 44–45.

66. Ibid., 46. Railroad officials frequently avoided trackage rights agreements, reasoning that the owning carrier would expedite its trains and not those of the guest road. And there were additional motivations. At times rental costs were high, but the expense of a wholly owned line could be amortized over time and captive shippers attracted.

67. C. Bouscaren, *Report on the Progress of Work and Cost of Construction of the Cincinnati Southern Railway* (Cincinnati: Wrightson, 1878), 3–20; Hollander, *The Cincinnati Southern Railway*, 46–48; Hall, *The Cincinnati Southern Railway*, 41–42.

68. *Poor's Manual of Railroads of the United States for 1885*, 494; Burke Davis, *The Southern Railway: Road of the Innovators* (Chapel Hill: University of North Carolina Press, 1985), 185; Stover, *American Railroads*, 133–35.

69. Hollander, *The Cincinnati Southern Railway*, 49.

70. *Macon Georgia Weekly Telegraph and Georgia Journal and Messenger*, March 26, 1880; *St. Louis Globe-Democrat*, March 23, 1880; *Frank Leslie's Illustrated Newspaper* (New York), April 10, 1880.

71. G. Bouscaron, *Report on the Progress of Work and Cost of Completing and Maintaining the Cincinnati Southern Railway* (Cincinnati: Wilstach, Baldwin, 1880), 90.

72. H. P. Boyden, *The Beginnings of the Cincinnati Southern Railway* (Cincinnati: Robert Clarke, 1901), 5.

73. Cincinnati Southern Railway public timetable, April 15, 1881.

74. Hollander, *The Cincinnati Southern Railway*, 49, 50–51; *Cincinnati Daily Enquirer*, n.d., clipping in CSRy papers; Davis, *The Southern Railway*, 182.

75. Hollander, *The Cincinnati Southern Railway*, 52.

76. *Report and Statements of Accounts of the Cincinnati, New Orleans & Texas Pacific Ry. Co. (Cincinnati Southern Railway) for the Year Ending December 31, 1882* (Cincinnati: Mallory & Webb, 1883), 45; *Fifth Annual Report of the Cincinnati, New Orleans & Texas Pacific Ry. Co. (Lessee of Cincinnati Railway Company) and Statement of Accounts for the Year Ending December 31, 1886* (Cincinnati: William A. Webb, 1887), 16–17; *Poor's Manual of Railroads of the United States for 1885*, 495; Davis, *The Southern Railway*, 183–84.

77. Hollander, *The Cincinnati Southern Railway*, 53; Greve, *Centennial History of Cincinnati and Representative Citizens*, 1:863–64.

78. *Poor's Manual of Railroads for the United States for 1897* (New York: Poor's Manual Company, 1897), 763–67; Davis, *The Southern Railway*, 25–27; Strouse, *Morgan*, 321–22.

79. Trelease, *The North Carolina Railroad*, 324–25; Davis, *The Southern Railway*, 184–87.

80. Since the late 1980s the lease agreement between Norfolk Southern and the City of Cincinnati has been a flat annual fee, indexed for inflation. Prior to that arrangement, the compensation from the railroad to the city was derived from a formula based on the line's gross and net revenues. See also Ron Flanary, "Rat Hole Revisited," *Trains* 73 (December 2013):24–33.

81. Charles W. Wood, "What Has Happened to Cincinnati," *Forbes* (May 15, 1928): 18–20, 52–53; Klein, *History of the Louisville & Nashville Railroad*, 102–122; Hoffman, *Building a Great Railroad*, 1.

7. WHAT MIGHT HAVE HAPPENED

1. *Proceedings of the Citizens of Charleston, Embracing the Report of the Committee and the Address and Resolutions Adopted at a General Meeting in Reference to the Proposed Railroad from Cincinnati to Charleston; Boston Courier*, November 28, 1838; Leila

Sellers, *Charleston Business on the Eve of the American Revolution* (Chapel Hill, 1934; reprint, New York: Arno Press, 1970), 7–16.

2. *Speech of Mr. Memminger,* 9; Scott Reynolds Nelson, *Iron Confederacies: Southern Railways, Klan Violence, and Reconstruction* (Chapel Hill: University of North Carolina Press, 1999), 23.

3. Norfolk Southern Railroad, successor to the Southern Railway, continues to provide freight service between Charleston and Cincinnati. With part of the more direct Spartanburg to Asheville line (Saluda Grade) out-of-service (but not abandoned), cars travel from Charleston to Cincinnati via Columbia, Charlotte, Salisbury, Asheville, Knoxville, and Harriman Junction, Tennessee.

4. See, for example, Broadus Mitchell, *The Rise of Cotton Mills in the South* (Baltimore: Johns Hopkins University Press, 1921), and Robert Royal Russel, *Economic Aspects of Southern Sectionalism, 1840–1861* (Urbana: University of Illinois, 1924); Walter J. Frazer Jr., *Charleston! Charleston! A History of a Southern City* (Columbia: University of South Carolina Press, 1989), 232.

5. *Speech of Mr. Memminger,* 14.

6. *American Railroad Journal,* March 3, 1851.

7. Robert N. Rosen, *A Short History of Charleston* (Columbia: University of South Carolina Press, 1992), 81, 135; Frazer, *Charleston! Charleston!,* 233, 235.

8. *Compendium of the Eleventh Census, 1890,* 98; Phillips, *A History of Transportation in the Eastern Cotton Belt,* 391.

9. *Proceedings of the Stockholders of the South-Carolina Rail-Road Company and of the South-Western Rail-Road Bank* (Charleston, S.C.: Miller & Browne, 1846).

10. Cleveland, *Controversy between John C. Calhoun and Robt. Y. Hayne,* n.p.

11. Ray Allen Billington, *Frederick Jackson Turner: Historian, Scholar, Teacher* (New York: Oxford University Press, 1973), 367–82.

12. Marc Egnal, *Clash of Extremes: The Economic Origins of the Civil War* (New York: Hill and Wang, 2009), 8.

13. John J. Binder, "The Transportation Revolution and Antebellum Sectional Disagreement," *Social Science History* 31 (Spring 2011): 20–57; *American Railroad Journal,* November 2, 1850; July 10, 1852; G. S. Callender, *Selections from the Economic History of the United States* (Boston: Ginn, 1909), 313–21. Binder uses numerous examples to demonstrate the impact that the transportation revolution had on rates between the Old Northwest and the South and the Old Northwest and the East. He shows, for example, that costs, in dollars per ton of freight, from Cincinnati to New York City via a northern route stood at $99.52 in 1816 as compared to a southern route cost of $30.30. But in 1853 the costs dropped to $10.48 for the former and $15.23 for the latter (table 3).

14. Theodore D. Jervey, *The Slave Trade: Slavery and Color* (Charleston, S.C.: State Company, 1925), 76–77; Balthasar Henry Meyer and Carolina E. MacGill, *History of Transportation in the United States before 1860* (Washington, D.C.: Carnegie Institution of Washington, 1917), 427; *Charleston (S.C.) Courier,* April 9, 1838; Van Deusen, *Economic Bases of Disunion in South Carolina,* 226.

15. N. Dwight Harris, *History of Negro Servitude in Illinois, and of the Slavery Agitation in That State* (Chicago: A. C. McClung, 1904), 235–36; J. G. Randall and David Donald, *The Civil War and Reconstruction,* 2nd ed. (Boston: D. C. Heath, 1961), 51; David M. Potter, *The Impending Crisis, 1848–1861* (New York: Harper & Row, 1976), 34–36; Andrew R. L. Cayton, *Ohio: The History of a People* (Columbus: Ohio State University Press, 2002), 26.

16. Majewski, *A House Dividing,* 136–37.

17. Albro Martin, *Railroads Triumphant: The Growth, Rejection, and Rebirth of a Vital American Force* (New York: Oxford University Press, 1992), 82.

18. Rippy, *Joel R. Poinsett,* 163.

19. *Washington, D.C., Daily National Intelligencer,* February 4, 1854; *American Railroad Journal,* June 26, 1845; June 5, 1852.

20. Wiltse, *John C. Calhoun,* 234–40; David Devine, *Slavery, Scandal, and Steel Rails: The 1854 Gadsden Purchase and the Second Transcontinental Railroad across Arizona and New Mexico Twenty-Five Years Later* (New York: iUniverse, 2004), 9–12, 37–43.

21. Cotterill, "Memphis Railroad Convention, 1849," 83–94; "Charleston," Ramsey Scraps.

22. John McCardell, *The Idea of a Southern Nation: Southern Nationalists and Southern Nationalism, 1830–1860* (New York: Norton, 1979), 270–71.

23. Charles Sellers, *The Market Revolution, Jacksonian America, 1815–1846* (New York: Oxford University Press, 1991), 392; Charles S. Sydnor, *The Development of Southern Sectionalism, 1819–1848* (Baton Rouge: Louisiana State University Press, 1948), 274; Ray Allen Billington, *Westward Expansion: A History of the American Frontier,* 3rd ed. (New York: Macmillan, 1967), 402. Other historians, too, reached similar conclusions. See, for example, Ambler, *A History of Transportation in the Ohio Valley,* 232.

24. For the irrepressible school of Civil War historiography, see Charles A. Beard and Mary R. Beard, *The Rise of American Civilization,* vol. 2 (New York: Macmillan, 1927), and Kenneth M. Stampp, *The Imperiled Union* (New York: Oxford University

Press, 1980). And for the repressible school, see Avery O. Craven, *An Historian and the Civil War* (Chicago: University of Chicago Press, 1964); David Hurbert Donald, *Lincoln Reconsidered* (New York: Alfred A. Knopf, 1956), and J. G. Randall, *Civil War and Reconstruction* (Boston: D. C. Heath, 1953).

Herbert E. Bixler, *Railroads: Their Rise and Fall: A Personal Observation* (Jaffrey Center, N.H.: Privately printed, 1982), 12; Henry C. Carey, *To the Friends of the Union throughout the Union* (Philadelphia: n.p., 1876), 2.

This is not to say that all scholars who have looked at the LC&C have reached similar conclusions that a completed road might have prevented the Civil War. In a thoughtful work, Richard L. Saunders Jr. reflects that "if there was any possibility that through rail connections might have altered the sectional alignments, it cannot be found in the case of the Louisville, Cincinnati and Charleston. Even if it had been completed, its influence would probably have been small." And he adds, "Perhaps the case of the LC&C shows that the economic watershed had already been passed and that the promoters were grappling with economic trends that were out of their control." See Richard Leroy Saunders Jr., "The Louisville, Cincinnati and Charleston Railroad and the Elusive Hope for Intersectional Unity, 1835–1845" (MA thesis, University of Illinois, 1964), 135–36.

Index

Page number in *italics* indicate presence of an illustration

A. Birdsall and Company, 126
Abbeville (locomotive), 112
Abbeville, South Carolina, 111
Abington, Virginia, 45, 48
Abington Rail Road, 46
Adams, Henry, 1
Address in Behalf of the Knoxville Convention, to the Citizens of the Several States Interested in the Proposed Louisville, Cincinnati and Charleston Rail Road (pamphlet), 66–67
Adrian, Michigan, 90
Alabama Great Southern Railway, 149–50
Alabama River, 10
Albany, New York, 108
Allegheny Portage Rail Road, 60
Allen, Horatio, 29, 33–34, 37–38, 47
Almond, North Carolina, 134, 136
Alpine, Texas, 120
Alston, South Carolina, 114–15
Altamaha River, 10
Alton, Illinois, 161
Aluminum Company of America (Alcoa), 136
American Society of Civil Engineers, 25
Anderson, Rev. Isaac, 64–65
Anderson, South Carolina, 111–12, 121–24, 127, 132, 136
Anderson Railroad Convention, 122–23
Andrews, Alexander Boyd, 135
Annals of Tennessee to the End of the Eighteenth Century (book), *The*, 52
Anson Bangs and Company, 125–26
Anti-Masonic Party, 44
Apalachicola River, 10
Asheville, North Carolina, 8, 46, 53, 63, 69, 75, 102–103, 112, 133–34, 155, 160
Asheville & Spartanburg Railroad, 134
Ashley River, 31, 117, 156
Athens, Georgia, 8, 46, 62, 70, 80, 84, 90, 125, 133
Athens, Ohio, 2
Athens, Tennessee, 126
Atlanta, Georgia, 84–85, 94, 134, 156–57
Atlanta & Charlotte Air Line Railroad, 133
Atlantic & Mississippi Rail Road, 170n6
Atlas (steamboat), 13
Audubon, John James, 15
Augusta, Georgia, 6, 10, 31, 41, 46, 62, 83–84, 90, 94, 107, 123, 137
Augusta & Eastern Rail Road, 46

Bache, Herman, 80
Baldwin, Mathias, 37–38
Baltimore, Maryland, 7, 30–33, 63, 87, 97, 137, 151, 156, 159
Baltimore & Ohio Railroad, 30–31, 33, 35–36, 60, 63, 72, 85, 87, *96*, 97, 137
Baltimore & Susquehanna Rail Road, 73, 88
Bangs, Austin, 126
Bangs, Eli, 126
Bank of England, 101
Barbour, James, 71
Battle of Bunker Hill, 24
Beacon Hill Railroad, 24–25
Beard, Charles A., 164
Beard, Mary R., 164
Beaufort, North Carolina, 31, 45
Belle (steamboat), 16
Belton, South Carolina, 111, 132
Best Friend of Charleston (locomotive), 35–37, *36*, *38*, *39*
Bierce, Lucius Verus, 2
Bill Creek (Tennessee), 76
Birmingham, Alabama, 146, 156
Black, Alexander, 30
Blanding, Abram, 56, 58, 60, 104, 160
Block House, Virginia, 8
Blue Ridge (locomotive), 131
Blue Ridge & Atlantic Railroad, 133
Blue Ridge Railroad, 120; Anderson Railroad Convention, 122–23; Advantages of, 121–24, 129–30; Construction, 126–28, 130; Contractors, 125–26; Corporate components, 121–22, 124; Financing and financials, 124–29; Freight and passenger service, 131–32, 179n34; Narrow-gauge proposal, 132; Opposition to, 124–25, 128; Post–Civil War lines (non-Blue Ridge Railroad), 134–36; Post–Civil War revival efforts, 131–33; Routes and surveys, 122–23, 125; Southwestern branch proposal,

126; Stump House Mountain Tunnel, 125, 127–29, *128*, *130*; Tunnels, 122–23, 125, 127
Blue Ridge Railroad [of Georgia], 121
Boone, Daniel, 8
Boonesborough, Kentucky, 8
Boston, Massachusetts, 24, 32–33, 108, 137, 152, 156, 158–59, 162
Boston & Providence Rail Road, 73
Branchville, South Carolina, 53, 95–96, 98–99, 106, 118, 121
Brisbane, Abbot, 73
Bristol, Virginia, 114, 134
Broad River, 19, 114
Brown, William Spence, 111
Brunswick, Georgia, 31, 153
Buchanan, James, 73–74
Buchanan, Virginia, 18
Buffalo Trace (Indiana), 2
Buncombe Turnpike, 75–76
Burnside, Ambrose, 138
Bushnell, North Carolina, 135
Butt Mountain Gap (North Carolina), 60, 75–76

Calderwood, Tennessee, 135–36
Caldwell, Joseph, 45
Calhoun, John C., 15, 51, 58, 62, 71–72, 78–85, *79*, 90, 104, 106, 111, 121, 157, 163, 171n29
Cambridge City, Indiana, 18
Camden, South Carolina, 16, 28, 31, 34, 47, 98–99, 116
Canals: Advantages of, 19–21; Scope, 17–19; Technology, 16, 19; Weaknesses and disadvantages of, 20–21
Cannon, Gabriel, 114
Canton, Massachusetts, 73
Canton, Mississippi, 102
Carbondale, Pennsylvania, 29
Carey, Henry Charles, 164
Carolina & Tennessee Southern Railway, 134
Carolina Gap (North Carolina), 80–82
Carroll, Charles, 97
Carrollton Viaduct, Maryland, 30
Carts, 5
Catawba River, 47
Central Rail Road & Canal Company of Georgia, 62, 83
Chambersburg, Pennsylvania, 67
Charleston, South Carolina, 7, 16, 18, 30–35, 40–41, 47–49, 51, 53–56, 61, 69, 81, 83–88, 91, 94–95, 98–99, 102–104, 107, 109–10, 113–14, 116–17, 119, 121–25, 127, 130, 134, 136–37, 139, 150–60, 162–64
Charleston & Savannah Railroad, 117
Charleston Chamber of Commerce, 30–32, 54
Charlotte, North Carolina, 116–17, 156
Charlotte & South Carolina Rail Road, 110, 116–17
Chattahoochee River, 10, 46, 62
Chattanooga, Tennessee, 62, 70, 85, 107, 126, 137, 140–44, 146, 149, 153, 157
Chatuga (steam locomotive), 131
Cheraw & Darlington Rail Road, 116
Chesapeake and Delaware Canal, 62
Chesapeake and Ohio Canal, 18, 30, 73
Chesnut, James, Jr., 116
Chester, South Carolina, 117
Chicago, Illinois, 53, 120, 137, 159
Chicago, Milwaukee & St. Paul Railway, 95
Chilhowee, Tennessee, 135
Church Street Methodist Church (Knoxville, Tennessee), 46, 58, 59, *59*
Cincinnati, Cumberland Gap & Charleston Railroad, 134
Cincinnati, Lexington & East Tennessee Railroad, 138
Cincinnati, New Orleans & Texas Pacific Railway, 149–50
Cincinnati, Ohio, 14, 17, 48–50, 53–54, 56, 76, 78, 87, 89, 93, 101–102, 119, 134, 136–44, 146, *147*, 149–51, 153, 155, 157–60
Cincinnati & Charleston Rail Road. *See* Louisville, Cincinnati & Charleston Rail Road
Cincinnati & Chattanooga Railway, 141
Cincinnati and Whitewater Canal, 17–18, 21, 89
Cincinnati Board of Trade, 137, 140
Cincinnati Chamber of Commerce, 54, 140
Cincinnati City Council, 140
Cincinnati Railroad, 149
Cincinnati Southern Railroad, 144, 149
Cincinnati Southern Railway, Advantages of, 138–40; Charters, 141–43; Chattanooga as southern terminal, 140–41; Completion celebration, 146–47, *147*; Construction, 143–46; Financing and financials, 139–40, 143–45; Freight and passenger service, 144, 146–47; Map of, *145*; Ohio River bridge, 142–45; Opposition to, 141–43; Origins, 137–40; Public timetable, *148*; Rental and lease agreements, 149–50, 180n80; Standardizing gauge, 149; Surveys, 143. *See also* Cincinnati, New Orleans & Texas Pacific Railway; Cincinnati Railroad; Cincinnati Southern Railroad
Cincinnati Superior Court, 140
Civil War, 116, 158, 160, 164, 182n24
Clark, James, 86
Clarkesville, Georgia, 133
Clayton, A. S., 58
Clayton, Georgia, 122, 133–34
Clemson, South Carolina. *See* Fort Hill, South Carolina
Clemson, Thomas Green, 81–82
Cleveland, John Bomar, 157
Cleveland, Ohio, 17, 137, 159
Clinton, DeWitt, 17, 108
Colhoun, James Edward, 81
Columbia, Pennsylvania, 42
Columbia, South Carolina, 8, 19, 31, 34, 53, 56, 69, 76, 85, 87, 89, 95–99, 105–106, 110–14, 116–18, 121, 123, 138, 155, 160
Columbia Canal, 19
Columbia Rail Road, 96
Columbus, Georgia, 46
Concord stages, 5–6
Conestoga wagons, 5
Congaree River, 12, 19, 31, 96
Coombs, Leslie, 58–59
Cooper, Peter, 35
Cooper River, 18, 31–32, 156
Coosa River, 10

Cornelia, Georgia, 133–35
Covington, Kentucky, 53, 76
Crab Orchard Gap (Tennessee), 81
Craven, Avery O., 164
Culp, John M., 135
Cumberland, Maryland, 7, 18
Cumberland Gap (Kentucky, Tennessee, Virginia), *9*, 53, 60, 69, 76, 78
Cumberland River, 11, 47–48, 81, 83–84, 93
Cumberland Valley Railroad, 67
Cycloped (locomotive), 27

Dahlonega, Georgia, 82
Daniel Crommelin and Sons, 88
Danville, Kentucky, 143
Darien, Georgia, 31
Dascomb, Marianne Parker, 7
Davis, Jefferson, 105, 163
Dayton, Ohio, 17
Dayton, Tennessee, 143
Dearborn, Henry, 108
Delaware and Hudson Canal, 28–30, 90
Detroit, Michigan, 159
Dismal Swamp Canal, 19
Documents to Prove the Superior Advantages of Railway and Steam Carriages over Canal Navigation (pamphlet), 28
Donald, David Herbert, 164
Drake, Daniel, 49–50, *50*, 53–54, 59, 61, 64
Drayton, Thomas, 73
Dudley, Edward Bishop, 92

East Tennessee, Virginia & Georgia Railway, 133–34, 149
East Tennessee & Virginia Rail Road, 114, 123
East Tennessee Historical Society, 52
Eatonton, Georgia, 45–46
Eddyville, New York, 28
Edisto River, 31, 34
Elizabeth City, North Carolina, 19
Elizabeth River, 19
Elizabethton, North Carolina, 2
Ellet, Charles, Jr., 118
Ellicott's Mills, Maryland, 30
Elliott, Stephen, 49
Emerson, Ralph Waldo, 103
Emile Erlanger and Company, 149
Emory Gap, Tennessee, 141, 143
Emory River, 141
Enterprise (steamboat), 13
Erie & Kalamazoo Rail Road Bank, 90
Erie Canal, 17, 19, 108, 155, 158
Erlanger, Frederick Emile d', 149
Erlanger Syndicate, 149–50
Estellville, Virginia, 47–48
Ewing, Thomas, 19
Express Mail (canal boat), 21

Fagg, F. B., 58
Falling Creek Rail Road, 25
Featherstonehaugh, G. F., 60
Ferguson, Edward, 137, 140, 142, 146
Ferguson Act (1869), 140, 142
Finley, William W., 135
Flat Rock, North Carolina, 65, 76
Flint River, 46
Florence, South Carolina, 116, 118
Fontana, North Carolina, 135–36
Fort Hill (locomotive), 131
Fort Hill, South Carolina, 78, 80–81
Fort Jackson, South Carolina, 116
Fort Sumter, South Carolina, 116
Fort Wayne, Indiana, 10
Foster, Rastrick and Company, 29
Frankfort, Kentucky, 56, 76–77
Franklin, Benjamin, 16
Franklin, North Carolina, 121, 133–36
Fremont, John C., 74–75
Fremont, Ohio, 40
French Broad River, 11, 33, 46, 53, 60, 69, 71, 75–76, 79, 81–82, 84, 91, 112, 124–25, 133, 160
Frost, Edward, 127–28
Fulton, Robert, 13

Gadsden, James, 58, 60, 73, 80, 84, 103–105, 163
Gadsden Purchase (1854), 104–105, 163
Gaines, Edmund, 72
Gallatin, Albert, 19, 71
Garlington, John, 113
General Survey Act (1824), 34, 71
George Collyer and Company, 126
Georgetown, District of Columbia, 18
Georgia & East Tennessee Railroad, 123
Georgia Rail Road & Banking Company, 62, 69, 83–84, 87, 90, 94, 107, 123, 126, 172n35
German Colonization Society of Charleston, 128
Gest, Clarissa, 101–102
Goodin, Samuel H., 139
Gourdin, Henry, 121
Grand Gulf & Banking Company, 90
Granite Railway, 24–25
Gravity Rail Road, 29–30
Great Britain, 23, 26–27
Green River, 33, 74–75
Greeneville, Tennessee, 2, 8, 65, 114
Greeneville & French Broad River Railroad, 114
Greensboro, North Carolina, 117
Greenville, South Carolina, 69, 110–13, 115, 157
Greenville & Columbia Rail Road, 110–15, 122
Greenville Rail Road, 111
Greenwood, South Carolina, 111–12
Gregg, William, 124–25
Guest and Company, 126
Gwynn, Walter, 129

Habersham, Richard, 58
Hamburg, South Carolina, 31, 34, 47, 69, 78, 83–84, 107
Hampton, Wade, II, 89
Harrison, J. W., 131
Harrison, William Henry, 54
Harrodsburg, Kentucky, 8
Hayne, Robert Y., 49–51, *51*, 55–56, 58–62, 64, 66, 68–69, 72–74, 82, 84–85, 87, 89–90, 92, 94, 97, 102–104, 109, 121, 157, 160
Hedley, William, 26
Hendersonville, North Carolina, 134
Hernando Rail Road & Banking Company, 90
Hiwassee Rail Road, 84, 106–107
Hiwassee River, 80
Hoboken, New Jersey, 28
Hodges, South Carolina, 111
Hollidaysburg, Pennsylvania, 42
Holston River, 11, 47, 130

Hone, Philip, 100
Honea Path, South Carolina, 112
Honesdale, Pennsylvania, 28–29
Horry, Elias, 160
Horses, 4
Hudson River, 13

Illinois Central Railroad, 88
Indianapolis, Indiana, 159

J. P. Morgan and Company, 150
Jackson, Andrew, 22, 85, 101
Jackson, Mississippi, 102
Jackson, William, 25
Jacksonville, Florida, 156
James River, 10, 18
James River and Kanawha Canal, 18–19, 21, 45, 73, 85
James River Company, 18
Jervis, John B., 29
Johnstown, Pennsylvania, 42
Jonesboro, Tennessee, 57

Kanawha River, 18
Kansas City, Mexico & Orient Railway, 120
Kansas City, Missouri, 120
Kentucky Central Railroad, 138, 143
Kentucky River, 12, 77, 143, 145
Keowee River, 78, 80
King, John P., 83
King, Michael, 46, 104–106
Kings Mountain Rail Road, 117
Kingsville, South Carolina, 116, 118
Knoxville, Tennessee, 13–14, 45–46, 51, 53, 57–59, 61–64, 70, 76, 79–81, 84, 87–88, 92, 105–107, 114, 119, 121–24, 130–38, 140, 155, 157, 160
Knoxville & Augusta Railroad, 133
Knoxville & Charleston Railroad, 121, 133
Knoxville & Danville Railroad, 123
Knoxville & Southern Rail Road, 46, 53
Knoxville Railroad Convention, 46, 48, 54, 57–67, 70, 79, 108–109, 121–22, 136, 160, 163; 175th anniversary, *68*
Knoxville Register (newspaper), *66*, *67*

La Grange & Memphis Rail Road, 81, 95
Lancaster, Kentucky, 60
Laurens, South Carolina, 111, 113
Laurens Rail Road, 113
Lavoinne, L., 146
Lawrenceburg, Indiana, 18
Lea, Pryor, 59, 64
Lewisburg, South Carolina, 98
Lexington, Kentucky, 53, 60, 63, 76–78, 119, 138, 141, 143, 155, 157, 160
Lexington, North Carolina, 45
Lexington & Ohio Rail Road, 76–78, 93
Licking River, 12, 76
Lincoln, Abraham, 138, 164
Little Tennessee River, 48, 69, 78, 80, 121, 134–36
Liverpool & Manchester Railway, 27
Locomotion No. 1 (locomotive), 26
Long, Stephen, 11, 53
Long Island Rail Road, 73
Louisville, Kentucky, 13–14, 53–54, 56, 76–78, 93, 119, 137–38, 141, 151, 157–58, 160
Louisville & Nashville Railroad, 136–38
Louisville and Portland Canal, 77
Louisville Bridge Company, 137, *138*
Louisville, Cincinnati & Charleston Rail Road, 46, 50; Acquisition of South-Carolina Canal & Rail-Road, 93–94, 99; Advantages of, 55–57, 60, 63, 65, 67, 72–73, 92; Branches proposed, 61–62, 64; Calhoun survey, 78–83; Camden branch, 98–99; Columbia line, 95–99, 107–108; Columbia railroad celebrations, 97–98; Deaths of Abram Blanding and Robert Y. Hayne, 103–104; Dual track, 97; Federal financing proposed, 62; Federal support, 72–74; Financing and financials, 62–64, 85–95, 99, 102, 106–108; Freight and passenger service on Columbia line, 99; If completed, 152–64; Merger with South-Carolina Canal & Rail-Road, 109; Origins of, 47–49, 53–57; Population en route, 68; Promotion of, 66–67; Rails, 96–97; Retrenchment, 105–106; Slave labor, 87–88, 174n43; State charters, 56, 64; Surveys, 56–57, 60, 69–70, *70*, 72, 74–76, *77*, 82. *See also* Knoxville Railroad Convention; Southwestern Rail Road Bank
Lovejoy, Elijah, 161
Low, James, 132
Ludlow, Kentucky, 144
Lula, Georgia, 133
Lumpkin, William, 172n35
Lynchburg, Virginia, 18, 45

Macon, Georgia, 10, 46, 62, 83
Macon & Western Rail Road, 83
Madison, Georgia, 84
Madison, James, 71
Manhattan, Ohio, 17
Marietta, Ohio, 10
Maryville, Tennessee, 130, 133–35
Massillon, Ohio, 6
Maysville, Kentucky, 56, 61, 78
Maysville Road (Kentucky), 22
McAdam, John Loudon, 9
McBee, Vardry, 58, 106, 111
McDuffie, George, 90
McNeill, William G., 60, 72–76, 78, 82, 84, 97, 146
Means, John, 124
Medical College of Ohio, 50
Memminger, Christopher Gustavus, 76, 91, 105, 130, 153
Memphis, Tennessee, 11, 65–66, 83–85, 95, 107, 134, 158, 163
Memphis & Charleston Rail Road, 85
Merthyr Tydfil, Wales, 26
Miami and Erie Canal, 17, 89
Miami Extension Canal, 17
Middle Cherokee Trading Path. *See* Old Federal Road (Georgia)
Military Academy of South Carolina (The Citadel), 122
Milledgeville, Georgia, 6, 10, 46
Millen, Georgia, 83
Miller, Ezra, 33–34
Mills, Robert, 1, 33, 58, 60
Mississippi Rail Road, 102
Mississippi River, 10, 13, 49, 137, 158–59, 164
Mobile, Alabama, 84, 139, 156, 158

Mohawk & Hudson Rail Road, 168n22
Monroe, James, 71
Morehead City, North Carolina, 31
Morgan, J. P., Sr., 133
Morris, Eastin, 81
Morristown, North Carolina, 134
Mount Vernon, Kentucky, 60
Murphy, North Carolina, 134
Muskingham River, 10
Myers, William, 99

Nashville, Tennessee, 11, 41, 81, 84, 92, 137–38, 140, 142, 156
Nashville & Chattanooga Railroad, 137, 141
Natchez, Mississippi, 102, 158
Natchez Trace (Mississippi), 3
National Road, 7, 10, 18, 62
Natural and Statistical View or Picture of Cincinnati (book), *The*, 50
Neponset River, 24
Neville, Morgan, 48
New Bern, North Carolina, 31
Newberry, South Carolina, 111–14
New Orleans, Louisiana, 13, 22, 42, 139, 156, 158–59, 162–63
New Orleans (steamboat), 13
Newport, Kentucky, 53, 76
New York, New York, 5, 31–32, 120, 137, 156, 158–59
New York, Pittsburgh & Chicago Railway, 120
New-York & Erie Rail Road, 39, 85
New York Central Railroad, 137, 155
Nicholasville, Kentucky, 60, 138
Nolichucky River, 47
Norfolk, Virginia, 19
Norfolk Southern Corporation, 150, 181n3
North Carolina Rail Road, 117, 124, 150
North-Eastern Rail Road Company (of Georgia), 125–26, 133
North-eastern Rail Road Company of South Carolina, 116, 118
Northeastern Railroad of Georgia, 133
Northern Pacific Railroad, 120
Northwestern Turnpike (Virginia), 8
Novelty (locomotive), 27

O'Barr Mine, 82
Ocmulgee River, 10
Oconee River, 10
Ogeechee River, 19
Ohio and Erie Canal, 17, 19–20
Ohio Rail Road, 39–40
Ohio River, 10–11, 13, 18, 49, 77, 137, 142–43, 145, 155, 158
Old Federal Road (Georgia), 8
Old Fort, North Carolina, 133–34
Old Northwest defined, 165n2
O'Neall, Belton, 122, 160–61
Orangeburg, South Carolina, 96, 98
Osborne, J. W., 58

Paint Rock, North Carolina, 134
Panic of 1837, 85, 88, 100–102, 107–108
Panic of 1857, 128, 136
Panic of 1873, 132, 143
Paris, Kentucky, 53
Pasquotank River, 19
Pendleton, South Carolina, 81, 122, 127, 129
Pendleton Messenger (newspaper), 81
Pendleton Rail Road, 122, 137
Pennsylvania Main Line of Public Works, 18, 42, 60
Pennsylvania Railroad, 120
Pensacola, Florida, 139
Pen-y-Darren Ironworks, 26
Perseverance (locomotive), 27
Petersburg Rail Road, 102
Pettigru, John, 58
Philadelphia, Pennsylvania, 5, 31–32, 42, 137, 158–59
Phoenix (locomotive), 37, 40
Phoenix (steamboat), 28
Pickensville (Easley), South Carolina, 80
Pittsboro, North Carolina, 45
Pittsburgh, Pennsylvania, 13–14, 67, 89, 158
Plan for the Construction of the Direct Railroad South, Connecting Cincinnati with the Southern System of Railroads (pamphlet), 139
Poinsett, Joel R., 48, 58, 162
Portland, Kentucky, 77
Poussin, Guillaume Tell, 12, 16
Prentiss, Georgia, 135
Pride of Newcastle (locomotive), 29
Proposed Rail-Road from Cincinnati to Charleston, The (pamphlet), 152

Queen and Crescent Route. *See* Cincinnati, New Orleans & Texas Pacific Railway
Quincy Railroad. *See* Granite Railway

Rabun Gap, Georgia, 61, 69, 80, 82, 121–22, 125, 131–36
Rabun Gap Route. See Blue Ridge Railroad
Rail-Road from the Banks of the Ohio River to the Tide Waters of the Carolinas and Georgia (pamphlet), 55
Railroad Advocate (newspaper), 53
Railroads, Advantages of, 22, 42–42, 71, 81, 113, 117–18; Financing and financials, 71, 117–18; Gauges, 38, 84, 112, 116–17, 132, 149; Inclined planes, 40, 47, 60, 75, 77, 82, 96; Origins of, 23–25; Piled roadbeds, 38–39; Railroad conventions, 45–48, 65, 85, 122, 132, 141–42, 163, 170n1, 170n3; Rails, 96–97; Scope of, 43, 67, 109, 115–17, 163–64; Steam locomotion, 26–30, 33–37, 47; Tunnels, 123; Wooden railways, 24–26
Rainhill trials, 27, 33
Raleigh, North Carolina, 45, 91
Ramsey, James Gettys McCreary, 49, 51–53, 52, 57, 61, 64, 106, 176n14
Randall, J. G., 164
Redfield, William C., 49
Reed, James, 73
Reedy Patch Creek (North Carolina), 60, 75
Report of the Secretary of the Treasury on the Subject of Roads and Canals (1808), 19
Rhett, Robert Barnwell, Jr., 130
Richmond, Virginia, 10, 18, 21, 25, 156

Richmond & Danville Railroad, 133, 150
Richmond Terminal Company, 133–34
Rivers: Boat types, 11–15, *15*; Costs of travel, 13; Scope of, 10–11, 16
Roads and travel: Better roads agitation, 1, 4–5, 9; Corduroy roads, 9; Federal support of, 1, 7; "Foot railroads," 4–5; Local support of, 8–9; Plank roads, 9–10; State support of, 7–8; Technological improvements, 9; Trails, 2–4; Travel on, 5–7
Roanoke Canal, 19
Roanoke River, 19
Rock Island, Illinois, 163
Rocket (locomotive), 27, 33
Rogersville, Tennessee, 52
Ross's Landing, Tennessee. *See* Chattanooga, Tennessee
Rotch, Charity Rodman, 6
Rutherfordton, Charlotte & Wilmington Rail Road, 124
Rutherfordton, North Carolina, 69, 114
Rutledge, Tennessee, 58

Saint Louis, Missouri, 53, 108, 137, 163
Saint Matthews, South Carolina. *See* Lewisburg, South Carolina
Salisbury, North Carolina, 133
Saluda Gap (North Carolina), 75
Saluda Mountain Grade, North Carolina, 134
Saluda River, 19, 53
Sandusky, Ohio, 162
Sans Pereil (locomotive), 27
Santee Canal, 18–19, 32–34, 118–19, 153
Santee River, 16, 18, 32, 34, 116
Savannah, Georgia, 31, 46, 62, 83–84, 107, 116–17, 124, 139, 153, 162, 164
Savannah and Ogeechee Canal, 19
Savannah River, 10, 14, 19, 31, 34, 47, 69, 78, 80–81, 84, 111, 124, 153–54
Second Bank of the United States, 101
Seneca River, 78, 81, 123
Sevierville, Tennessee, 65
Simpson, Maria Louise Garlington, 113
Sketch of the Geographical Rout[e] of a Great Railway (pamphlet), 49
Slavery, 160–63, 174n43
Sloan, William, 80
Smedberg, John, 75
Somerset, Kentucky, 143–44
South Carolina (locomotive), 37
South Carolina & Georgia Railroad, 150
South Carolina College, 97
South Carolina Rail Road, 81, 103, 109–10, 116–18, 123, 157, 169n45, 174n43. *See also* South Carolina & Georgia Railroad
South Carolina State Bank, 49, 90
South Western Rail Road, 83
South-Carolina Canal & Rail-Road, 30–31, 33–43, 45, 47, 53, 57, 69, 84–87, 93–96, 98–99, 107, 121, 153, 160
Southern and Western Theological Seminary, 64
Southern Railway, 133–36, 150, 153
South-western Rail Road Bank, 89–95, *93*, 104, 107–108, 110
Spartanburg, South Carolina, 69, 113, 115, 134, 157
Spartanburg & Union Rail Road, 110, 113–15, 134
Specie Circular (1836), 101
Spencer, Samuel, 150
Stagecoaches, 5, 20
Stampp, Kenneth M., 164
Statistics of South Carolina (book), 33
Staunton and Parkersburg Road (Virginia), 8
Steam Boat (steamboat), 13
Stephenson, George, 26–28
Stephenson, Robert, 27
Stephenson and Company, 27, 29, 37
Stevens, John, 28
Stilwell, Arthur, 120
Stockton & Darlington Railway, 26–27, 31
Stourbridge Lion (locomotive), 29–30
Stump House Mountain, 127, *130*. *See also* Blue Ridge Railroad
Stump House Mountain Tunnel, 125, 127–29
Surplus Revenue Act (1836), 63, 86, 110
Symington, William, 26
Symmes, Frederick, 80

Tallulah Falls, Georgia, 135
Tallulah Falls Railway, 133, 135
Tampa, Florida, 156
Taunton & New Bedford Rail Road, 73
Telegraph, 160
Tennessee & Carolina Southern Railway, 135
Tennessee Historical Society, 52
Tennessee River, 11, 13–14, 16, 46–48, 52, 62, 70, 78, 80, 83, 93, 107
Tennessee River Railroad, 121
Tennessee Valley Authority, 136
Terre Haute, Indiana, 10
Texas Railroad & Banking Company, 90
Thomas, Ebenezer, 48–49, 59
Thomas Salmond (steamboat), 16
Thomson, J. Edgar, 69–70, 80
Tocqueville, Alexis de, 23
Toledo, Ohio, 17, 90
Tom Thumb (locomotive), 35–36
Topolobampo, Mexico, 120
Trenholm, George, 121, 131
Trevithick, Richard, 26
Tuckasegee River, 80
Tugallo River, 80
Turner, Frederick Jackson, 158
Turnley, Parmenas Taylor, 2
Tuscumbia, Courtland & Decatur Rail Road, 83–85
Tuscumbia Landing, Alabama, 83, 95
Twelve Mile Creek (South Carolina), 78

Union, South Carolina, 113, 115
University of Pennsylvania, 50–51
U.S. Military Academy, 71, 73
Utica & Schenectady Rail-Road, 87

Virginia & Tennessee Rail Road, 45

Wabash and Erie Canal, 10, 17, 80
Wabash River, 10, 12

Wagons, 5
Walhalla, South Carolina, 128, 130, 132–33, 136
Walker *v.* City of Cincinnati (1871), 142
Walking, 2–4, 3
War of 1812, 72
Warm Springs (Hot Springs), North Carolina, 75
Warwoman Creek (Georgia), 130
Washington, D.C., 7, 22, 87, 134
Washington College, 51
Wateree River, 16, 96, 98
Weldon, North Carolina, 19
West Point (locomotive), 37
West Point Foundry Association, 35–37
West Portsmouth, Ohio, 17
West Quincy, Massachusetts, 24
West Union, South Carolina, 130
Western & Atlantic Rail Road, 62, 84–85, 107, 144, 157
Western North Carolina Railroad, 133–34
Western Rail Road of Massachusetts, 33, 73, 108
Wheeling, Virginia (West Virginia), 7, 30
Whitewater Canal, 17–18
Whitney, Asa, 49
Whyte System, 169n37
Wichita, Kansas, 120
Wickliffe, Robert, 58
Wilderness Road, 8
William Norris Works, *96-97*, 133
Williams, John, 58–59
Williams, William G., 60, 72–74, 82
Wilmington, North Carolina, 31, 73, 91, 116, 153
Wilmington & Manchester Rail Road, 116, 118
Wilmington & Weldon Rail Road, 43
Winchester, Virginia, 2, 8
Wolf Creek, Tennessee, 134
Wood, Nicholas, 41
Wynatt, William, 57

York (Yorkville), South Carolina, 69, 117

Zanesville, Ohio, 10–11

Books in the Railroads Past & Present Series

Landmarks on the Iron Road: Two Centuries of North American Railroad Engineering
William D. Middleton

South Shore: The Last Interurban
(revised second edition)
William D. Middleton

Katy Northwest: The Story of a Branch Line Railroad
Don L. Hofsommer

"Yet there isn't a train I wouldn't take": Railway Journeys by William D. Middleton
William D. Middleton

The Pennsylvania Railroad in Indiana
William J. Watt

In the Traces: Railroad Paintings of Ted Rose
Ted Rose

A Sampling of Penn Central: Southern Region on Display
Jerry Taylor

The Lake Shore Electric Railway Story
Herbert H. Harwood Jr. & Robert S. Korach

The Pennsylvania Railroad at Bay: William Riley McKeen and the Terre Haute & Indianapolis Railroad
Richard T. Wallis

The Bridge at Québec
William D. Middleton

History of the J. G. Brill Company
Debra Brill

Uncle Sam's Locomotives: The USRA and the Nation's Railroads
Eugene L. Huddleston

Metropolitan Railways: Rapid Transit in America
William D. Middleton

Perfecting the American Steam Locomotive
J. Parker Lamb

From Small Town to Downtown: A History of the Jewett Car Company, 1893–1919
Lawrence A. Brough and James H. Graebner

Limiteds, Locals, and Expresses in Indiana, 1838–1971
Craig Sanders

Steel Trails of Hawkeyeland: Iowa's Railroad Experience
Don L. Hofsommer

Amtrak in the Heartland
Craig Sanders

When the Steam Railroads Electrified
(revised second edition)
William D. Middleton

The GrandLuxe Express: Traveling in High Style
Karl Zimmermann

Still Standing: A Century of Urban Train Station Design
Christopher Brown

The Indiana Rail Road Company: America's New Regional Railroad
Christopher Rund

Evolution of the American Diesel Locomotive
J. Parker Lamb

The Men Who Loved Trains: The Story of Men Who Battled Greed to Save an Ailing Industry
Rush Loving Jr.

The Train of Tomorrow
Ric Morgan

Built to Move Millions: Streetcar Building in Ohio
Craig R. Semsel

The CSX Clinchfield Route in the 21st Century
Jerry Taylor & Ray Poteat

The New York, Westchester & Boston Railway: J. P. Morgan's Magnificent Mistake
Herbert H. Harwood Jr.

Iron Rails in the Garden State: Tales of New Jersey Railroading
Anthony J. Bianculli

Visionary Railroader: Jervis Langdon Jr. and the Transportation Revolution
H. Roger Grant

The Duluth South Shore & Atlantic Railway: A History of the Lake Superior District's Pioneer Iron Ore Hauler
John Gaertner

Iowa's Railroads: An Album
H. Roger Grant & Don L. Hofsommer

Frank Julian Sprague: Electrical Inventor and Engineer
William D. Middleton & William D. Middleton III

Twilight of the Great Trains
(expanded edition)
Fred W. Frailey

Little Trains to Faraway Places
Karl Zimmermann

Railroad Noir: The American West at the End of the Twentieth Century
Linda Grant Niemann

From Telegrapher to Titan: The Life of William C. Van Horne
Valerie Knowles

The Railroad That Never Was: Vanderbilt, Morgan, and the South Pennsylvania Railroad
Herbert H. Harwood Jr.

Boomer: Railroad Memoirs
Linda Grant Niemann

Indiana Railroad Lines
Graydon M. Meints

The Indiana Rail Road Company: America's New Regional Railroad
(revised and expanded edition)
Christopher Rund, Fred W. Frailey, & Eric Powell

The CSX Clinchfield Route in the 21st Century
(now in paperback)
Jerry Taylor & Ray Poteat

Wet Britches and Muddy Boots: A History of Travel in Victorian America
John H. White Jr.

Landmarks on the Iron Road: Two Centuries of North American Railroad Engineering
(now in paperback)
William D. Middleton

On Railways Far Away
William D. Middleton

Railroads of Meridian
J. Parker Lamb, with contributions by David H. Bridges & David S. Price

Railroads and the American People
H. Roger Grant

The Electric Pullman: A History of the Niles Car and Manufacturing Company
Lawrence A. Brough

John Frank Stevens: Civil Engineer
Clifford Foust

Off the Main Lines: A Photographic Odyssey
Don L. Hofsommer

The Rock Island Line
Bill Marvel

H. ROGER GRANT is Kathryn and Calhoun Lemon Professor of History at Clemson University. He is author of twenty-nine books, including *Railroads and the American People* (Indiana University Press, 2012), *Visionary Railroader* (Indiana University Press, 2008), and (with Don L. Hofsommer) *Iowa's Railroads* (Indiana University Press, 2009).